Happy Birthday Dad,

back many happy

All our love God Bless
Myra John & Billy

X X X X X X X

FINNEY

– a football legend

by Paul Agnew

Carnegie Press, 1989

To Elisabeth

Erratum — p12.
The author would like to apologise for a mistake on page 12. Tom's father Alf did not spend his latter years in an old folks' home. In fact, he lived at home with his wife on the Larches estate of Ashton Preston.

Finney: A Football Legend
Paul Agnew

Copyright © Paul Agnew, 1989

First published, September 1989

Published by Carnegie Press, 125 Woodplumpton Road, Fulwood, Preston PR2 2LS. Tel (0772) 728868.
Typeset in 10½pt Times by Carnegie Press.
Printed by Mather Brothers (Printers) Ltd., 1 Garstang Road, Preston
(a member of the Pindar Group of Companies)

ISBN 0 948789 29 8

Contents

Foreword

T HERE can be no greater tribute than to refer to someone as the best in the world. As a footballer Tom Finney was precisely that – the reason why it has never been possible to assess the true membership of his unofficial fan club.

Tom was a brilliant player. No, even more than that, he was a genius and I am honoured to be handed the opportunity to write the foreword to this, his first biography.

I believe that Tom and I were fortunate in the fact that we played our football at the game's peak. We were England colleagues in a glorious era after the last war and I was always in awe of his ability.

As a defender in the England side, my job was to win the ball as quickly as possible, get it out to Tom and then let him get on with it. Yes, it was that easy and he was that good. As an international, he was equally impressive home and away. It made no difference whether we were at Wembley or in Rio, Turin, Lisbon or Montevideo.

He was regularly asked to withstand, let's say, 'physical treatment' from opposing defenders, especially in South America, but he never allowed anyone the satisfaction of getting the better of him.

A lovely man, quiet by nature, he was a totally different proposition out there on the pitch. He had a ruthless streak and, believe me, he was a master tactician. Once he had beaten you and left you stranded on your backside, there was no recovery.

Tom made wonderful use of his body; swerving from side to side, with the facility for moving the ball from one foot to the other and back again before you could blink.

Our careers hold many parallels. We were both one-club men and established internationals at the same time. He was synonymous with Preston North End and I was much the same at Wolverhampton Wanderers. As 'local products', our success brought immense personal satisfaction. Indeed, there was a line of similarity running right through our lives. I was born in 1924, a couple of years later than Tom, but, like him, I joined my club around the time of the war and went on to spend my entire career there.

Together, we totalled more than 400 League games and managed 181 England caps between us. Funnily enough, I played in all but two of Tom's internationals, the exceptions being against Wales in 1950 and Portugal in 1951.

Another 'link' is that we were both chosen to win the Footballer of the Year award. You could say, therefore, that although we were never club colleagues, I got to know this fellow fairly well!

His ability was extraordinary and he could make established top-ranking players look amateurish. I occasionally saw someone mark him well but never did anyone blot him out of the picture completely. You just couldn't do that to Tom and, in my experience, he never had an off day.

He had a wonderful easy attitude and mental awareness. His shrewd football brain allowed him to draw maximum results from his colleagues. Many men owe him a debt of gratitude.

He was popular in the dressing room but when Tom 'talked Lancashire' with Nat Lofthouse and Bobby Langton the rest of us might as well have been playing in a different team. Seriously, though, we all understood every word of his football vocabulary and I am proud to count Tom Finney among my dearest friends.

He encouraged people to pay their hard-earned money at turnstiles right across the soccer globe and never gave less than value for money. Consistently outstanding – the hallmark of a true great – I doubt whether world football will ever see his like again.

Billy Wright

Chapter One

Boyhood Dreams

L ANCASHIRE in 1922 was a county battling against insurmountable social and economic difficulties, still reeling from the after-effects and devastation of the First World War. Preston, in common with so many other Lancashire towns, was highly dependent upon the prosperity of the cotton industry, and had suffered badly. The community was again asked to display the kind of collective spirit which had been evident so often throughout a turbulent history.

Preston at that time had around 100,000 inhabitants; it was – and is – an industrial town with proud traditions. The Romans and Vikings had been here, and the town had been ransacked at the hands of the Scots on more than one occasion. During the Civil Wars Preston was captured on no fewer than three occasions by rival armies; even Oliver Cromwell and his Roundheads paid a visit; and, more recently, the ravages of the Industrial Revolution of the nineteenth century had left a stark legacy of cotton mills, factories and some of the worst living conditions in the North of England.

It was into this tough but close-knit environment that Tom Finney was born on 5 April 1922. Preston had in the past boasted several famous personages, some of whom acquired world renown – poets Francis Thompson and Robert W. Service, astronomer-cleric Jeremiah Horrocks and inventor Richard Arkwright to name a few. In terms of national prominence, however, Tom Finney, the Preston Plumber, rose above them all, his achievements probably eclipsing all others.

Tom was the son of Alf and Margaret Finney, a hard-working couple who lived in St. Michael's Road, just across Deepdale Road and, amazingly, just a few hundred yards away from the football stadium which he was later to grace for so many years.

Appropriately, perhaps, everyone in Preston was throwing a party when Tom Finney arrived on the scene. He was born in the year of the Preston Guild, a time of great community festivity and civic celebration. Held once every twenty years since medieval times, the Preston Guild is an occasion when Prestonians keep open house for the country with a unique mix of entertainment, pageantry and spectacle. No one realised at the time, but the birth of Tom Finney was reason enough for the town to throw a party!

The Finneys were football minded and a happy unit. Along with Joe and Tom there were four daughters, Madge, Peggy, Doris and Edith.

Father, Alf, was a conscientious and family-minded man who had spells working as a clerk in local government and for the Electricity Board. Frequently, however, Alf found himself unemployed. These were very difficult years and few working-class families could ever be sure that there would be a job for the breadwinner from one week to the next. Mostly Alf Finney's take-home pay from the jobs he could find was a pittance but he waited on in local pubs and at nearby Blackpool during the summer season to keep the money coming in and the children clothed and fed.

Tom was little more than a toddler when his parents decided to move to Daisy Lane in the Holme Slack area of town – still within earshot of the roar of the crowd at Deepdale.

In spite of quite obvious hardship, the Finneys were battling bravely and successfully until, in 1926, tragedy threatened to split them apart. Quite suddenly Mrs Finney was taken ill and Tom, aged just four, can remember the ambulance arriving to whisk her to Preston Royal Infirmary. Initially it was thought she had appendicitis but that diagnosis proved innacurate and within the short space of a few days the Finney children were mourning their mother's death. Margaret, or Maggie as she preferred, was 32.

Her passing cast a cloud over the household and the very future of the children might well have been thrown into jeopardy but for the determination of Alf and the support of the neighbours. At that time many youngsters who lost their mothers found themselves sent into special care or, alternatively, handed on to foster homes. Some, indeed, were taken under the wing of charities who shipped them to 'better lives' abroad, never to see their relatives again.

Alf was adamant that such a course of action would never be required for his beloved children. With the unstinting assistance of friends and adjoining families – Tom recalls with affection the Fish, Cross and Mashiter clans – Alf's persistence proved unbeatable.

There were problems and difficulties, of course, and there was considerable strain for Alf, but Tom has always insisted that his childhood was happy. On many a winter night Alf would take Joe and Tom upon his knee by the sitting room fire and relate the wonderful games and great players he had seen. Through those memories he harboured a secret desire that one if not both his sons might one day make the grade. Thus, from the very cradle, the young Joe and Tom were immersed in the whole culture of a society almost unanimously keen on the game of soccer.

In the 1920s, football had virtually become a way of life in northern England. From its roots in the public schools and universities of mid-Victorian Britain, it had grown to be a hugely popular sport, especially in the towns and cities of the North. Public school men were behind the setting up of the Football Association in 1863, and the earliest winners of the FA Cup, first contested in 1871-72, include such seemingly unlikely names as Old Etonians and Wanderers. In the 1883 final, however, Blackburn Olympic, a side composed mainly of working-class players, defeated the Old Etonians, a victory that symbolised the arrival of soccer as a key part of northern popular culture.

The game reached 'ordinary people' by a number of routes. Sometimes clubs were started for them by clergymen or teachers who were anxious to improve the health and fitness of the race at a time of massive expansion of the British Empire. Alternatively, others grew up within the community at large, as working men sought to find interesting ways of spending the free Saturday afternoons that increasing numbers enjoyed from the 1870s onwards. The cotton districts of central and southern Lancashire were at the heart of the development of the game, boasting no fewer than five founder members of the Football League in 1888 (Accrington, Blackburn, Bolton, Burnley and Preston).

Soccer was never a purely 'working-class' game. For one thing, one half of that social group played very little part in events; football was decidedly a masculine preserve. Similarly, much of the crucial financial and organisational input came from the industrial and commercial middle classes, while a significant number of spectators and even a few League players were also drawn from the middle classes. Nevertheless, the better-off members of the working class formed the backbone of the game as both players and, above all, spectators. By 1914, football had become a major feature of their lives.

Attendance figures were not recorded in a systematic way until the 1930s (Preston North End were one of the few happy exceptions in this respect), but we have enough information to show the great growth of interest in this period. In 1888-9 the average attendance at First Division games was 4,600. By 1905-6 it had risen to 13,200, by 1913-14, 23,100. Leading members of society came to realise the importance of the game. As Lord Roseberry commented when presenting the FA Cup in 1900, 'This is the second year running that you have had a distinguished Cabinet Minister amongst you to preside over this sport. It is good for football, and it is not bad for the Cabinet Minister.'

The inter-war period saw continued large-scale growth of interest in the game. Attendances continued to rise, the First Division average reaching 30,500 in 1938-39. The twenties and thirties were, of course, profoundly difficult ones for many sectors of the working class. From 1920, unemployment was never below one million, and at the height of the depression in January 1933, almost three million people were out of work. Unemployment and the associated problem of low wages, however, did not dampen people's enthusiasm for the game. Although attendances were badly affected in towns with particularly high unemployment, people showed a willingness to make sacrifices in order to watch their team, especially at 'big matches'. In January 1933, for example, as unemployment in Sheffield reached its peak of 60,000, a crowd of 66,000 gathered at Hillsborough to see Sheffield Wednesday take on Arsenal. The *Preston Herald* commented in 1930 that 'the directors are obtaining splendid support from the public in these most distressed times.'

Among schoolboys, football became almost an obsession. Although not always able to attend – the breadwinner's leisure came first when money was short – they followed the game with a passion that even the school authorities came to admire and to use as an encouragement. In 1922, the headmaster of St. Luke's Boy's closed the school to allow some boys to go and watch a cup-tie at Deepdale. In 1938, when Preston Boys reached the English Schoolboys final, a special holiday was granted for some schoolchildren.

It is possible to speculate for pages about the reasons for soccer's hold on the imaginations of so many working lads. Some of it, no doubt, was due to the ever-increasing coverage that the game received from the media. Newspapers devoted ever more space to the game while the BBC began commentaries on the wireless in 1927. (For the fortunate 10,000 with receivers, the first TV commentary was screened in 1938, featuring Arsenal *v.* Arsenal Reserves. Maybe 'fortunate' is the wrong word!). Players were increasingly taken up by companies to advertise and endorse products, ranging from football boots to Oxo, Phospherine Tonic and cigarettes. The massive expansion of the pools in this period also put many in touch with the game for the first time. By the mid-1930s, over seven million people spent over thirty million pounds a year on the pools.

In the final analysis, though, the game and the sheer excitement and expectation it generated was what really mattered. In a real sense football offered a sense of release. Big matches in particular were like great popular festivals, with rattles, favours, songs and, as the *Green 'Un* noted in 1928, people behaving 'in a manner they would never think of doing at any other time.'

As the historian Nigel Fishwick has recently claimed, this was particularly important at a time when there was much pressure for more 'decorous' public behaviour. In Fishwick's words, football was 'a rebellion against a society in which such boisterous behaviour was increasingly seen as an invasion of other people's right of peace and privacy'.

It was not the case, however, that football was simply about 'escape' from a hum-drum existence, for that is far too negative. It had so many attractions of its own. To watch an exciting game, to witness the skills of a Matthews or a James – or for later generations, Finney or Best – was to experience something special and a matter for real joy. There was genuine sadness when these figures were lost. The football correspondent of the *Lancashire Evening Post* was probably not exaggerating too much when claiming that Alex James's departure from Preston to Arsenal was 'to me and to thousands of others [including young Tom] . . . a sort of football tragedy'.

Football's all-time popularity in terms of attendance was reached in the period immediately after the war when an entertainment-hungry public sought compensation for the deprivations of war. In 1948-9, a record 41 million attendances were recorded at the season's League matches. Numbers have fallen steadily since then, reaching the lowest point of 16.5 million in 1985-6. In the last two years, despite all the negative images of the game that have been presented, attendance has climbed, albeit slowly, for the first time in almost forty years.

In terms of attendance, soccer will never again achieve the levels of the 1930s and 1940s. Safety regulations alone will ensure that. At the same time, it has been challenged by a variety of social and economic changes. Many other pursuits now rival it for the time, money and commitment of the populace. Nevertheless, the game still has a huge place in popular social life, watched (on TV if not on the terraces), played and discussed by millions. Particularly in the North East and the North West, those early centres of football, the game still has the capacity to capture popular affection to a remarkable degree.

This was nowhere more apparent than on the final day of the 1986-7 season when the whole of Lancashire (and perhaps the whole of footballing public outside of Torquay and Lincoln) willed once-mighty Burnley to avoid the humiliation of relegation to non-League football. After the game, when Burnley were safe, some people cried, all celebrated. Irrational, maybe, to get that worked up about twenty-two men chasing a ball. Then again, it's always been about a lot more than that.

The Finney home, 20 Daisy Lane, was a council house; three-bedroomed with a sitting room and kitchen, on a typical Lancashire council estate. Facilities were basic but there was a large back garden in which Alf grew a selection of vegetables to supplement the children's diet.

Evidence of just how poor the Finneys were comes from the fact that the family qualified for help through the town's 'Clog Fund' – a charitable organisation which undertook to send under-privileged youngsters on special holidays. Tom's first taste of the seaside came as a result of the Fund, when he accompanied brother Joe to a hostel in Lytham St. Annes.

The struggle he and his family endured in the '20s is etched on Tom's brow when he recalls the early years:

'I barely remember my mother but my father was a tremendous inspiration to us all. I have often looked back and marvelled at the way he fought to keep us together. More often than not he put together a survival package funded on 50 shillings a week, but, after my mother died, my eldest sister, Madge, gave him a lot of help. My two grandmothers also figured a lot in my upbringing. Sometimes I would sleep over at Grandma Finney's on a Friday night and be treated to a fish and chip supper!'

Tom's life took considerable influence from the example set and the lessons taught by his father and elder brother. When they both died in the same year, 1964, it came as a devastating double blow. Alf, who lived to be 73, spent his latter years in an old folks' home. He died after a long illness. Joe, struck down by cancer, followed within six weeks, aged 47. Tom can remember the emotion of the period vividly:

'Joe was so ill when father died that he was unable to attend the funeral. It hurt him deeply not to be present. Those two months were the saddest of my life. My father was such a strong man, high in principles and I always looked to him and Joe for guidance. My sisters were always there and very supportive but all the encouragement for my football came from dad and Joe.

'I have endeavoured to live my life by their standards. Many times when faced with a problem or a big decision I have sat back and thought about what my dad would have done.'

I t was not long before football began to creep on to Tom's daily agenda. The 'back fields' became a second home and the pitch which sloped down to the brook behind Metcalfe's Farm played host to some classic confrontations. In the colourful imaginations of the youngsters this was Deepdale; the thrill of scoring equal to any sensation experienced by the professionals between 3 o'clock and 4.45 on Saturday afternoons.

Everyone who remembers Tom agrees that he was quite delicate as a young boy and the other lads often considered him too small to figure in the main game. As a consequence he was regularly left on the touchline to wait patiently in the hope that someone would fail to turn up. Then, and usually only then, would the older boys grant Tom his chance. For the most part, with varying degrees of politeness, he was ordered to get from under their feet.

Tom and Joe were always supported in their football by their father. Alf played in the local Sunday School League for a team called St Jude's and he and many other enthusiastic fathers were delighted to see so many friendships born and nurtured on the back fields.

Nearby Moor Park and 'Stoney Moor', adjacent to the Corporation Tram Shed, also provided the young chums with their first taste of soccer . . . rubber ball style. The skinny kid who no one could ever have imagined was one day destined to hit the heights world wide, kicked the toes out of many a pair of shoes on those very fields. One of Tom's early duties was to act as a 'go-fer' and he was sent along to the local shop, clutching a handful of pennies from a Saturday morning whipround, to buy a ball.

He remembers vividly the run-up to Christmas 1927 when he prayed long and hard for a new pair of football boots. On the big day he awoke to find the gleaming new boots at the foot of his bed and, for good measure, a pair of Preston North End stockings alongside. Dressed to kill in his new kit, Tom proudly displayed himself to the rest of the gang; Joe, Stan Else, George and Arthur Fish, Bunny and Jimmy Bell and Ronnie and Doug Cross.

Holme Slack Fields were about fun, carefree enjoyment and camaraderie. School caps, either lost or left lying overnight, made for suitable goalposts, as did jackets. Many times Tom would get up in a morning unable to find his coat before remembering he had left it on the field. When the garment was discovered after a school journey via the previous night's pitch, it was sopping wet with morning dew.

One young girl with vivid recollections of those days was Gertrude Lawrence (née Giddins). Gertrude and her brother Frank regularly visited the home of their grandparents whose neighbours were the Finneys. Still living in Preston, on Woodside Avenue, Ribbleton, Gertrude explains:

'I was a wee small girl and grand-dad had made a gate at the end of the garden which led on to the back fields. Along with Frank, I would run out there on a Sunday afternoon and soon get invited by Tom to kick a ball about with him until the big lads arrived.

'When they came I was content just to sit on the grass and watch the game of football that ensued; little thinking how many times I would watch Tom's dazzling football in years to come.

'I remember meeting up with him on a couple of occasions as adults. Years later I was standing on Skeffington Road, a small baby in a pram and two toddlers alongside, waiting for the arrival of the bus carrying the Preston North End team back from Wembley. Tom spotted me in that huge crowd and gave me a special wave. I still tell my grandchildren of the days I played football with Tom Finney on the Holme Slack back fields.'

There was football talent in abundance living on the estate in those days and the sheer passion for the game among the young lads inspired Alf and several of the neighbours to start up a club of their own. By this time Alf had re-married – uniting with a young Irish woman called Mary who inherited a ready-made seven-strong family. Mary easily adjusted to the motherly duties and, eventually, bore Alf two further sons, Roy and Dennis.

The Finney clan moved again, this time to a bigger house in Rose Lane and every Friday night without fail Alf, along with Harold Sharples, Bill Colley, Jack Heaney, old Uncle Tom Cobley and all, would meet in the front room to pick the team and arrange fixtures. Eventually, with burgeoning enthusiasm, the ever-increasing gathering decided that the front room was inadequate for their needs and meetings were transferred to the local barber's shop, owned by Wally Gabbott.

In their wisdom, the committee decided to charge 6d a week for kit and to play friendlies only. Mr Metcalfe, a friendly approachable local character, agreed to the use of part of his farm land for a pitch. Sawdust was used to mark out the pitch and the lines usually resembled a dog's hind leg!

Freckleton village, several miles away in the Fylde to the west of Preston, also had a team run on similar lines and they approached Holme Slack FC about the possibility of a fixture, thus beginning a long and happy association between the two sides.

Freckleton's challenge was accepted, a coach was hired for the afternoon and battle commenced. Holme Slack forced a draw. This represented an excellent result, delighting the Preston team and the spectators who had loyally followed them to the game. More importantly perhaps, a thoroughly enjoyable afternoon out was had by all. But it was the hospitality of the hosts – including a meal – which really impressed Alf and his colleagues.

Holme Slack felt obliged to extend the hand of friendship and threw out the invitation for a return game. The football? Well that did not present a problem. But what, oh what, were the Holme Slack to do about after-match entertainment? Holme Slack had no village hall and, even worse, there were few coppers in the club kitty to pay for the necessary refreshments.

House-to-house collections were often made to the local residents and, once again, the HSFC footballers decided to rely on such a source of goodwill and generosity. They were not disappointed. Players' parents were asked to 'adopt' a Freckleton player, official or supporter and cook him a dinner.

Boxing Day was selected for the fixture and Freckleton, the visitors, specifically requested a kick-off in the morning so as to allow their party members the chance of watching the professionals at North End in the afternoon. A well-known local builder, Mr Croft, allowed the use of his hut as a temporary 'village hall' and the event proved so successful that the game became an annual fixture until much later when Holme Slack opted to join the Preston and District League, playing in such prestigious local competitions as the local Guild Hall Cup.

Tom was always closely involved, albeit at spectator level, and he remembers some of his first experiences of organised football at around that time:

'Holme Slack was a typical local side and for that game at Freckleton we couldn't afford the bus fare so a local coal merchant, Bill Collier, allowed us to travel in his cart. We arrived covered in dust, but it was great fun!

'Those days were terrific – the spirit was excellent, despite the fact that most of us hadn't got two ha'pennies to rub together.'

Some time later, when Tom had begun his own playing career, his old friends at Holme Slack clubbed together to buy him a travelling kit as a present.

However, at around this time, Tom's progress in football, as in simple day-to-day living, was impaired by the development of an infected gland in his neck. The hospital in which his mother had died was soon to become more and more familiar. He was often seen with a large bandage wrapped around his neck to protect an unsightly and obtrusive swelling.

Twice a week every week for eight years Tom went along to Preston Royal. He was subjected to revolutionary sun-ray treatment until, at 14, it was decided to operate and the gland was removed.

'They told my father that it was a T.B. gland and the lump protruded quite a long way, which caused me a lot of discomfort. Prior to the operation, I had to go for specialist treatment. Believe it or not, this involved two candles strategically placed on a small machine to produce a sun-ray effect. I was made to stand there naked, an hour at a time, with a large pair of wooden sandals on my feet.'

Tom was born a natural left hander and, at school, wrote with that hand. The teachers never tried to affect his preference and it was understandable that, when it came to football, he should automatically choose the left wing as his prime position.

Tom attended Deepdale County Primary School before moving on, in the fullness of time, to the adjoining Secondary Modern. He was academically average, tolerating school rather than enjoying it. All he really wanted to do was to play football or, like so many other youngsters then and since, to leave and get a job.

'I did not hate school by any means but I certainly wasn't college or university material. I remember some of my teachers at Deepdale Council; Miss Bibby, Mr Duckworth and Mr Yates, who we christened Gumpy for some reason which now escapes me.

'Deepdale Modern, the alternative to the local Grammar School, was built to a new design, including glass walls and umpteen windows. Because of that, we were not allowed to kick a ball about the schoolyard!'

Such minor impediments didn't stop Tom and his schoolfriends from their daily football fix.

'During joinery classes we would drop bits of wood about three inches square and use them as make-shift balls. We all kicked the toes out of many a pair of shoes in that way!'

One of his old schoolmistresses, Mrs Marshall, was not impressed when Tom wrote in an essay that his aim in life was to become a footballer. Mrs Marshall relates the incident:

'We had just finished a P.E lesson and, as usual, Tom had practised dribbling a ball with considerable concentration. He was about eight at that time and wrote in the essay that on leaving school he would become a footballer.

'He was a small, frail-looking boy, quiet and thoughtful and never giving a single moment's trouble and I remember saying that he simply wasn't strong enough for the job.'

Tom paid little attention to such talk. He was acutely keen on all aspects of football and the game was never far from his mind, even at that early age. His interest and enthusiasm was unbounded, although, paradoxically, his visits to Deepdale to watch the professionals in action were few and far between. The cost of the ticket was the main restriction but, besides, the boys preferred to play than spectate anyway.

Going on North End was always considered a special treat and, on occasions, the turnstile attendant would allow Alf to hoist his young son over the barrier free of charge.

Tom was fascinated by the whole scene – a packed ground, electric atmosphere, great players – he was enveloped in the sheer aura of it all.

His early hero was Alex James, a legendary ball player who was idolised by the Preston football-watching public and considered much too good to be playing at Second Division level.

The close ball control, excellent dribbling and speed made James the perfect star for young Tom. All youngsters go through a copy-cat stage and Tom imitated James in both style and mannerism. He even tried to dress like him, allowing his pants to flap around his knees and slicking down his hair, complete with centre parting. He tried to play like James, juggling the ball from left to right foot with a swiftness which left many an opponent on his backside.

Significantly, Tom insists that his attempted impersonation of James had much to do with his own later successes. And, naturally, when he worked his way into the school team there was only one position for Tom Finney – inside left – James' position. As we have seen, there was a considerable local outcry among the fans and in the press when James left for Arsenal but Tom, for one, continued to follow his career with keen interest.

'James was different and I used to be in awe of the way this little, rather insignificant guy in the long, baggy shorts, could torment the big defenders.

'He was my boyhood idol and, when North End transferred him to Arsenal, I was in tears.'

Funnily enough, Tom, who was only seven when James left Preston, met up with his hero many years later – and the roles were reversed.

'We were playing a game in London and Alex James was in the Press Box in his capacity as a correspondent with the *News of the World*. I approached him and when I told him of those early days at Deepdale he wrote his report about it. That was quite a thrill.'

As a youngster, when Tom went to matches without his father, he would sometimes join in the prank of trying to gain entry by crawling under the turnstiles. Attendants soon got wise to the mischievious tactics and a large size-ten shoe was left across the passage to prevent unofficial entry.

The gang of friends would congregate outside the main entrance after the match with the sole intention of rubbing shoulders with the big-name players and collecting autographs. The steam from the huge baths would bellow out when the door opened but the youngsters were still able to recognise their favourites. Elaborate books were uncommon but many a famous PNE name from those days – Russell, Nisbet, Craven and Reid – were treasured on the back of a used tram ticket.

When for some reason Tom and his friends had failed to find a way in to a home game – by fair means preferably but foul means if necessary – they would hang around until the last ten minutes . . . the time when the gates were thrown open and youngsters gained free entry.

S chooldays were dominated by soccer. Tom played in the school teams at primary and secondary level. He soon won a reputation as a nippy little inside forward and a representative honour came his way in 1936 when he was selected as reserve for the Preston Town Team for the prestigious All England Schools Shield knockout tournament.

Reserve he started and reserve he stayed, never playing in the knockout rounds. But, despite his frustrating role of onlooker, he shared in the glory Preston experienced when they won through to the grand national final – a date with West Ham at Upton Park.

Thirteen youngsters – Finney was one of only two who had been selected while still in short trousers – were chosen for the trip to London for a weekend to remember. The Preston youngsters were not given much of a hope against their stronger opponents, but a full sight-seeing excursion around the capital was laid on, perhaps in an attempt to soften the blow of expected defeat.

In the event, however, the Preston schoolboys played their hearts out to force a draw and share the shield with the much-fancied Londoners. They were All England Joint Champions and when the party returned to Lancashire the town of Preston threw a blue and white carnival in celebration. A large crowd lined Fishergate, the long main street, and packed around the Town Hall where the Mayor had granted a civic reception.

Tom had not kicked a ball in anger throughout the competition but he shared the limelight. Furthermore, he claimed that he had been worth at least one goal through his unrelenting verbal encouragement from the touchline.

The youngster who had been responsible for keeping Tom on the sidelines – for the first, but certainly not the last time – was Tommy Hough. A pupil at St Augustine's, Hough had made the town team when he was 11 and had kept his place at inside forward for three seasons. He represented Lancashire and also won selection for the full England squad. Much bigger in physique than Finney, Hough later joined North End and kept Finney out there too.

Good judges reckon that Hough had everything needed to be a great footballer and Finney describes him as one of his most difficult opponents. Alas, the Second World War saw to it that Tommy never really satisfactorily fulfilled his immense potential and, consequently, left the field open for Finney.

Until the war Hough had seemed destined to work his way right to the top. After a sparkling start as a schoolboy, he signed professional terms for North End, his home-town club, despite the attentions of both Blackburn and Liverpool. His debut came during war-time competition against Everton but, within weeks, he was called up to serve as a Royal Marine. When he came out after four arduous years, he was not the same player.

A fine up-standing gent who still lives within walking distance of Deepdale, Hough has every reason to harbour a degree of bitterness. He doesn't:

'I was in my middle twenties when I came home from the war and the services had really taken their toll on me. I had lost the best years and Preston allowed me to leave.

'I dropped into the then Third Division North with Barrow before drifting into non-League football with Fleetwood. I always believed in my ability but the war was the opponent I just couldn't beat.

'Football has always been in my blood and I have a season ticket with PNE. I don't have any grudges but I often sit there in the stand and wonder what might have happened if the war had not got in the way.'

Finney's sportsmaster at Deepdale Modern was a certain Bill Tuson, destined to become well known in the educational field in the town, and after whom a local college was later named. Tuson was noted for his caring approach and the helpful advice he willingly handed over to young soccer players.

One day he pulled Tom to one side and enquired: 'Well, young Finney, you're coming along very well. Have you ever thought about becoming a professional?'. Quite a question for a 13-year-old! And one upon which Tom would dwell often during the next phase of his early life.

More pragmatic thoughts attended the following months, however, as Tom prepared to leave school. Shortly after his 14th birthday, Tom joined the local plumbing firm of Pilkingtons at Fulwood.

Here, not for the last time, the influence of his father was of great importance. Through his contacts at the Electricity Board, Alf had already secured an electrician's apprenticeship for Tom's brother, Joe.

Now it was Tom's turn. He had a word with Harry Pilkington and his friend, full of admiration for Alf's undoubted courage, decided to give the younger Finney son his chance. Tom recalls: 'Harry was a smashing bloke. He knew we had been through a rough time as a family and I am convinced he took me on a little out of sympathy.'

He began, as many do, as an errand boy. Also on his first day, however, while he was all dressed up in his best short-trousered suit, he was asked to accompany a senior workman to remove a backboiler from a local terraced house. Dirty work in anyone's book and, the following day, Tom's suit made way for overalls!

Tom soon took to plumbing, the trade which was to remain a major part of his life, but football occupied his thoughts and he continued to dream of the chance making his mark in his favourite sport. The words of Bill Tuson would be remembered often over the coming months and years.

Chapter Two

The Ladder to Stardom

PPARENTLY settled in as a plumber's apprentice, the 14-year-old Tom was to find opportunity knocking on his door quicker than he could ever have hoped – an opportunity to place a first tentative foot on the ladder towards a career in football. These were the days of the Great Depression but spirits in the Finney household were set to get a timely lift through the pages of the local newspaper.

The source of all the excitement was that Jim Taylor, then chairman of Preston North End, had decided to run some junior teams at Deepdale. Recruitment took the form of an advertisement in the local paper, the *Lancashire Evening Post*. It read:

Wanted: Young boys between the ages of 14 and 18 to join PNE as juniors. Interested parties should write in for a trial.

Tom spotted the ad and thrust the copy under his father's nose. This was the moment he had been waiting for. In Tom's mind it was the first step to heaven. He could barely contain his joy and, if truth be known, Alf was almost as excited himself. That very night, with his father's backing, Tom wrote off to Deepdale, listing his height, weight, age and all other necessary details.

Perhaps there was an oversight; perhaps the club had had an overwhelming response. Whatever the reason, the application labelled under the name of T. Finney failed to make any impact on the North End staff . . . they didn't even bother to send a reply!

When it became obvious that his written plea had prompted nothing in the way of a response, Tom was devastated. Alf did his best to offer consolation. After all, he explained, North End had probably received hundreds of similar applications and the administration process would take some considerable time. But the postman kept on passing by the Finney house and Tom grew convinced that his small physical appearance had stunted his progress. At just four feet nine and weighing less than five stone, he was certainly no heavyweight. But, then again, neither was Alex James – and he had made it.

Tom's progress had already won him a place in the Holme Slack junior side, playing in the Preston and District League against the likes of Middleforth and Leyland Motors. The disappointment suffered from his PNE rebuff was beginning to heal but his father remained determined to try and open a few doors for his talented son.

At this particular time, Alf was working as a waiter in The Sumners Hotel in Fulwood, which was, by pure coincidence, being used by North End to house their then trainer, Will Scott. Alf was nothing if not shrewd, and he made himself known to Scott before relating the story of Tom's unsuccessful application. Scott, a thoughtful and trusting man, was impressed by the waiter and said: 'So he can play a bit, can he? Well, send him along and we'll have a look for ourselves.'

Shortly after this fortunate meeting, a letter duly arrived asking Tom to report to Ashton Park for a trial match. On the summer evening in question Scott pulled the lads to one side to offer encouragement before selecting two teams – the blues and the whites. Tom turned out at inside left for the former and, although disappointed not to have figured on the scoresheet, he was reasonably happy with his display. That eventful evening at Ashton Park is forever implanted in Tom's memory:

'Will Scott told me to play number 10 for the blues but when I got over to where the shirts were laid out on the grass a much bigger lad had already pulled on the inside-left jersey.

'When I asked him for it he told me what to do in no uncertain terms. I was close to tears but one of the men running the trial came over to settle the matter. He turned to the big lad and said "Give the kid your shirt, son – he won't be on long anyway!" '

Unlike many of the others, however, he was actually allowed a full game, not simply substituted at half-time. Scott and his chairman looked on from the sidelines. They were suitably impressed with the general standard but one lad had really caught their eye – a fragile but skilful inside forward who had prompted every attacking move made by the blues.

At the final whistle both men beckoned Tom over and the chairman took his breath away by offering him a place on the groundstaff. He was speechless and much of the verbal detail, including the offer of a wage of £2 10s a week, passed right over his head. Mr Taylor advised Tom to talk things over with his father before making a decision. Tom agreed but knew that his father would have no objections; after all, Alf had masterminded the opportunity in the first place.

But Tom was wrong and, to his utter amazement, his father's clear response was an unambiguous and definite 'No!' Alf reasoned that Tom should concentrate on learning his plumbing trade. His future as a footballer as yet rested on no more than one man's speculation and he should, for the time being at least, enjoy his soccer as an amateur and re-assess the situation in a few years. Joining the groundstaff represented a gamble and it wasn't worth the risk. Quite frankly, there were too many pitfalls.

Tom listened in disbelief. What was his father trying to do – ruin his life? Here was the chance he had always wanted and the only person standing in his way was his own father. His anger soon turned to tears but Alf was not for relenting.

The following morning Tom decided to seek the opinion of his employer, but Harry Pilkington offered little in the way of consolation. 'Sorry lad, but your father's right. Finish your time and play as an amateur', said Harry. When most of his workmates shared the same view, Tom began to realise that perhaps his dad was acting in his best interests. He remembers these agonising days well:

'The prospect of joining the groundstaff was almost too good to be true, even if the job did mainly comprise of cleaning boots and sweeping terraces.

'When my father blocked it on the bus ride home I thought he had taken leave of his senses. He reckoned that if I failed to make the grade I would be tossed out like an old rag. I thought my father to be selfish at the time but I have since realised the opposite to be the case. He wanted me to become a footballer as much as I did. To be negative was difficult for him – especially as we needed the money too.'

Indeed, long after his playing days were over, Tom repeated that very same advice to promising young footballers whose minds are rarely capable of seeing any further than the glory attached to joining a professional club.

As it happens, Tom took well to his plumbing and enjoyed its variety and interesting workload. Had his football career backfired, he would have had no qualms about making it a full-time job in due course.

North End were happy enough to accept Tom's reasoning when he called in at the ground to reject their offer. Instead, they signed him on as an amateur. Financially, he was turning his back on £2 10s to go back to his 6s-a-week plumbing job. Such a move made him eligible for the North End B team, however, and, as well as turning out in matches, he trained on Tuesday and Thursday evenings – usually reporting in straight from work.

As in all League clubs, there was enormous rivalry between the A and B sides, mainly because the lads in the A team were from the groundstaff and so considered themselves superior in every way to the 'working-class' B brigade. But both teams enjoyed great success and some of their winning margins in District League fixtures underlined the immediate success of the PNE 'nursery'. For example, Tom can remember being on the right side of a 22-0 drubbing and then on another memorable occasion scoring seven goals on his own.

After one such victory Tom was asked to report to Will Scott. He had played well and presumed he was in for a pat on the back. He could not have been more wrong. Scott boomed: 'It seems to me, Finney, that you want a ball all of your own. You have forgotten that there are other players in the forward line. Stop being so greedy.'

Tom's move to the right wing, the position in which he was eventually to play most frequently, came completely by chance. His form had won him promotion to North End's under-18 team for the 1938 season. The youth team was the place youngsters were groomed for future League stardom but Tom was consistently denied his favoured inside-left position through the outstanding form of the lad who had already denied him a place in the Preston Town Team – Tommy Hough. Even Tom's level temperament and placid nature were tested to the limit by sheer frustration. Match after match, he would turn up at Deepdale full of hope, only to see Hough slowly killing his dreams.

Then, right out of the blue, came an unexpected opportunity. Preston youths were getting ready for a mid-week home match against Manchester United (including the likes of Johnny Aston and Charlie Mitten) and Tom reported in as usual for his role as twelfth man-cum spectator. A crowd of around 7,000 was gathering when Tom received the news that he was playing. Eddie Burke had been unable to shrug off an injury and Tom was to take his place . . . on the right flank.

The prospect caused him immediate distress. He had never played there before and convinced himself it could prove the beginning of the end. He would look a fool, a left footer on the right wing – how ridiculous, how unfair.

But play he did and, after heeding Will Scott's advice of 'be as direct as you can, get crosses over clean and fast with your right foot and have a go at goal with your left cutting in', Tom turned in an excellent performance. Preston won 3-0 and Tom was instrumental in setting up two of the goals.

Chairman Taylor, who rarely missed a match of any level at Deepdale, was the first man to greet Tom in the corridor afterwards. Taylor was adamant that the right wing was going to be the position Finney was to make his name. How right he was but, initially at least, Tom was not so sure. He would have to learn a whole new ball game, a different style of play altogether. From being a foraging footballer working to lay on thoughtful goal chances for his colleagues, he had to change emphasis to concentrate on high speed, the knack of passing a defender on the run and, most importantly, he had to become completely two-footed.

The theory in the late '30s was that no one could possibly succeed at the top if one foot was only good for standing on. Tom practised improving his right-foot ball control for hour after hour, day after day and week after week. He recalls those early, formative days:

> 'Most footballers then were extremely dedicated. Preston was a big club with some big name players and, in the likes of Bill Shankly, we had people who oozed enthusiasm.
>
> 'It was no hardship for me to put in extra hours and I worked on the right foot until it became as strong as my left. That involved many afternoons but I was always in the company of the senior players, who regularly stayed behind for a spell of head tennis.'

B ill Shankly had arrived at Deepdale from Carlisle United in 1933 when he was eighteen. He celebrated his nineteenth birthday in December of that year by earning promotion to the first team, in which he made 85 consecutive appearances before being dropped for one game – in September 1935.

The best of his 17 seasons as a North Ender was 1937-8, when he gained a Cup winner's medal and an international cap and would have been playing in the League constantly but for being chosen to play for Scotland against England at Wembley. Apart from war-time football, during which he contributed to Preston's winning of the Regional League and War Cup double in 1940-41, Shankly appeared in the North End first team 341 times. The Scottish international wing half left in early April 1949 to become manager of Carlisle, in succession to Ivor Broadis. It was to be the first rung of a ladder which took him right to the top in management at Liverpool.

Tom insists that the attitude of Shankly was a source of general encouragement to everyone at the club and himself in particular:

> 'Shanks was unique, a complete one-off. He lived for the game. He caused a great stir many years later when he described football as more important than life or death, but it was a statement that didn't surprise me. And he certainly meant it.
>
> 'He was great with the kids and the theory he used to hammer home to us was that no opponent is better than you until he proves it out on the park.
>
> 'He didn't know what defeat meant and he kept the very same

principles right through his soccer life. A fitness fanatic, he set
the example that everyone followed. He frowned upon smoking
and drinking and had no time for cheats or dodgers, no matter
how skilful they might have been as players.

'I had a lot to thank Shanks for – and so did scores of other
players."

The departure of the great Scot seemed sure to leave a hole, not only
in the Preston team but also in the very foundation of the club. Within
a matter of seven months, however, Shankly's void had been well and
truly filled by another, equally enthusiastic, ebullient and effervescent
Scot – Tommy Docherty.

Like his predecessor, Docherty was to carve out a special place in
the Deepdale annals and also make his mark in management. He
never found Shankly's recipe for success, but certainly made his
presence felt, especially at Manchester United.

Docherty was 21 and a reserve wing half or inside forward at
Glasgow Celtic who arrived for a fee of £4,000 on the eve of Bonfire
Night, 1949. He had come through the Scottish club's junior ranks
before, in 1946, he was conscripted and served for two years in
Palestine with the First Battalion of the Highland Light Infantry. He
made his initial appearance with the North End first eleven at Leeds
on Christmas Eve as an emergency outside left. It was not until the
Hull City game at Deepdale a month later that he first shared in his
best position at right half. He earned the description of being a
'Shankly type' and it was coincidental that more than 16 years before
his first game at right half against Hull, Shankly himself had made his
senior debut also at Deepdale and also against Hull. Docherty, rated a
first-class team man, strong in both attack and defence, was an all-
action player whom Finney liked and admired.

Capped for the first time against Wales in 1952, he also went on to
captain his country. He left Deepdale in 1958 to join Arsenal for a fee
of £20,000. Doc had become unsettled at North End and had registered
at least half-a-dozen transfer requests. One instance concerned a time
when his wife was due to have a baby and the Dochertys were living in
a club house with an outside lavatory. Doc thought it wasn't good
enough and told the club in no uncertain terms. As a result of this and
other frictions with the club, he went on the list.

Docherty was to return – as a North End manager – in the early
1980s. He arrived to an emotional welcome on the main entrance steps
from Finney but he was unable to turn the club's fortunes around and
got the sack after just a few months.

Being surrounded by such strong and able personalities when he
was growing and developing as a footballer undoubtedly helped Tom.

All the youngsters were motivated to work and train hard, but none more so than he. Will Scott came to his support by agreeing to stay on late to help him get his game together. His play was becoming more and more polished and impressive and he won a regular place in the youth team.

Tom won four trophies, two cups and a couple of medals playing in the B team and took part in several curtain-raisers to Central League action at Deepdale. It was at this point that Tom began to believe, for the first time, that he was making progress towards the ultimate goal of becoming a professional.

The atmosphere enveloping the B team was akin to senior status. They trained in the same gymnasium as the first-team players, stripped in the same dressing room and wallowed in the same plunge bath. Even the kit came perfectly, precisely and professionally packaged. The youngsters were also allowed access to the inner sanctum – the Boardroom – to hear tactical talks from the management. Blackboards and lessons had never been quite so popular during school days.

Brother Joe was by this time playing on a regular basis for Netherfield in the Lancashire Combination and rumour was rife that Tom would also join the Cumbrian outfit. Soon, however, an offer was to come from a different quarter, Preston's neighbour and arch-rival, Blackburn Rovers. Tom's father had stayed close friends with Reg Taylor, a former Deepdale employee who had joined the staff at Ewood Park. He had already arranged for Joe to train with Rovers twice a week and thought it would be a sound, sensible idea if his two sons joined the same club. Rather fortunately for Preston, North End just managed to get in first. They contacted Tom by post to offer him a trial before any firm plans could be laid down. Without a doubt, had that letter been delayed for just a couple of days the whole shape of English football might have taken a different route and Rovers, rather than North End, would have reaped the benefit of having Tom within their ranks.

His patience and dedication, coupled with that special brand of determination inherited from his father, had made the young Finney a footballer of considerable maturity and polish well ahead of his years and on New Year's Day 1940, four months after the outbreak of the Second World War, came the most important step in his career so far.

North End's Chairman, Taylor, contacted Alf to request a meeting. Alf met up with Tom, still in his overalls, straight from work and they made their way to Taylor's rather grand residence on Victoria Road, Fulwood. After a short discussion it was unanimously agreed that the time was ripe for Tom to turn professional. Tom offered to pop over to Deepdale the following morning to sign the necessary forms but such a suggestion failed to meet with the chairman's approval. Quite unbeknown to the Finneys, Taylor had laid on a taxi and arranged for Deepdale secretary, George Howarth, to work late on what he had termed 'a special assignment'.

The trio drove to Deepdale in style – sharing a silence born out of common satisfaction – before Tom put his name on the dotted line. He was to repeat that very signature thousands of times over the next 20 years. The smallness of the reward – 10 shillings a week – did not dampen the enthusiasm of the moment. Money hardly seemed relevant; Tom had begun a new stage in his life and, for him, that counted for everything.

Tom Finney never played for North End reserves – an unusual omission caused by force of circumstance. When the time came for promotion from the junior to the Central League side, there was a slight problem . . . the country was at war. Like many of his generation Tom had to wait several years for the hostilities to cease before making his full Football League debut.

Not that he ever looked back in frustration or annoyance at his inability to graduate through normal peace-time channels. He was usually able to find plenty of opportunity to play and he benefited greatly from playing with and alongside some of the country's top players; besides, he also considers service life to have been of great value.

Tom had been to morning service at St Jude's Church in Preston on the morning of Sunday September 3 and had called at the home of a plumbing colleague, Tommy Johnson, when he heard that war had been declared. Football thoughts disappeared from mind immediately, although he did wonder what might happen. Was his career doomed for disaster before it had even started? He has often thought since that his father was wise to block North End's initial move to take him on as a full timer – for when war broke out the lads who had signed and who had served on the groundstaff quickly found themselves out of a job.

At first, Tom had assumed that he would begin his professional career carrying out the menial chores around the club and staying in the background to master his craft. The arrival of war seemed to complicate matters, especially when the Football League itself was disbanded. Nevertheless, the Government decreed that soccer would provide a useful source of entertainment for war workers and a significant boost for morale and, within a matter of months, Tom found that he was playing first-class football rather sooner than he had anticipated.

The opening date of the 1940-41 season saw Tom at Anfield, selected on the right wing against Liverpool in what was to become known as Regional War-Time Soccer. Air raids and a multitude of restrictions failed to dampen enthusiasm on the pitch or on the terraces. War-time soccer was to prove immensely popular, with a high standard of play and player on offer. Clubs, struggling to field many of their regular and registered stars, introduced 'guests' but, with players unable to confirm their availability until the very last minute, games were often left in considerable doubt right up to kick off.

On his debut at Anfield, Tom found himself up against the likes of guests Don Welsh and Stan Cullis, both of whom were England internationals. Cyril Done scored twice for Liverpool 'United' to leave Preston pointless. On the short journey home the North End coach party was caught in a massive air raid, flashes lighting up the Merseyside skyline and bombs dropping all around.

Preston's performances improved match by match until, in a shorter season than normal, they won 18 out of 29 games to finish up as Northern Section champions. That achievement was as surprising as it was outstanding for, when war was declared, North End had been struggling in nineteenth position in the old First Division.

The club followed up its triumph by an even more dramatic and exciting campaign to claim the War-Time Cup to complete a notable 'double'. Finney was enjoying it all thoroughly. Here he was, still adjusting to the rigours of first-team football, yet all set to play at Wembley – a venue later to become his second home.

The cup ran on a two-legged, home-and-away basis and North End's record went:

Round One: v Bury (home) 4-4, (away) 2-1.
Round Two: v Bolton (home) 4-1, (away) 2-0.
Round Three: v Tranmere (home) 12-1, (away) 8-1.
Round Four: v Manchester City (home) 2-1, (away) 3-0.
Semi-Final: v Newcastle (home) 2-0, (away) 0-0.
Final: v Arsenal: 1-1, replay 2-1.

It was a striking performance by any standard, made yet more remarkable by the absence of players like Shankly, Hughie O'Donnell and Andy Beattie. The trio missed several matches after consistently failing to obtain leave from their units.

The Cup contest opened in February and in the first game, a 4-4 thriller at Bury, Finney began in sparkling form, with two goals. His scoring prowess was to continue throughout but it took a couple of goals from Shankly, in a rare appearance, to see off Newcastle United and make sure of a Wembley showdown with Arsenal.

Earlier, the massacre of poor old Tranmere – in which teens of goals made up the aggregate difference – didn't go down at all well among the opposition's elder brethren. As North End trooped from the field

with an aggregate total of twenty goals under their belts after the
second leg, one Tranmere player, clearly annoyed and doubtless
embarrassed, turned to Finney and uttered: 'There was no need to
score so many. You shouldn't have rubbed it in like that in front of our
supporters.'

Returning from the Newcastle semi-final the Preston party stayed in
Carlisle and it was while out for an early evening stroll with his good
friend Andy McLaren that Tom first felt the impact of the imminent
trip to Wembley. He went weak at the knees.

He shared a room with McLaren and neither had ever been to stay
at a large hotel. This was their first season as professionals and both
were apprehensive about the accommodation. The first taste of
football luxury was sweet, but strange. The very question of leaving
their shoes outside the bedroom door for overnight cleaning gave
instant cause for doubt. They were informed that the hotel staff would
gladly polish the footwear but Tom and Andy were unimpressed,
fearing that they would awake to find the shoes had been stolen. After
a long discussion on a matter of apparent trivia, they decided to err on
the side of caution. A pair of shoes to a lad of nineteen earning just ten
shillings a week represented a considerable item of expenditure. But
Finney and McLaren found themselves the odd men out at breakfast
the following day when all their team-mates turned up with shoes
gleaming!

The decision to stage the final at Wembley was hardly geographi-
cally fair to Preston. The venue, intimidating and awesome at the best
of times, seemed certain to provide Arsenal with a distinct psychological advantage, especially as tickets were only on sale at the stadium
itself or at Highbury, Arsenal's home. Indeed, the partisan 65,000
crowd included just 600 Preston followers.

Fortunately, Andy Beattie, a great Deepdale favourite, was available
after missing much of the season. North End decided to use his
expertise and, most important, his inside knowledge – Beattie had
guested for Arsenal and was therefore well placed to give a calculated
assessment of the Gunners' likely style and formation. In spite of the
fact that Preston were Northern champions, however, few outsiders
gave the Lancashire lads much of a prayer and it was thought that
Finney was likely to be overshadowed and out-thought by his direct
opponent Eddie Hapgood, the England full back and skipper.

The teams lined up as follows. Arsenal: Marks, Scott, Hapgood,
Crayston, Joy, Collett, Kirchen, Jones, Compton (L), Bastin and
Compton (D). Preston North End: Fairbrother, Scott, Gallimore,
Shankly, Smith, Beattie (A), Finney, McLaren, Dougal, Beattie (B),
O'Donnell.

Finney, who had been to the stadium as part of Preston's 1938 Cup

Final party, was nervous but not over-awed. Tom Smith, his captain, had got the northern troops in a combative frame of mind just minutes before the kick-off. Smith, a proud man, had rallied his men by saying: 'Look here, lads, there is no cause for worry. Arsenal or no Arsenal we can win this Cup. I know it, and so do you. So let's get out there and prove it!'

Fighting talk, but the signs looked ominous for North End as early as the third minute when Arsenal won a penalty for handball. Fortune favoured the underdogs, though, when Leslie Compton's shot cannoned against an upright and bounced out to safety.

Inspired, North End swept on to the offensive and took the lead as Finney left Hapgood for dead (the international admitted afterwards that he had been amazed to see a right winger dribbling so brilliantly with his left foot) and, when the cross came over as accurately as always, McLaren supplied the finishing touch.

Preston stayed comfortably in control but failed to find the necessary second goal, despite a series of swift and penetrating raids into enemy territory. They paid the price for misgivings in front of goal when the more famous of the Compton brothers, Denis, stole clear to equalise. Preston left Wembley a little aggrieved but their disappointment was tempered by the knowledge that the replay would be staged at the far friendlier Ewood Park, just ten miles from home, in Blackburn.

Arsenal recalled Ted Drake and Preston introduced Cliff Mansley for the injured Bill Scott. It was quite an occasion, too, for goalkeeper Jack Fairbrother, then a policeman in the Blackburn Constabulary. The attendance was limited to 45,000, though the game was played before an audience 10,000 down on capacity. Numbered among the spectators were Polish airmen, Canadian military and Czech soldiers.

After Drake had twice threatened early on, North End assumed control with a goal from Bobby Beattie, whose very inclusion had been shrouded in uncertainty; Beattie failed to team up with the North End coach when it left Deepdale for the short drive across to East Lancashire and most of the conversation on board revolved around how Preston would re-organise in his absence. They need not have worried, for the first man to greet them on arrival at Ewood was none other than Beattie, who had arrived early after being released on leave from the RAF.

The opening goal came on 50 minutes when Finney set up a move for Jimmy Dougal and McLaren to continue before Beattie toe-poked the ball home. Arsenal's cause was further hampered by an injury to Drake, who was forced to leave the field, but they found a way back when Bernard Joy's speculative shot caught a cruel deflection off an unwitting Len Gallimore and nestled in the back of the North

End net.

Arsenal's joy was shortlived. Within a minute and without a Highbury player having touched the ball, North End were ahead again. A sweeping attack, with Finney one of five men involved, ended with Beattie again popping up in the right place at the right time.

The Cup belonged to Preston and skipper Smith's delight was obvious as he led North End up the steps to receive the trophy from Everton chairman, W. C. Cuff.

Finney's own contribution to the final had been ordinary, certainly by his high standards, but one week later in a game which North End needed to win to clinch the Championship, he was back to his dazzling best.

North End secured their double with an emphatic 6-0 victory over Liverpool. McLaren, a quick and mercurial inside forward with a nose for goals, scored all six and Finney had a match to remember. Some say that the wing play that day was as good if not better than anything he ever produced.

North End's Championship record read: Played 29, Won 18, Drawn 7, Lost 4, For 81, Against 37. Finney did not miss a single fixture – League or Cup – and the following season he again started in superlative form. He had made 33 appearances when, in April 1942, he received his call-up papers from the Army.

Initially, Trooper T. Finney 7958274 of the Royal Armoured Corps, managed to stay closely involved in the game, albeit away from Preston. He spent three months on intensive training at Bovington before being 'transferred' (for the only time in his life!), to Catterick. He soon blew the dust off his boots to join the 'guest' circuit. Few people are aware that 'one-club Finney' actually turned out in the colours of Newcastle, Southampton and Bolton.

There was rarely any opportunity for training; escaping for Saturday afternoon action was hard enough, but the toil and sweat of working a double shift proved well worthwhile.

Tom's service opponents included Raich Carter and Len Shackleton. Impressive showings led to the Preston star winning his first representative honour – selection for a Football Association XI for a challenge fixture against the RAF. Also named in the FA side was the Deepdale goalkeeper Jack Fairbrother. Listed for the RAF . . . Eddie Hapgood, Bill Shankly and a right winger Tom was to cross swords with on many future occasions . . . Stanley Matthews!

The game, played at Stoke City and won 4-3 by the FA XI, was a thriller, with Matthews turning on the magic in front of his own home fans. Indeed, that very afternoon saw the beginning of the Finney-Matthews controversy which was to rumble throughout the following twenty years and more. Neither player liked the comparisons which were being drawn between them but they were powerless to prevent the speculation.

In early December 1942, Tom was ready and trained to travel overseas. He was instructed to join a troop ship and the only clue given as regards destination was the issue of a tropical kit. The 'troop ship' turned out to be the converted *Queen Mary* and the 7,000 servicemen were bound for Egypt.

Chapter Three

Love . . . and war

ALANCASHIRE teenager's social life in the years leading up to the Second World War tended to be divided fairly evenly between dance halls, night classes and cinemas. Preston seemed to boast a picture house on every street corner and, besides the established ballrooms like Worsley's and the 'AD', most churches in the town held regular weekend dance nights. St Jude's, St Ignatius' and St Mary's were typical of these, with St Jude's considered the best because of its 'posh' brick-built exterior. On a Saturday night St Jude's was the place to be seen – a teenage heaven in an environment free from the watchful gaze of parents.

Alcohol was forbidden at St Jude's and the only liquid refreshment on offer to the youngsters was of a soft variety. Many of the more daring lads, frustrated by this state of affairs and fuelled by mischievous excitement, would obtain a special pass out for an hour or so to call in at a couple of adjacent pubs.

Drink proved neither a fascination nor an attraction to the young Finney. Indeed, he was getting on towards his twenty-first birthday before he as much as sampled the taste of beer for the first time. He didn't like it much then and doesn't care for it much now.

The dance gang at St Jude's comprised the same faces every week; familiarity often led to friendships, from which romances often developed. So it was that at St Jude's in 1938 Tom met up with a 16-year-old girl by the name of Elsie Noblett – now Mrs Tom Finney of 44 years' standing.

Tom and Elsie were aware of each other's existence long before verbal contact was eventually struck. Elsie, the youngest of four children belonging to Jim and Ruth Noblett, lived on Barlow Street in Preston. After leaving Moor Park Methodist School at 14, Elsie had taken up employment at a local company called Margerisons Soap Factory.

Along with her close friend, Olive Poole (later to act as her bridesmaid), Elsie was noted for her prowess on the dance floor. Tom, despite his remarkable skills at football, had two left feet when the band struck up; nonetheless, one particular weekend, he and Elsie were thrown together. . . by accident! Elsie takes up the story:

'Olive was especially keen on Tom and she persuaded me to go over and find out whether he was free or dating the girl we had seen him with on occasions. We knew he was interested in football but that meant little to either of us and was no great attraction. I didn't come from a sporting background and Preston North End was little more than the name of a club down Deepdale way as far as I was concerned.

'I went over to chat with Tom and when it became clear that he and his friend were both available Olive insisted that we should make a positive move.'

At the dance with his boyhood friend and choir colleague, Alf Lorimer, Tom explains:

'I had known Elsie and Olive for about six months through seeing them at the Saturday dances. Elsie was a few months younger than me and I had chipped in for the odd "excuse me" but, quite frankly, I was something of an embarrassment on the dance floor. I could just about get round, whereas the two girls were excellent dancers.

'That Saturday we made our acquaintance and afterwards Alf took Elsie home and I escorted Olive!'

The four teenagers then decided to make a date for the following night at the cinema. Tom remembers:

'We met up as planned and made our way to the Rialto which used to stand on St Paul's Road. We were a little on the latish side and when we got in the film had already started and the place was in darkness.

'Elsie followed me down the aisle and into our row with Alf and Olive tagging on right behind. When we got to our seat numbers we discovered they were "doubles" and, like it or not, Elsie was obliged to sit by me. It wasn't planned but that incident sparked off our courtship.'

The young couple agreed to a six-month trial but the relationship proved a great success, with Tom being particularly well received by his prospective in-laws. Indeed, Ruth Noblett, saddened on learning that Tom had lost his mother so young, became a source of great inspiration and help. Jim, meanwhile, played his part by becoming increasingly interested in the affairs of the town's football club and in the developing career of young Tom.

The dawn of war brought immense strain on young lovers the nation over and when Tom received his call-up for active service in 1942 he managed to see Elsie just twice in three years. Elsie recalls:

'When we realised that Tom was going away and likely to be away for some considerable time we decided to get engaged. It was Easter 1942 and Tom really wanted us to get married there and then. Mother blocked that idea by stating that she considered me too young.

'Of course it was a wrench to lose your fiancé to the other side of the world but everyone was in the same predicament and you had to accept the facts and get on with your life. We kept in touch through letters but neither of us was a particularly good writer and there was often quite a gap between contact.'

As we have seen, Tom did play war-time football before being called up; after he set sail for Egypt, however, Tom felt that other affairs would necessarily take precedence:

'I must confess that I thought my soccer was over for a while, except, that is, for the friendly banter in the barrack room. We were posted to a camp directly under the Pyramids and almost within earshot of the famous Mena House where Churchill, Stalin and Roosevelt used to meet.

'Learning the profession of soldiering was tough enough and football occupied only a minor part in my thoughts, except for the times I would lie awake at night thinking of home and how war was robbing so many of us of the chance to develop our soccer careers. We did manage occasional kickabouts on rock-hard make-shift sand pitches near the billets but football was very much a bottom priority.

'The desert campaign had started in earnest and we had plenty of supply work to do, not to mention the rigours of day-long manoeuvres which left you drained and close to exhaustion. The heat alone was a killer.'

Tom then received a surprise posting to Abbassia and it was there, right out of the blue, that he was invited to travel to Cairo for a trial with a forces side called The Wanderers. The team, organised exclusively to provide a source of light entertainment for the weary troops, included a host of top-class players including Bolton's Tommy Woodward, Middlesborough's Mickey Fenton and the Newcastle trio of Ted Swinburne, Harry Clifton and Don Kelly.

Tom's trial went well and, after he had played a starring role and scored a couple of goals for good measure, his place in the Wanderers' line-up was guaranteed. He travelled extensively across Palestine and Syria, playing against service teams and Egyptian national elevens.

One opponent, albeit on the substitute's bench, during an Egyptian fixture was none other than Omar Sharif, later to find fame as an actor of international stature.

The game itself differed completely from what the Englishmen had grown used to back home but it was the attitude of the supporters which Tom remembers best:

'Talk about fanatics – those people were unbelievable. They would take along their prayer mats and kit themselves out in fezes and white robes. Then they would crouch down in the area behind our goal and go absolutely crazy whenever their team attacked. But, if we had the audacity to try and get across the half-way line or, heaven forbid, even score a goal – well, they would fall to their knees, face Mecca and pray for an equaliser.'

Not quite Old Trafford or Deepdale but the football at least brought some respite:

'To be brutally frank it was a relief to get out there onto the pitch, irrespective of conditions underfoot or crowd behaviour. It was fun, or at least that is the way we all looked upon it. I can't speak for the others but I know I often had a terrible guilty complex about playing. It seemed grossly unfair that football was offered to those talented enough to make the team while the others were left to get on with the fighting.

'I even went so far as to express those sentiments to the Commanding Officer but he was far from sympathetic and stressed that the footballing soldiers were playing a major role in maintaining morale.

'All the Unit and Depot sides were named after famous British clubs and I regularly played against the likes of Huddersfield Town, Glasgow Rangers and Arsenal! My own club was not that well known – Bovington United – and we didn't fare too well. Our main claim to fame was in reaching the semi-final of the Cairo Cup. It turned out to be a humdinger of a game with Rangers but we lost by the odd three goals in 13!'

With The Wanderers Finney derived great satisfaction and he recalls one particular tour, right across Jerusalem, Beirut and Tel Aviv, which took in 13 matches in 23 days.

'We were transported around on the back of lorries or on trains and the travelling was gruelling. When I hear modern-day players talking about the effort involved in sitting on a luxury coach up and down the country's motorway network once a fortnight . . . my heart bleeds for them!

'But no one dared to complain for there was no doubt in anybody's mind that the good footballers were very much in the highly privileged minority. There was plenty of skill and no shortage of endeavour in the matches and everyone was treated as professionally as possible.'

Finney, who was later to speak out in favour of the 'plastic' pitch which Preston North End laid amid great controversy in 1985 when the hallowed Deepdale turf was uprooted and sold off to supporters, reckoned that his experience on rock hard surfaces in Egypt improved his game.

'I am convinced that my touch got better and better and I certainly gained a yard of pace out there. Many other players blossomed too and I understand that there were instances of players who were unknown prior to army service getting tempting offers to turn professional when they returned home some years later.'

George Davis, another Lancastrian posted overseas, remembers trudging for miles to see Finney in action for The Wanderers. 'As soon as we heard of a game being staged, we couldn't get there quickly enough', said George who now lives in Lostock Hall, just outside Preston. The date was March 17th 1943, the venue Aleppo and the game Wanderers versus the British Army.

George still holds a copy of a single sheet programme produced for the afternoon contest and the Wanderers line-up read Rayner (Doncaster Rovers), Duckhouse (Birmingham), Cox (Sheffield United), Bell (West Ham), Kelly (Newcastle), Telfer (Falkirk), Finney (PNE), King (Liverpool), Burgess (Army), Galloway (Glasgow Rangers) and Vickers (PNE).

Tom's posting to Italy took him down to the southern tip and a township called Foggia. Encouraged by his Egyptian experience he immediately made moves to set up a team, only to receive a dressing down from the base captain. The officer in question had no time for soccer or the 'dodgers' who played the game and he wasted no time in despatching trouble-maker Finney to the 9th Q. R. Lancers and, within a day, Tom found himself literally in the firing line. He drove with a squadron of Honey tanks and faced month after month of gruelling action with the Eighth Army. Soccer was all but forgotten.

'I was mainly a tank driver or a mechanic and found myself thrown into immediate action as a replacement for lads who had been killed the previous day. The danger and loss of life was constantly with you. You sensed it and feared it but you hadn't time to worry over much. It became a job of work.

'The most distressing part came when you returned to base at night to discover that some of your pals had gone down that day. Nevertheless, the army experience was an invaluable one for me. It taught me the true value of companionship and friendship. There were men from all walks of life, but everyone was on an equal footing. Backgrounds of wealth or title counted for absolutely nothing.

'It was a real eye-opener. The heartache of listening to grown men, hard men, sitting up in bed crying at night; the empty feeling when a death was announced.

'When I was called up to go overseas I can recall my father walking down to Preston Railway Station with me and trying to cheer me up. When the time came to say our goodbyes, he just broke down and cried on the spot.

'It was my first stint away from home but I wouldn't have missed it and I was one of the fortunate ones. It taught me the lesson of life and my fitness was never greater. When I was demobbed I was around 10st 3lb and as wick as a whippet.'

Finney was considered a competent soldier who was always keen to play a full and active part in the collective effort. But, through football, he was blessed with consistent good fortune. The Allies had made good progress in Italy and the commanding officers decided to reward the efforts of the men with some relaxation. Comfort packages arrived and football became part of Tom's life once again.

Ironically, the man in charge of the Eighth Army side was Andy Beattie, captain of Preston and Scotland and the line-up had enough star names to warrant an international status all of its own. Tom was handed the opportunity to get involved and, once again, the chance to sharpen his skills under the guidance of established players like Frank Squires, Charlie Adam, Beattie and Willie Thornton.

Thornton, one of the greatest players in the history of Glasgow Rangers, was one of the soldiers pulled out of the front line in 1944 to play in the touring forces team led by the legendary Stan Cullis. A wireless operator in the Scottish Horse Regiment, he met up with Finney for a game in Rimini. The forces side received a sound beating. Thornton, decorated during the Sicilian Campaign and involved in the battle in which renowned cricketer Hedley Verity lost his life, remembers the occasion well.

'Tom and I were fortunate to get a break from the fighting and so relieved, but, before the game could start, engineers had to sweep the pitch for mines! We should have been on danger money for those mines were capable of blowing your foot clean off. You might say that we all went into the fixture with a certain degree of apprehension!"

'Cullis and Beattie were both Sergeant Majors and they pulled in George Hamilton of Aberdeen, Charlie Adam, Tom and myself to tour around Italy to teach the finer points of football to the troops.

'Tom and I became good chums and after the war was over we played against each other in a Scotland versus England international at Hampden Park.'

That day, April 10 1948, the big Eighth Army chief, Field Marshal Lord Montgomery of Alamein, was the guest of honour: 'Monty came up to me beforehand and wished me well, telling me not to let the English win. Little did I know that he had just come from giving the same command – in reverse of course – to Tom!'

During the half-time interval a knock came on the England dressing room door and in walked Monty, who made a direct line for Finney, scorer of the game's opening goal.

He said 'Congratulations on that goal. It was a fine effort from a man who fought alongside me.' A few days later a letter from the famous Field Marshal arrived at Tom's Preston home and read: 'My Dear Finney, I was delighted to meet up with you once again in Glasgow and especially to see you score. May you score many more. I send you my programme from the game which I have signed and a photograph you may care to have.' The photograph, also signed, showed Montgomery in his famous beret and said: 'To T. Finney, left wing for England at Hampden Park on April 10th 1948 and scorer of England's first goal.'

Thornton and Finney had been opponents before, in 1941, when Preston and Rangers had met at Ibrox in the match organised between the restive English and Scottish League champions. The trophy room at Ibrox still houses the special silver casket awarded to Rangers following their victory.

Thornton had joined Rangers in 1936 and on the second day of the following year had become the youngest player to pull on a first-team jersey at the club. He was just 16. An outstanding centre forward who went on to play 300 games despite losing six years to the war, he was capped eight times by Scotland. Now employed on a part-time basis with Rangers entertaining visitors in the Ibrox executive suite which carries his name, he lost contact with his new-found friend after the Rimini game but renewed contact when the Central Mediterranean Forces instigated soccer's first ever soccer coaching school. His opinion of Finney remains unchanged:

'It was Tom's unassuming nature which most appealed to me. As a footballer he had no equal and I was lucky to play with the two finest wingers in history, Finney of England and Willie Waddell of Scotland. Willie was a wizard and so was Stanley Matthews who once guested for Rangers, but neither could match Finney's aggression. That killer instinct made him the tops.

'He was a fitness fanatic – not many men could have been called away from war and placed straight into an international match and then done themselves justice. Finney did. He had a stunning turn of pace, great balance and two devastating feet. If anyone had an excuse to become big-headed it was Tom.

'He was also an inspiration as a soldier . . . a tougher man than many realise. We both owed a debt to Beattie who would get us up at six o'clock in the morning every morning for special training before the heat became overbearing.'

Beattie, another highly successful manager in later life, with Huddersfield Town, also became a great ally and trusted advisor to Tom. When the war was drawing to a close he would escort Finney, Thornton and others around Italy and Austria to play competitive matches against service sides. Interest in the game had been re-kindled. Crowds were turning up in their thousands just for inter-army games.

Tom's outstanding memory centres around an appearance for the CMF against at Army XI.

'Matt Busby captained the opposition who also included Frank Swift, while we had three internationals in our line-up. The game was staged in Naples and 30,000 turned up. It was all treated so seriously that they even went so far as to sign up the services of a neutral referee.

'Busby, 13 years my senior and one of the veterans on view, was magnificent and we had to settle for a 2-2 draw after holding the lead twice. It was thrill-a-minute stuff.'

Following another service game in Austria some weeks later Tom was given a rude awakening.

'It was the middle of the night. I was brought out of my slumber and told to report post haste to the duty officer. I was handed a telegram from the English Football Association who were requesting that the Army should release me to play for England in an unofficial international in Switzerland.

'I could hardly take it all in. All the way back to the billet, still in a semi-conscious state, I remember thinking I must be dreaming. Here I was, a footballer without much in the way of experience, stationed in a foreign country miles from my home and family, being told that I was to play for my country. It was absolutely unbelievable.

'There wasn't much time for it all to sink in and I was escorted to the Austrian-Italian border where I met up with Andy Beattie who accompanied me on the first leg of my long haul back to England via a flight from Naples.

'On the plane I thought there might just be a chance of a quick visit to Preston to see Elsie but the governing bodies would not permit such an interruption to what was a hectic schedule. The Swiss didn't allow uniforms so, for the first time in what felt like a lifetime, I was able to discard the khaki and pull on some civvies.

'We boarded another plane to Zurich and went on to play the game in Berne, losing 3-1. Frankly, the Swiss were far more prepared and just too good for us.'

Within a few days the FA party headed back to London and Tom managed to secure a fortnight's leave. It was the chance at long last to see Elsie and be re-united with family and friends.

'It is always a funny feeling to return home, even after a fortnight's holiday, when everything seems so different. So you can imagine what I felt like after being away for three years. I felt a bit of a stranger but the feeling soon disappeared. Popping into Deepdale was another treat, although, with it being the summer, it was fairly quiet.'

The Army seemed a little at a loss as to how to employ Tom once his leave expired. He was sent to a transit camp in Folkestone and built up hopes of a home posting. His luck was out and he was sent back to Italy but, prior to his return overseas, he did manage to figure in the North End side for a game at Barnsley. Much had changed and there were many unfamiliar faces in the dressing room when Tom made his entrance. The new-look side gelled from the word go and he celebrated his homecoming with a 5-1 victory.

Back in Italy he re-joined his old unit and was given a job with the newly-formed Sport Control Board, organised by the CMF, with special duties involving the teaching of ball control and the merits of team play.

Having spent so long fighting abroad, Tom had plenty of leave time at his disposal and he came back to Preston to figure in an 8-2 victory over Leeds prior to his marriage to Elsie on November 1st 1945. A third spell in Italy followed but his days as a soldier were numbered and he won an eagerly-awaited exit through the B Release regulation.

'Builders and plumbers were in great demand in England and I was allowed to return home on the understanding that I took up immediate employment at my old firm, Pilkingtons. By day I was a plumber and in the evening I reported for training with PNE.'

It was at this time that Finney ran into one of his rare disputes with the club. During the war he had talked at great length to Willie Thornton, who revealed that Rangers had paid their army players a retainer amounting to a couple of pounds a week. Finney, who had signed as a Preston professional at 10 shillings a week – later increased to a war-time maximum of 30 shillings – got precisely nothing during his service days.

'After three years in the Army I was still a Preston player yet I was asked to re-sign on part-time wages of £5 per week.

'It was an insult, especially as the recognised first-team money was around twice that sum. I felt let down and made my feelings known. Deep discussions followed and, thankfully, I won the case, with Preston upping their offer to the full amount.'

Tom and Elsie's wedding was held at Emmanuel Church, Brook Street, Preston, but domestic life was made difficult through a shortage of funds. They moved in with Elsie's parents and stayed there for 18 months before gathering enough money to buy a small bungalow on Victoria Road, a smart Victorian residential area not too far from North End's ground across Moor Park.

The Nobletts made the young couple welcome and comfortable but neither Ruth nor Jim had much knowledge of football. Indeed, Ruth was totally naive on the matter, a point emphasised by a humorous incident. Tom recalls:

'I was due to play one afternoon for North End at Deepdale and, after lunch, I got up from the table and went upstairs to change for the match. After a wash and brush up I came back down only for Elsie's mother to look round in a state of shock. She said, "Tom, surely you don't intend to go and play football in your best suit, do you?"

'We just fell about laughing, but it was a genuine question. She really did think that I was going out to play in a League game dressed in jacket and flannels!'

Chapter Four

Pride of Preston –
North End, 1946-52

Y OU cannot talk about golf without giving mention to Jack
Nicklaus, tennis without Bjorn Borg, cricket without Gary
Sobers, horse racing without Lester Piggott . . . all are synonymous with success in their field. In the world of soccer, you
cannot discuss Manchester United without mentioning Bobby Charlton, Liverpool without Bill Shankly, Nottingham Forest without Brian
Clough, Wolverhampton Wanderers without Billy Wright. By the same
token, but with a slight change of emphasis, you cannot talk about
Tom Finney without mentioning Preston North End.

Finney only ever played League football for Preston North End. He
spent the years from 1946 to 1960 at his home-town club. They were
years which can certainly be reckoned to be among the greatest in
North End's history – the very year after Finney retired, Preston left the
First Division and they have never been back and in 1948-49, when
Finney was injured for a significant part of the season, Preston were
relegated.

In the fabulous 1950s, when the English game was at its peak and
the domestic game was littered with stars and enjoying its boom,
Finney literally *was* Preston North End. He was arguably football's
biggest draw at the time and, naturally, North End gained immensely
from his wonderful achievements and consequent acclaim. They say,
quite correctly, that no single individual performer is ever bigger than
his club. In the case of Finney and Preston North End, however, it was
a close run thing.

That is not to make out for a moment that he was the club's only
claim to fame . . . anything but. Indeed, the Deepdale outfit – the only
club in the land to occupy the same home venue throughout its entire
history – had been a considerable football force long before Finney
was born. As one soccer commentator once put it: 'Preston North End
rolls from the tongue like no other; it is the club which epitomises

English soccer.'

Preston North End had been formed in 1881, turning professional four years later and becoming founder members of the Football League following an open letter despatched by Aston Villa official William McGregor on 2nd March 1888. McGregor's persistence led directly to the League's formation at a special meeting at Manchester's Royal Hotel some six weeks later. The 12 founders were Preston North End, Everton, Blackburn Rovers, Wolverhampton Wanderers, Accrington Stanley, Derby County, West Bromwich Albion, Aston Villa, Bolton Wanderers, Notts County, Burnley and Stoke City.

In the first season of competition (1888-89) it was North End who were unstoppable, with a notable and truly remarkable 'double'. They took the Championship with a record reading: Played 22, Won 18, Drawn 4, Lost 0, For 74, Against 15, Points 40, and followed it by a 3-0 FA Cup Final victory over Wolves at Kennington Oval. They won the Championship without losing a game and won the Cup without conceding a goal – a unique record which will almost certainly never be equalled in the modern game. They had reached the final the previous year too but, on that occasion, lost 2-1 to West Bromwich Albion. The very next season they were Champions again, but missed out on the Cup, losing a quarter-final tie to Bolton.

In all of the next three seasons, 1890-91, 1891-92 and 1892-93, they finished runners-up. In 1900, however, they suffered the indignity of relegation, only to bounce back to take the Second Division Championship in 1903-04 and earn a First Division runners-up slot in 1905-06.

After a further period of relegation, Preston took the Division Two title and runners-up spot respectively in 1912-13 and then in 1914-15. Throw in another Second Division promotion season in 1933-34, an FA Cup Final win over Huddersfield at Wembley in 1938, plus Cup Final appearances as losers in 1922 (lost to Huddersfield 0-1) and 1937 (lost to Sunderland 1-3) and it becomes clear that Preston North End was a football club of national significance well before the days of Finney.

Since at least the eighteenth century, and perhaps earlier, the town has been widely known as 'Proud Preston', partly because of the 'P.P.' which appears on the town's crest and partly, so the story goes, because of the elevated gentility of some of its inhabitants! It was an epithet which was widely used in Preston and one which could certainly have been applied with justice to that first North End football team and, later, with even more reason, to Preston's most famous football son. For, what no record and reference book, however faultless in detail and statistics, can ever relate accurately is the atmosphere of a club and the nature of public feeling for the game. In that regard there can be little doubt that PNE 'arrived' when Finney came to the forefront. Finney was already an international before he made his official Preston First Division debut at the age of 24. During the war many representative honours and some sparkling performances had made him a household name. He was one of 36 professionals on the Deepdale books for the start of the first post-war campaign.

T he long-awaited re-start of League football arrived on August 31 1946 and North End, entertaining Leeds United, kicked off with a win before a crowd numbering more than 25,000. Preston's line-up on a quite historic day read: Fairbrother, Beattie (A), Scott, Horton, Shankly, Watson, Finney, McIntosh, Dougal, Beattie (R), Wharton. Finney remembers:

'It was a day of great excitement, on and off the field, with everyone in good spirits. I suppose the general feeling of goodwill was brought about by sheer relief.

'But as professionals we were determined to open with a win. The Deepdale crowd has never been easy to satisfy and I say that without wishing to appear critical. It is borne out of the club's traditions. The club has long been known as Proud Preston and the "Old Invincibles" of the previous century set some incredible standards.

'We were always aware of a special reputation and the demand of the supporters reflected the tradition. But we did reach the required standard on that opening day against Leeds. It was a carnival sort of afternoon and I was lucky enough to score one of our goals in a 3-2 win.'

As usual, however, modesty prevents him from telling the full story of his own contribution. The local newspaper headline was less diffident, claiming: 'Finney "Made" All The Goals, Scored One' and reporting that, without his cunning and bewildering craft, North End would have struggled to break Leeds down.

This was the first game after the war but already the journalists had begun to wax lyrical. Typical of the printed word was this extract:

'Preston's opening performance was too much a one-man show, with Finney excelling in his first game since being demobilised. His composure, mastery, artifice and tantalising finesse made his match-winning scheming the talk of the town.'

Finney's goal, Preston's second, was described thus:

'He had a defender baffled, leg-locked and deceived by a slow fascinating dribble. He took the full back to the line and then, with a quick turn and side flick, sent his opponent stumbling and reeling off his balance into space; left himself with a clear opening and planted a beautiful shot just inside the far post. Storming applause greeted a brilliant solo effort.'

Finney was, of course, no stranger to North End fans. They had watched him blossom during the previous few seasons, but it was not until the late 'forties that his genius was truly recognised and appreciated. Possession of the ball was all that he needed to become immortal. Bewitching balance and supreme control were his hallmarks. As one local journalist once penned:

'Every facet of the game was mastered by the most perfect player ever to grace an English pitch. He had immense athleticism, was majestic in the air and possessed clinical finishing power.

'If all the brains in the game sat in committee to design the perfect player then they would come up with a reincarnation of Tom Finney.'

The 1947-48 season saw Preston begin well, with an early sequence of five straight victories and then, on Saturday December 6, came a game in a million; a match still rated by many observors as the greatest ever seen at Deepdale. Even Finney himself, not noted for needless exaggeration, shares that opinion. Derby County provided the opposition, making the short trip in high spirits and with confidence, for at that moment they shared third place in the First Division with . . . North End.

The Deepdale match-day programme, selling for 2d, welcomed the Rams as '. . . very strong and attractive opposition, the first team in the land to lower the Arsenal colours, and unbeaten in 10 games. They are chock full of star appeal, notably England's silver-haired Raich Carter . . .' The team line-ups read as follows:

Preston North End: Gooch, Gray, Robertson, Shankly.
Williams, Horton, Finney, Beattie,
McIntosh, McLaren, Anders.
Derby County: Townsend, Mosley, Howe, Ward, Leuty,
Musson, Harrison, Carter, Morrison,
Steele, Oliver.

But no build up could ever have foretold the 90 incredible minutes which lay in store for the spectators. North End had hardly settled into their stride before Derby went two up, with Carter spinning a web of mesmerising deception to eclipse his illustrious England team-mate on the home right flank. First, Howe capitalised on a defensive blunder to rifle home a penalty and then, with North End wobbling, Morrison ran between Shankly and Williams to score with a shot which crossed the line after clipping an upright. A humiliating defeat looked a likely prospect until Preston decided to begin a steady fightback.

Harry Anders, normally Finney's understudy (more of that later), but on this occasion his left-wing colleague, began to weave his own brand of wing magic and before long North End had pulled themselves round on to level terms. Anders was up-ended in the box and, after the referee and linesman had deliberated for some time, Shankly scored with a spot kick. The game developed into a humdinger and, under the stress of fast driving raids, mistakes were inevitable.

Both sides remained totally set on attack and the 34,000 crowd roared a united appreciation as the thrills came at one per minute, first in one penalty area and then in the other. Preston's pluck was rewarded with the equaliser when McLaren timed a run to perfection to score with a copybook header from a Finney corner.

Derby regained the lead after 32 minutes when Morrison beat two defenders before drawing Gooch off his line and then shooting into an empty net. North End's determination could not be extinguished, though, and they levelled at 3-3 just before half-time thanks to Shankly's persistence.

On the hour, Derby pushed their noses ahead yet again, when Morrison capitalised on a rare error of defensive judgement from Shankly to complete his hat-trick before the home side produced another equaliser from the boot of Beattie after quite brilliant work from the tireless Finney. Eight goals scored . . . and Preston not once in front!

The atmosphere was at fever pitch and non-stop pressure from the home ranks produced a grandstand finale. Derby just had to crack – and they did. Pandemonium broke loose when, 15 minutes from time, North End took the lead through McIntosh before the same player hit number six in a goalmouth scramble.

But, not for the first time, it was Finney who was to have the final say to write the last chapter on an epic game. With the final whistle imminent Finney took up possession on the half-way line before embarking on a zany run, leaving defender after defender floundering in his wake, to supply the simplest of opportunities for a gleeful McLaren. *The Lancashire Daily Post*, in its Saturday Football Edition, said:

'North End will never give a finer exhibition of determination linked with skill. One hesitates to single out any player, but

Finney, surely, must be given special credit for his grit and amazing match-winning powers.'

In his Monday night considered piece the newspaper's football reporter, writing under the pseudonym of 'Viator', wrote:

'A remarkable performance which was truly heroic. What spurred North End into such action after falling behind 2-0 I cannot say. There could have been half a dozen psychological factors, one of them not unconnected with a collective resolve. The outcome was a thriller and a classic rolled into one, a game chock full of incident, excitement and high endeavour and coloured by the sort of individual brilliance one expects from players of the Finney, Beattie, Steele and Carter stamp. Finney's dazzling runs were sheer artistry and it was fitting that the wingman should end it all by creating a goal in a million.'

Tom recalls events of that December afternoon with a mischievous twinkle in his eye, the passing of forty-one years doing little to tarnish a golden memory.

'Simply to come from behind three times and then to win by three clear goals was truly amazing. They still call it Deepdale's match of the century and I wouldn't argue with that.

'It was unbelievable and the crowd noise was deafening. The famous radio commentator Raymond Glendenning was there that day to provide live coverage, but even he got his words jumbled up in the excitement.

'Angus Morrison got a hat-trick for us that day. You could say that the Preston officials were impressed with Angus for a few weeks later they bought him!

'I can honestly state that of all the many many marvellous matches I took part in the Derby game of 1948 was the best. For sheer incident and excitement I doubt whether it could ever be bettered.'

T he season continued in successful if less spectacular form. The next campaign, however, for no apparent reason, deteriorated into a complete and unmitigated disaster resulting in relegation. It was a catastrophe precipitated by misfortune and injury, notably to Finney, who managed to make just 25 appearances. When Finney didn't play, it would appear, neither did North End! By Christmas North End had won just five out of 24 games and the spectre of demotion loomed large. On the final day North End upset the applecart with a most unlikely win at Anfield, but their rivals-in-distress, Huddersfield Town, beat Manchester City in a case of much too little, far too late for the Deepdale men.

The prospect of Division Two was too grim to contemplate and Finney decided that his very future lay on the line. Money was one consideration and equally important was his international status. He explains:

'I was not picking up much in wages as a player and international duty with England provided a vital part of my income. I was deeply concerned that playing in the Second Division would hamper my England chances, for the selectors rarely looked outside the top flight in those days.

'My heart was at Deepdale, no doubt about that, but I didn't re-sign immediately and news got out. As often happens people got hold of the wrong end of the stick. There was a burst of transfer rumour and speculation, linking me first with Blackpool and then with Manchester United.

'I can also admit that I was offered an under-the-table payment of £2,000 from a mystery agent acting on behalf of a First Division club. And I must also admit that the offer was extremely tempting, especially for someone earning summer wages of £10 a week!

'I was out taking a walk in Preston one summer afternoon when I was approached by a chap who first asked about my welfare and then commiserated with me over the club's relegation. In the famed cloak and dagger style, he leaned over and whispered that he would arrange for me to get a tax-free cash payment of £2,000 . . . in return for getting myself on the transfer list.

'Although money provides many of life's pleasures, it does not guarantee happiness and while I was not carried away with the prospect of Division Two soccer I was still in love with my club.

'I would be a hypocrite, though, to say I didn't give the £2,000 a great deal of thought. I tried to convince myself that I would be doing nothing wrong if I accepted. After all I had been approached; I hadn't sold myself to the highest bidder. Somehow, at the back of my mind, it just wasn't the right thing to do.'

Finney was confused. He wanted a transfer if that was the only way to remain in First Division soccer and because it seemed to be the sensible career move but, then again, he wanted to stay with North End. Eventually he decided, not for the first time, to seek the view of Deepdale chairman Jim Taylor. His old friend, who could always be relied upon to be straight with him, was as candid and forthright as ever. The chairman was furious over the issue of an illegal approach but sympathetic with Finney's fear that the Preston squad wasn't capable of an immediate promotion.

Taylor promised new signings – Charlie Wayman was soon to arrive from Southampton and Eddie Quigley made the move over the Pennines from Sheffield Wednesday for a then British record transfer fee of £26,500 – but he stressed, in what sounds very much like a heartfelt plea: 'You should never ever leave Preston, Tom. Preston needs you.'

He stayed and, although a heated newspaper controversy over an alleged feud with Quigley threatened to impose itself on his career, Finney went from strength to strength.

'Some people claimed that Quigley and I were constantly at loggerheads and that I was determined not to make space for another "star" in the forward line.

'It was all blown up by the media with the sole aim of selling more newspapers. A wedge had been driven between two players and I feared that the unrest would backfire on the club. Again I turned to Jim Taylor and he promised to investigate the troublesome press campaign. When the chairman begged a quiet word with an editor or two the whole thing settled down.'

Quigley, a robust inside forward and dead-ball specialist, brought with him a reputation for power shooting and he was able to fill a variety of roles. He was a Finney fan and remembers well his Deepdale days:

'I was top scorer with Wednesday at the time when Hillsborough was regularly holding crowds of 60,000 and Preston were duly impressed with my record. I also had a choice of Everton or Wolves but chose Preston mainly because my wife wanted to move back to the area. I was born and brought up in Bury. I recall North End paying a record fee, for the previous holder of the record was former Manchester United Johnny Morris, my nephew!

'We had a good spell at North End and my family has always held a special relationship with the town. My son became a practising solicitor there.'

Quigley eventually joined Blackburn Rovers before turning to a successful career in management, but his Deepdale days were the warmest.

'Finney was brilliant and it was a privilege to play in the same team. We really took the game seriously. Tom would train as hard as anyone and I remember practising free kicks for hours on end.'

With Quigley and Finney in harmony the team began to get its act together and the re-birth of Preston North End as a soccer force was just around the corner.

I t is perhaps rather ironic that Finney and North End enjoyed one of their most mutually successful seasons in the Second, rather than the First Division. Season 1950-51 was memorable for a variety of reasons, not least the fact that North End claimed the Second Division Championship.

Equally notable, perhaps, was Preston's remarkable winning sequence during the latter stages of the campaign. A phenomenal run of fourteen consecutive victories stands to this day as a club record. In fact, records were crashing everywhere. Preston North End

1. Equalled the Bristol City record of fourteen successive wins.
2. Beat the Invincibles' record of thirteen successive wins.
3. Established a new club record of eight successive away wins (League).
4. Established a new club record for points gained in a season (fifty-seven).
5. Established a new club record for most wins in a season (twenty-six).
6. Played in twenty consecutive matches without defeat (18th November 1950 through to 7th April 1951).

Little wonder, then, that Finney-inspired Preston enjoyed a turnstile boom, with a Deepdale average crowd of 31,256 . . . and that for Second Division football!

Finney's outstanding overall contribution to the club's performance is underlined by the fact that, when he missed the start of the season through injury, sitting out the opening five matches, three of them were lost. The great man's value could never be gainsaid. Then, typically, when he came back North End celebrated with a 4-1 win over Chesterfield.

A relatively uneventful period followed until Christmas Day when another 4-1 victory, this time at Queens Park Rangers with Wayman scoring all four, set North End off on their remarkable winning run. That capital show was just the start. The following day in the Deepdale return with QPR, North End triumphed again, 1-0, and went on to win their next dozen games. The amazing fourteen-victory sequence went like this:

1. QPR, away, 4-1.

2. QPR, home, 1-0.
3. Cardiff, away, 2-0.
4. Birmingham, home, 1-0.
5. Grimsby, away, 4-0.
6. Notts County, home, 3-1.
7. Bradford City, away, 4-2.
8. Luton, home, 1-0.
9. Leeds, away 3-0.
10. Barnsley, home, 7-0.
11. Sheffield United, away, 3-2.
12. Blackburn Rovers, home, 3-0.
13. Leicester, home, 3-2.
14. Leicester, away, 3-2.

It amounted to 28 points out of a possible 28, 42 goals hitting the back of the opposition net and just ten being conceded. The run ended with a 3-3 draw at Southampton, although consolation came from the fact that the point gained at The Dell was enough to guarantee promotion five games in advance of the season's end.

During the record-breaking spell Finney was an ever-present force on the right wing. He himself scored seven goals and set up Wayman for fifteen and his old friend Ken Horton for a further eleven. It led to inside-right Horton saying:

'We used to get the ball out to Tom as quickly as possible and then run into the box and wait for it to come across. It invariably did, just at the right height and the right speed, and we simply had to sidefoot it over the line. It was as easy as that, for we were playing with a superman.'

Horton had come through the schoolboy ranks at the same time as Finney, signing on in the same week along with Tommy Hough. He has remained a close friend and worked for thirty years in Finney's plumbing business.

'I even had Tom as best man at my wedding,' recalls Horton. 'During that promotion season I got twenty-two goals and I can also remember boasting a run of scoring in seven successive away games. But nearly everything we achieved was down to Tom.

'I had started book-keeping at the plumbing business and a typical day in the early 'fifties saw us work from 8am-10am, go along to Deepdale for training until the early afternoon and then return to the business until evening.

'You might say that we were only part-timers, but the comradeship and atmosphere within the dressing room was wonderful then. I was just an average player who gave it everything he had but Finney was in a different league. He was a wizard.'

The twenty-match undefeated run came to an end in the match after the draw at The Dell when Preston, already assured of elevation to the top flight, relaxed and lost by a single goal at home to West Ham. Willie Cunningham had the misfortune to miss a penalty.

Managers consistently talk about the merits and advantages of fielding a 'settled side' and North End proved the point during their fourteen-game spell of victories. Ten players wore the same shirts throughout – the only change coming at centre half, a role shared by Harry Mattinson and Joe Marston (the former breaking his leg in January in a Cup-tie at Huddersfield). Therefore, only a dozen men were involved, namely Jimmy Gooch, Willie Cunningham, Bill Scott, Tommy Docherty, Harry Mattinson, Joe Marston, Willie Forbes, Tom Finney, Ken Horton, Charlie Wayman, Bobby Beattie and Angus Morrison. Docherty, Forbes and Morrison never missed a game all season, and Finney took part in thirty-four and scored thirteen goals. The marvellous Championship record reads: Played 42, Won 26, Drawn 5, Lost 11, For 91, Against 49, Points 57.

I t was hardly surprising that North End opened their 1951-52 season game at Fulham with a team of Gooch, Cunningham, Scott, Docherty, Marston, Forbes, Finney, Horton, Wayman, Beattie and Morrison! – exactly the same as at the end of the previous season. That game resulted in a 3-2 win and Finney was in irrepressible mood. One watching journalist, Scott Hall, saw it like this:

'The last packed seconds of the opening Craven Cottage game are ticking off. I am standing at the players' run-in with the proudest man in London – manager Will Scott of Preston North End.

'Fulham's last, loneliest forward fling is smothered around the fringe of Preston's penalty box. Out comes the watch and from the terraces the crowd shuffling noise that unfailingly forecasts the end. Then the whistle and the scrum for handshakes. They run past us to the dressing room and Will Scott has a word for them all. To one, knuckling wayward sandy hair from his eyes, Scott says: "Thank you Tom". It was the end of Tom Finney's almost perfect day.

'The soft lights and tones, the wit and chuckles of his soccer, almost turned this game into the opening of Finney's football fête. He did things in a way no one else could. He prompted twice-behind Preston to their fightback and, in the end, splendid victory. He showed how, unaided, he is an entire soccer coaching school – its principal, brightest pupil and greatest unpaid advertisement. He conjured up memories and images of unforgettable, unforgotten wingers of the past.

'When, after some 15 minutes, he really stepped into his game, Fulham stepped out of it.

'Finney really makes football seem (*vide* J. B. Priestley) "that altogether more splendid type of life, hurtling with conflict and yet passionate and beautiful in its art". Fulham had no answer.'

Another Press Box onlooker, also over-awed by the Finney charisma, offered:

'Finney bluffed and blazed his way through. He will win many more games for Preston against stronger opposition. Big Reg Lowe began well enough against him, then made the mistake of laying off instead of tackling, and for the rest of the afternoon was chasing rainbows. Fulham won't meet any more like him and for that you will hear a sigh of relief all around Craven Cottage.'

North End went on to finish seventh, with a 3-0 home victory over arch-enemy Blackpool on the 10th of September, producing a capacity crowd – 40,809 – a record mid-week attendance. Finney missed nine games through injury, plus a couple of England internationals, but still managed thirteen goals . . . a figure which was to prove his overall club average.

As we shall see, the 1951-52 season was also a time when Tom was excelling for his country, travelling abroad and putting in many an outstanding performance for a national side which was itself taking the world by storm with some terrific displays of football skill. It was also a time when an unknown figure threatened to turn Tom Finney's entire career upside down.

Chapter Five

The offer of a lifetime

F inney knew no other football home than Deepdale. Apart from a few war-time appearances, he played for no other club. While this certainly says something about the loyalty of the man, it is also indicative of a far less fluid transfer market than today. Nevertheless, given Tom's position at the top of his profession, it would have been surprising if no offers or approaches had been forthcoming. In fact there were more several and 'one-club Finney' came close to leaving North End on more than one occasion.

Moreover, it can be argued that, had he been born say 20 years later, he would almost certainly have spearheaded the exodus of British footballers to the Continent. Europe has long provided an alluring challenge and good financial rewards for the likes of Denis Law, Jimmy Greavse, Glenn Hoddle, Kevin Keegan, Ian Rush, Mark Hughes and Gary Lineker. It could so easily have been Finney who led the way for them all. His chance to move into Europe came before Rush, Hoddle and Hughes were even born and followed a quite astonishing run of events in 1952.

Tom was approached by an Italian prince and offered a king's ransom to try his luck overseas and sign on a two-year contract for an Italian side. At the time, it sounded incredible and, even today, the sheer scale of the offer which was handed to Tom is staggering.

Finney was 30 years old and at his prime, universally regarded as the most valuable footballer anywhere in the world. Even allowing for all that, however, the approach made by Prince Roberto Lanza di Trabia, millionaire president of the Sicilian team, Palermo, is still considered the most sensational transfer bid ever put together for an English player.

Prince Roberto was determined to secure Tom for his team and the contract on the table was beyond the wildest dream of even the most ambitious star performer. The package he drew up to tempt Tom was:

£10,000 as a personal signing-on fee.
£130 a month in wages.
Bonuses for results of between £30 and £100.

A villa on the Mediterranean.
A brand new, top of the range continental car.
Free travel to Italy for his family.

In short, Palermo, who were at that time fighting to become Italy's top club were prepared to give Tom the earth . . . and all he had to do in return was to agree to play there for two years! The prince was also ready and willing to pay substantial compensation to North End for the loss of Finney for two years or, if they preferred, a £30,000 direct transfer fee.

The whole incident had come about in May while Tom was on tour with England in Florence. The game ended all square at 1-1 and the visitors were invited to an official banquet laid on in the most lavish manner imaginable by the host country's Football Association. Tom spent much of the time consoling his old friend Nat Lofthouse, who had been subjected to a real gruelling by the notoriously physical Italian defenders, when England skipper Billy Wright interrupted to say that a fan was waiting to see him.

The 'fan' was none other than Prince Roberto and, after a short, rather vague chat about the international soccer scene, Tom good-naturedly invited his admirer back to the room he was sharing with Ivor Broadis, ironically England's goalscorer in the Italy clash.

It was then that Tom was turned to stone by the bombshell offer. His initial reaction to what he felt sure was a practical joke was to hide quickly behind a smokescreen of humour.

'If the money's right I'll consider signing!', he cracked, but the Prince was not laughing and simply said, 'How much will it take to get you to Palermo. I am prepared to offer you £7,000.'

Tom, now realising that the situation was deadly serious, hesitated and stared across at Broadis in absolute disbelief. His delay in replying was interpreted as dissatisfaction and the Prince jumped in, 'All right then, £10,000, so when can you get everything sorted out and fixed up?'

When the villa and the car and all the extra perks and bonuses were brought into the conversation, Tom's legs turned to spaghetti! He was unable to muster much of a response and the Prince left the room with the matter still up in the air. It was then that Finney and his room-mate realised that he could in fact land himself in deep water.

At that time it was illegal for any club to approach a player directly without first going through the procedure of contacting his club. In England in the 1950s, clubs still ruled the roost. Unlike today, contracts were binding and, consequently, players had little if any freedom of choice.

'I'll never forget Ivor's face when the Prince made the offer. He went white and kept repeating over and over again that it was a dream and all too good to be true. We talked about nothing else that night but when the Prince came back again the following morning I knew it was more than just pie in the sky.

'I must admit that the offer began to dominate my thoughts and I remember promising to put the offer to my directors on returning home . . .'

The Deepdale Board were unimpressed and they shrugged off the prospect of losing their star attraction by refusing Palermo's approach point blank. There was, they claimed, nothing to discuss.

'To be quite honest I didn't expect North End to react any other way so I accepted the decision without too much fuss and decided that the best thing to do was to try and put the whole business out of my mind.'

That was not quite the end of the matter, however, for Palermo were nothing if not imaginative. They made preliminary moves aimed, not strictly at 'transferring' or 'buying' Finney, but at 'borrowing' him for twelve months instead. This would have been the first known example of the use of the 'loan' system which now operates so widely in the game.

The whole idea was too new, though, and the Football Association verdict read, 'Finney is registered in this country and under the Federation of International Football Association's rules he cannot move to Palermo in any circumstances without a clearance certificate. Anyway', they added significantly, 'temporary transfers will not be approved.' The North End chairman, Nat Buck, had his own, slightly cheeky way of indicating the club's determination not to lose Tom – by placing a value of a staggering £50,000 on his star player. Tom sent a telegram to Palermo which stated 'Sorry. Unable to accept your offer owing to club refusal to negotiate for transfer'.

Thus, instead of heading for a sumptuous Mediterranean villa, Tom, Elsie and the two children, Brian and Barbara, headed for their favourite guest house – in Blackpool! Tom felt ready for a get-away-from-it-all break, a return to sanity and normality after all the palaver of Palermo. At least that was the intention. But news of Palermo's offer had leaked out and, within a couple of days, Tom was besieged by the nation's Press.

'I remember quite clearly sitting with Brian on my shoulders watching the Punch and Judy show on the sands when suddenly we were confronted by a posse of reporters. It was embarrassing to say the least but, as I had always had a good working relationship with many of the national newspapermen, I took a couple of journalists back to the hotel to put them in the picture.'

But Tom's honesty did not prevent him from becoming a target for abuse. He was termed 'greedy' and a 'traitor' for even considering leaving Deepdale. But, within the criticism, there emerged a weight of opinion that Finney was being unfairly done to and that North End had no right to deny him such a glorious chance of providing his family with financial security.

Tom has always held very definite views on the subject of individual wages in sport. In a book, *Finney On Football*, published in 1958, he wrote:

'No soccer topic causes more argument than the wages earned by professional players, but need the contents of a man's weekly pay packet caue so much recrimination? I believe that every man, be he a footballer, farmer or foundry-worker, should be paid what he is worth. To revive an old comparison an artist like Stanley Matthews is permitted to earn not a penny more than an ordinary player with a Fourth Division club. Imagine Rex Harrison appearing in *My Fair Lady* at the Theatre Royal Drury Lane for £20-a-week maximum wages (winter of course!). Ridiculous, of course it is. Yet Stanley Matthews, in his own field, is as great a star as Rex Harrison and he should be paid accordingly.'

Strong words in the days prior to the maximum wage being abolished in professional soccer but Finney's sentiments are the same today.

'People say it is crazy and unfair for a footballer to be earning £2,000 or £3,000 a week. But if that is what a club is prepared to pay out to a star then I say good luck to him. The money is most definitely there for the top players nowadays and they should grasp the opportunity. The whole deal was so wrong in the '50s and when Jimmy Hill and Co. managed to bring about some changes later on they were labelled as money-grabbing.

'What is wrong with a free market place? I remember saying years ago that, while I thought Preston North End was the greatest club in the world, if Newcastle United had come in to double my wage I would have certainly signed.'

One hypothetical question that Tom has never properly answered is whether he would have taken up Palermo's offer had the situation been different and had he been in the position to decide for himself without domestic contractual difficulties. He has had 37 years to ponder the question:

'I must admit that the Palermo business has drifted across my mind more than once and the more I think back the more astonished I become about the sheer magnitude of the offer.

'It would have taken me the best part of a decade at Deepdale to earn what Prince Roberto was prepared to pay me for simply signing on the dotted line. I knew what English wages were all about, having earned just £5 for a 46-hour week as a plumber just after the war and £14 a week as a professional footballer.

'In many ways I would have liked to have gone across to Italy and given it a whirl. Apart from the obvious attraction of financial security and the prospect of making myself a very wealthy young fellow, it was an intriguing and exciting thought. I have often wondered how I would have fared in the Continental game.

'I would never try to deny that there was a great and obvious temptation but, set against those advantages, were my roots, my family, my business and my affection towards Preston North End. The kids were settled at school and moving abroad would have totally disrupted our lives. Elsie, like me, has always been a home bird and all our friends lived nearby.

'All in all it was a difficult situation, a very delicately poised issue. To be perfectly honest, perhaps I was lucky in some respects that the decision was never really mine to make. Clubs were the rulers over players and, when you signed on, you effectively signed on for life – unless, of course, they wanted rid of you. In this instance, my club made it plain that I was leaving for nowhere and I had to accept it. It provided me with an easy way out if you like.

'But, if I had been in a position to make a choice at the time, I would probably have turned Palermo down. That might shock and surprise a lot of people but I have tried to explain my reasons and be realistic. Money isn't everything by a long chalk.'

As it was, no Palermo meant no overnight fortune. If Tom was to make money it was to be over a long period of time. Well before the end of his North End playing days – unlike so many of his colleagues – he had already begun to map out his future by building up his Preston-based plumbing business. By settling down so early in his career, he was securing his future in a far more effective way than the get-rich-quick lure of foreign football could probably ever have provided.

Chapter Six

Pride before a fall – North End, 1952-54

I N the very next season, 1952-53, Finney was to come within slide-rule distance of a League Championship medal. This was the season in which Sheffield Wednesday striker Derek Dooley lost his right leg in a collision with North End goalkeeper, George Thompson. An amputation was required when gangrene set in. To this very day – and the record books and accounts of the incident bear him out – Thompson insists that it was all a pure accident.

For the last 28 years George has run a fish and chip shop in the Lancashire village of Whalley and of that tragic afternoon he recalls:

'I could see Dooley homing in and I simply got there first and whipped the ball away. He followed through and there was a horrible crunch as his shin smashed against my knee. There has never been any ill feeling and I appeared as a guest when Derek was honoured with a *This Is Your Life* television special.'

This was also the season when Will Scott's long run as manager came to a close with the appointment of Scott Symon; the season North End toured Switzerland beforehand and Austria afterwards; the season during which PNE inside forward Derek Lewis died, aged 24, of a brain haemorrhage; and the season that a stocky little winger by the name of Harry Anders waved a fond farewell to Deepdale to join Manchester City for £10,000.

Harry Anders is, in fact, the source of one of the most amusing and revealing aspects of Finney's Deepdale career. For five seasons the diminutive Anders, who wore size-four boots, played the role of Finney's direct understudy.

On the occasions when the great man was injured, North End management went to great lengths to keep the fact a secret. Local press reporters were asked not to mention Finney's absence in Friday night preview pieces and the team was not announced publicly until just

minutes before the kickoff, by which time and all the supporters had
paid their admission money and taken their places.

Then and only then would come the dreaded announcement over
the tannoy system: 'For number seven, read Anders, not Finney.'
Booing and jeering would follow immediately, leaving poor old
Anders to tackle the hardest job in football – enough to reduce any
man to a jibbering wreck. But 'Arry, one of sport's most cheery
characters, was far too busy making the most of his moment of glory.
He says,

> 'Actually, I never heard much of the booing – I was in the
> dressing room getting stripped at the time. But I like to look back
> and think that they were jeering because Tom wasn't playing, not
> because I was.'

A miner at St Helens Colliery until signing professional terms with
North End soon after the war, he made the first team on the opposite
flank to Finney until Preston moved into the transfer market for
England forward Bobby Langton.

> 'People would say I was too good to be in the reserves but I was
> competing against two English internationals and one of them
> just happened to be the greatest player of all time!
> 'It wasn't easy to just flit in and out of the side every now and
> again but Tom was good with me and success never changed him
> one scrap.'

Anders never reached anything like the level achieved by his mentor
but he most certainly carved out his own niche in the Deepdale hall of
fame.

North End finished the '52-'53 campaign on equal points with
Arsenal before having to settle for runners-up spot because of a
marginally poorer goal average. In a thrilling finale North End
won their last three games: Manchester City away 2-0, Arsenal home
2-0 and Derby away 1-0, with Finney keeping remarkably cool to net a
couple of crucial penalties.

In that vital end-of-season tussle with Arsenal, tributes poured in for
Finney's 'one man wonder show'. One eminent journalist, Maurice
Smith, reckoned the Gunners had failed to find a cure for an acute
attack of 'Finneyitis'. He reported that,

> 'From the moment he was brought down before converting a
> penalty Finney became an Arsenal obsession, a bogeyman, a
> ghost they trapped but could never lay.
> 'The Arsenal defenders – not one but three or four of them –

dithered like old women on a zebra crossing when Finney took up possession. As for man of the match – need you ask? Finney was that man as everyone at Deepdale would confirm.'

The following win at Derby, gained thanks to another Finney penalty, prompted more eulogies from the press, this time from David Williams, who had predicted before-hand that Finney's groin strain was likely to affect his contribution. Afterwards, Williams conceded: 'Finney was half the Preston side. He could, if necessary, have beaten the Derby defence on one leg.'

But, alas, 'Finneyitis' was not enough. When Preston had completed their fixtures, Arsenal still had one game left, against Burnley at Highbury. The Clarets did their utmost to provide a helping hand for their county cousins but the Gunners scraped home 3-2 to clinch the tightest of title races. The respective records read:

Arsenal: P 42, W 21, D 12, L 9, F 97, A 64, Pts 54.
North End: P 42, W 21, D 12, L 9, F 85, A 60, Pts 54.

Finney recalls:

'It was a sickener because we had played so well and worked so damned hard. To lose out on goal average was a real kick in the teeth. We felt we had done enough to take the Championship outright and I am sure every player on the books and every supporter spent the early part of the summer tracing back through the matches to find where we might have got that one missing point.

'The English League was – and probably still is – the hardest to win in the world and consistency is the only real route to success. You need nerve, too, for even in the middle of a good run you find yourself worrying whether the very next game will prove your undoing and push you onto the slippery slope.

'Our management at that time always preached that we should endeavour to win with style, to play an attractive brand of football. We played the ball along the ground and employed short passing movements.

'But such standards are difficult if not impossible to sustain week in and week out and some players reckoned that our 'Proud Preston' tag sometimes worked against us. The fans were sometimes impatient, forgetting that often you can only play as well as the opposition allows.'

The club geared itself up to go one better next time around, but few teams manage to lift themselves and recover after such a setback. Indeed, North End had to settle for a mid-way position in the 1953-54 season. Finney, despite the satisfaction of his 100th PNE senior goal at Cardiff, missed a large slice of the action through injury.

But if League form was decidedly ordinary, then the supporters were to find compensation and consolation through Preston's showing in the FA Cup. Ultimately it turned out to be another last-minute cliffhanger, with a defeat in the final, but how the supporters were to be entertained along the road to Wembley!

All the ingredients for the ultimate in soccer entertainment were to be found on 1st May 1954 when Tom Finney captained Preston North End in the FA Cup Final against West Bromwich Albion. Tom's career seemed to have been moving relentlessly towards this final pinnacle of achievement – to his captaining his home-town team in soccer's ultimate showpiece game at Wembley. When Tom, chest expanded, led out the North End team on that afternoon, he was visibly bursting with pride.

But the day which promised to provide the highspot of his club career turned out to be the exact opposite. The match was a personal disaster – North End lost 3-2 – and Finney, not to put too fine a point on it, had a stinker!

In fairness, there had been considerable advance pressure, aside from the usual level of expectancy and anxiety associated with a Wembley showpiece. The previous year his old adversary Stanley Matthews had almost single-handedly set up Blackpool for a memorable triumph over Bolton Wanderers in one of the competition's greatest ever encounters. Indeed, it was dubbed 'The Matthews Final'. Would 1954, asked the media, throw up 'the Finney Final'? However, although many times Finney emulated and eclipsed his great wing rival, he certainly came out a poor second in terms of the FA Cup.

The Cup campaign which led to Wembley had been long and hard. Derby County provided the third-round opposition at the Baseball Ground during the second week of January when Finney, troubled by a groin strain, had not figured in the side for eight weeks. Nevertheless, he came back to share the glory and the goals with Charlie Wayman as North End recorded a 2-0 victory. Finney's strike came from an acute angle fifteen minutes from time to settle a tense contest.

A training injury to an ankle caused Tom to sit out the next couple of matches but he was nursed through in time for the next Cup outing at Lincoln City. The Sincil Bank tie was notable, not only for North End's 2-0 victory, but also for Wayman's 100th PNE goal and a fine penalty save from goalkeeper George Thompson.

In round five North End were in rampant form and Ipswich left for the long drive back to Suffolk smarting from a heavy 6-1 defeat.

1. *Tom's mother Margaret, or 'Maggie' as she was known, who died, aged 32, when Tom was only four.*

2. *Alf Finney with his second wife Mary. Alf was a tremendously important influence on the young Tom and encouraged his football from an early age.*

3. *A family snapshot from 1928. On the back row are Aunt Florrie, great grandfather Riley and grandma Mitchell. On the front are Billy Shufflebottom, a somewhat mischievous looking Tom and his elder brother Joe.*

4. *A young Tom Finney, aged 13, with a ball at his feet! Although chosen as reserve in the Preston Town Team while still in short trousers, Tom was considered a delicate, fragile lad, and often had to sit on the sidelines because the older lads would not let him join in. His small stature and slight physique were probably partly responsible for North End's initial failure to respond to Tom's letter of application for a trial.*

5. *A young Tom proudly sporting a North End jersey.*   6. *A slightly older Tom, this time in an England strip.*

7. *Tom pictured with his father Alf. No one followed Tom's career more keenly than Alf and, when Tom lost his father and his brother Joe in the space of six months, it came as a tremendous blow.*

8. *Tom (centre, in short trousers) pictured with some other team-mates at the station leaving for the All-England Schools Shield when Tom was 14. Tommy Hough, Tom's early rival and friend, is standing at the back, holding on to the engine. Though Tom was only chosen as reserve, he shared in the limelight and glory of a drawn final.*

9. *Tom (front, fourth from the left) with Deepdale Modern School Team. On the far left of the back row is Bill Tuson, later education chief in Preston, and an important influence on Tom's schooldays.*

10. **Above** *One of a series of cartoon strips which were published in the local paper to illustrate Tom's career. This one tells of his schooldays and the news of his trial for North End.*

11. **Left** *Tommy Hough today. It was Hough who quite often kept Tom out of the town team and, later, when he had joined Preston, he kept him out of the team there, too. Unfortunately, Hough's football career was cut short by the war.*

12. *The only way is up . . . Tom pictured during his early days as a plumber. Unlike so many players, Tom followed the sound advice of his father and others who stressed the importance of pursuing a career other than football. Thus, Tom continued with his apprenticeship and turned down North End's initial offer of a place on the groundstaff. The good sense of this was brought home at the outbreak of war in 1939, when all those on the groundstaff were dismissed. Besides, Tom has made good use of his trade in later life.*

13. *On one of the many trips to foreign lands with the England party. Tom played in three-quarters of the England internationals in the twelve years after the war and, to date, there are only two or three major countries he has not visited. This photograph was taken on board* The R. M. S. Alcantara.

14. *Break time during war service in Venice. Left to right are a driver, Willie Thornton (of Glasgow Rangers), George Hamilton (of Aberdeen) and Finney.*

15. *Finney, front left, along with 'The Wanderers', a service team for which he played in Egypt during the war. The team travelled all over the Middle East providing entertainment for the troops. In one game, one of his opponents, albeit on the substitute's bench, was none other than Omar Sharif.*

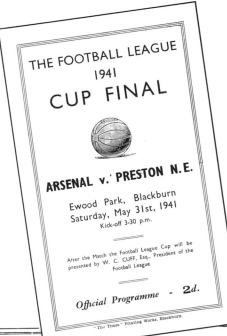

16. *Preston had beaten Bury (6-5 on aggregate), Bolton Wanderers (6-1), Tranmere (20-2!), Manchester City (5-1) and Newcastle United (2-0) to reach the final against Arsenal.*

The game for which this is the programme was actually the replay, the previous game at Wembley having resulted in a 1-1 draw. Preston went on to win the Cup 2-1.

PLAN OF THE FIELD OF PLAY

BAND OF THE LOYAL REGIMENT (By kind permission of Lt.-Col. C. V. Moberly Bell, O.B.E., and Officers).

ARSENAL

COLOURS : Shirts Red with White Sleeves and Collar. Knickers White.
Stockings Blue with White Rings.

(1)
Goalkeeper
MARKS

(2)
Right Back
SCOTT

(3)
Left Back
HAPGOOD

(4)
Right Half Back
CRAYSTON

(5)
Centre Half Back
B. JOY

(6)
Left Half Back
COLLETT

(7)
Outside Right
KIRCHEN

(8)
Inside Right
JONES, L.

(9)
Centre Forward
~~COMPTON, L.~~
DRAKE

(10)
Inside Left
BASTIN

(11)
Outside Left
COMPTON, D.

(11)
Outside Left
O'DONNELL, H.

(10)
Inside Right
BEATTIE, R.
2

(9)
Centre Forward
DOUGAL

(8)
Inside Right
McLAREN

(7)
Outside Right
FINNEY

(6)
Left Half Back
~~BEATTIE, A.~~
MANSLEY

(5)
Centre Half Back
SMITH

(4)
Right Half Back
SHANKLY

(3)
Left Back
~~SCOTT~~
A. BEATTIE.

(2)
Right Back
GALLIMORE

(1)
Goalkeeper
FAIRBROTHER

PRESTON NORTH END

COLOURS : Shirts White. Knickers Blue.

Referee :
F. S. MILNER (Wolverhampton)
Linesmen
H. HARTLES (Runcorn)
E. PLINSTON (Warrington)

17. & 18. *Two more cartoon strips, showing one incident when Tom was whisked away to play a friendly game against Switzerland during the war and (bottom), the resumption of League football in England in 1946.*

19. *Tom wearing his first England cap in 1946, a picture he sent to his aunt and uncle.*

20. *November 1st, 1945. Tom and Elsie on their wedding day. The couple got married almost as soon as Tom was de-mobbed; they had seen practically nothing of each other for three years.*

21. & 22. Cartoon strips depicting part of Tom's immediate post-war England career.

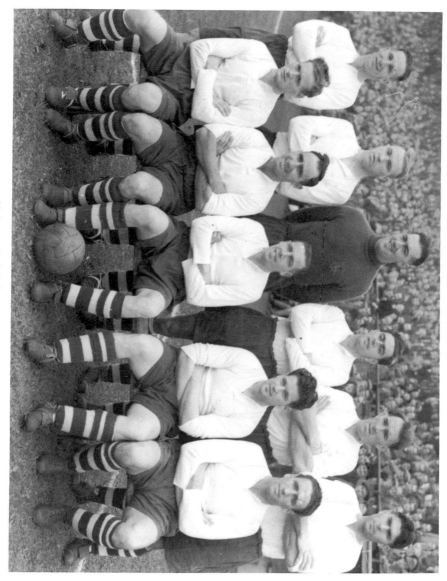

23. Preston North End team group, 1946-47.

24. Preston North End, 1947-48. Finney is seated front left. With the ball at his feet is Bill Shankly, such an important figure in Tom's early North End career. On the right is Harry Anders, Tom's understudy and the man they used to boo whenever he came on for the injured Finney.

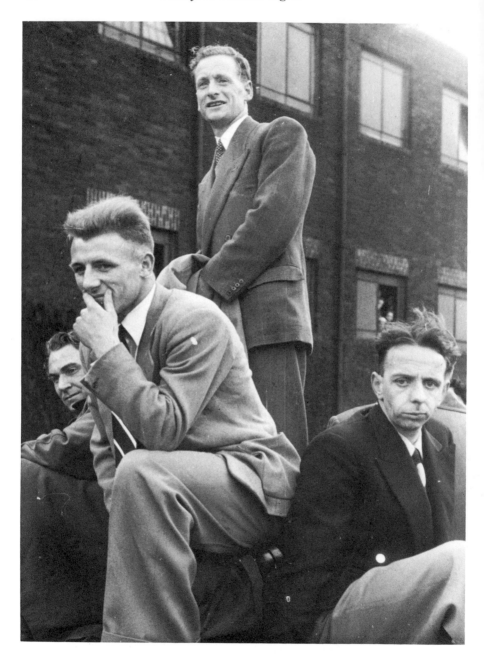

25. *With PNE colleagues Charlie Wayman, Tommy Docherty and Jimmy Baxter.*

26. Training was always a priority with Tom. Here he is pictured with Tommy Docherty, Joe Marston and Bobby Foster. Here, again, Tom's relative slightness of frame is evident compared with his colleagues. Some maintained that his manoeuvrability, stability and great acceleration came at least in part from this low centre of gravity, strong legs and light upper body.

27. Weights formed part of the regular training schedule, then as now.

28. *During a lighter moment in training at Deepdale. Tom is standing second from the right.*

29. *Yet another work-out, this time for England. Tom is on the extreme right.*

30. *Injuries, though rarely serious, were a constant worry for Tom and he was often asked to play when not fully fit. Speculation was rife prior to the 1958-59 season about his fitness and he is seen here with Jimmy Baxter gently jogging when a Press photographer caught up with them.*

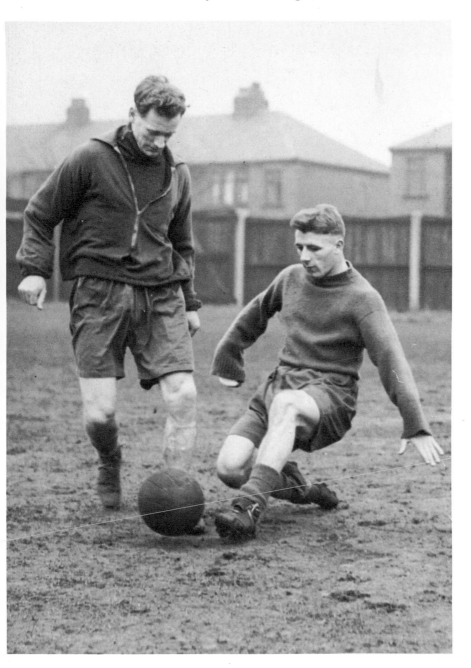

31. *An excellent and rare photograph of the two North End internationals, Finney and Docherty, training together at Deepdale.*

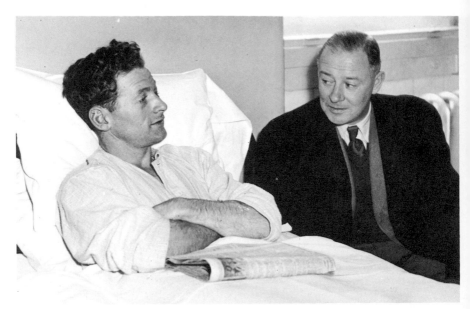

32. *Recovering in hospital in Leicester Royal Infirmary after breaking a jaw in a game against Leicester City in 1948.*

33. *This time in Manchester Hospital after a leg operation.*

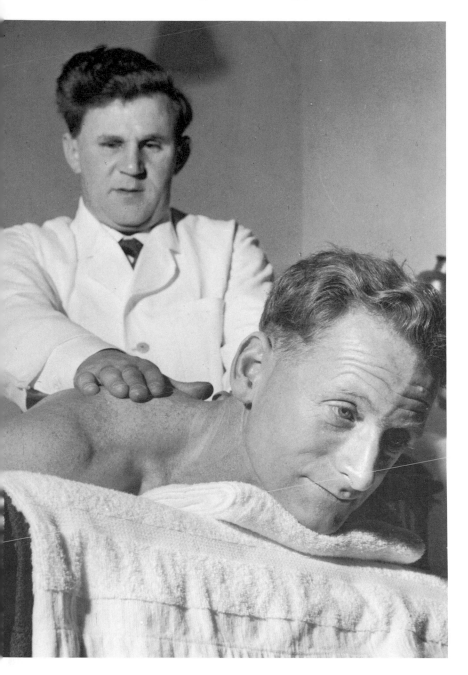

34. *Des Coupe, who was blind, gives Tom a massage, part of the continuous struggle to keep him fit for action.*

35. A Preston North End Directors Meeting at Deepdale, with, left to right, W. Onda, Mr Cross, Mr Holt (Vice Chairman), E. Bradshaw, Mr Howarth (Secretary), J. L. Taylor (Chairman), J. Melling, W. Lucas and Nat Buck.

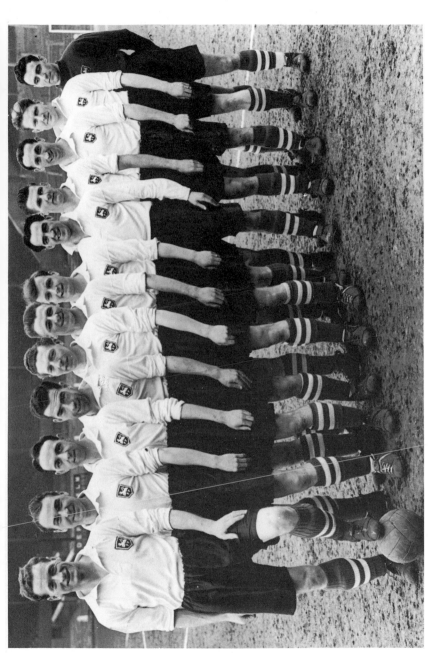

36. Captain Finney with PNE squad of Finney, Wayman, Baxter, Cunningham, Walton, Docherty, Foster, Forbes, Marston, Morrison, Mattinson and Thompson.

37. Posing for the photographers in a North End strip at Deepdale. A good portrait of the man.

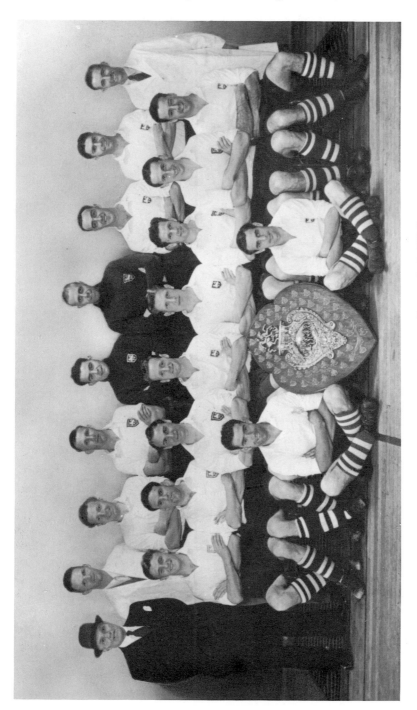

38. The team that took the Second Division Championship in 1950-51.

39. *The incredible height and power which Tom could attain in the air is well shown in this photograph.*

40. Ouch! Who said goalkeepers deserve better protection?

41. *A famous picture which became known as 'The Magnet' shows Finney winning the attractions of three Blackburn Rovers defenders at Deepdale.*

42. *This time two Manchester City defenders are given the slip at Preston.*

43. *And again, this time against Sunderland at home.*

44. *Finney near the end of his career, in 1957-58, lets loose a ferocious shot on goal.*

45. *Pictured with his trophy as Footballer of the Year in 1954.*

Ipswich had never met North End before in a competitive fixture and in the second half, trailing by 4-0, they tried rough-house tactics on Finney, who scored once and helped lay on most of the others for Wayman (two), Jimmy Baxter (two) and Angus Morrison. The Ipswich tactics, exceeding the limits of robust vigour, were based exclusively on obliterating Preston's outside right, the man everyone feared most. But Finney could not be tamed. Local newspaperman Walter Pilkington reported,

'Eight successive free kicks were awarded for tackles against Finney and rarely have I seen this lion-hearted forward take so much unpardonable punishment in the heat and stress of even the most vital game.

'Most of the 35,000 crowd had paid to enjoy Finney's skills but he was subjected to the tyranny of uncouth reprisals. Recognising his craft, Ipswich tried to wreck it but the plan recoiled, with Finney's brilliance responsible for all the four first-half goals.'

Quarter-final opponents were Leicester City in a tie which eventually needed two replays and which was, once again, a hard, physical encounter. Leicester made their intentions obvious and Finney regularly found himself face down in the Filbert Street mud during a bruising opening game in which a strike from Morrison earned a 1-1 draw. Receipts from a crowd of 40,065 were a Leicester club record of £8,300.

Morrison was on the mark again, as was Wayman, in a 2-2 replay at Deepdale in front of 38,130 spectators who this time paid Deepdale record takings of £5,114. In truth, North End were fortunate to survive for a third bite at the cherry, but that came at the home of Sheffield Wednesday – Hillsborough – the stadium which now carries the scars of a terrible crowd tragedy earlier in 1989 when 95 Liverpool supporters lost their lives in a terrace crush at a Cup semi-final tie.

On the 27th of March 1954, however, the focus of attention was on the events on the field of play and, this time, North End made no mistake, winning 3-1. Finney shared a scoresheet with Baxter and Bobby Foster.

It had already become apparent that North End had decided to put all their eggs in one basket; with each step towards Wembley in the Cup, the interest and enthusiasm for League encounters diminished. Between the two quarter-final replays North End sacrificed a League game at home to Wolves. Willie Forbes, Foster and Wayman were all 'rested', while Finney could not feature due to a pulled muscle.

The drawn-out saga with Leicester meant that North End had just five days' grace before their semi-final clash with Sheffield Wednesday at Maine Road, Manchester. Finney was far from 100 per cent fit but

he came through a late test. The magnificent stadium was packed with
the maximum permitted attendance of 75,000, of which a third were
North End followers.

Preston were without craggy Scottish defender Willie Cunningham
but, with Finney in sparkling mood, they demoralised a bewildered
Wednesday through skill and resource; a 2-0 victory which was made
possible through a total team effort. The result was never really in
doubt; Preston had forced no fewer than twenty-two corners as
Wednesday struggled to get on the positive side of the half-way line.
One watching journalist described it thus:

> 'Seemingly, the Wednesday defence played Finney fairly and to
> the utmost of their ability but, even with united assistance, they
> just couldn't cope with the wiles, tricky dribbling and changes of
> pace of this master footballer.
>
> 'The full back and other defenders were constantly flound-
> ering as Finney swerved this way and that in stamping his skill
> on the game. He excelled in luring defenders out of position and
> deceiving them with the unexpected, dexterous move.
>
> 'When Wayman scored Finney centred first time when a
> dribble was anticipated and when Baxter coolly shot a second
> goal Finney put three or four opponents in a tangle before
> centring with perfect precision.'

Wayman's goal came on the hour, with Baxter making sure four
minutes from time. Victory was glorious and if the prospect of a May
Day at Wembley wasn't enough, Finney was immediately named as
Footballer of the Year by the Football Writers Association, an
achievement he was to repeat three years later.

Finney had reproduced top class form with such ease during the
Cup run – despite the handicap of various niggling injuries – that it
was suggested in many quarters that Preston were little more than a
one-man band. One wag went as far as to say, 'Tom Finney should
claim income tax relief . . . for his 10 dependants'.

Finney was not impressed and he was the first to scotch such claims.
Looking back he states,

> 'I had enjoyed a particularly successful run and was playing well.
> But the one-man-team tag really stuck in my throat. It had all
> started a few seasons before when I missed most of the matches
> and the club went down. I had to withstand the allegation several
> times after and I was never flattered by it.
>
> 'A one-man team has never existed anywhere. We had an
> international goalkeeper in George Thompson, the Scottish
> grafter in Tommy Docherty, the best centre half in Britain at that

time in Joe Marston, a winger on the fringe of international recognition in Angus Morrison and a striker who scored goals for fun in Charlie Wayman. That is not to mention several other quality performers who helped make up a good all-round team.'

T he final itself had the makings of an epic. Preston were renowned for flowing football and West Bromwich Albion had only missed out on the Championship, finishing runners-up to Wolves, because of a succession of late-season injuries to key men. And, in the shape of Ray Barlow, Jimmy Dugdale and particularly Ronnie Allen, they had some outstanding individuals at their disposal. But they had no one to rival Finney and all eyes were certain to come to rest on the Preston ace. Few soccer stars have ever approached a big occasion under such intense scrutiny.

On the previous Thursday he attended the Press Club to receive his Footballer of the Year statuette from journalist J. G. Orange. Some in the audience joked that Tom could use the 'trophy collecting' exercise as practice for Wembley. In presenting the statuette, Mr Orange said, 'Finney has never got himself involved in any act on the field for which he has ever needed the least regret. He has measured up completely to the qualification of sportsman and I am almost as honoured in presenting as Tom is in receiving.'

On the eve of the final *The Daily Herald* forecast that North End would win the Cup with a degree of comfort. But Old Moores stated that Finney would be subdued and so allow a mere mortal to take the individual glory.

Finney was no stranger to Wembley, nor to the thrill of playing before a capacity crowd, and he had seen North End's previous appearance in 1938 when they had overcome Huddersfield. But, to be leading his side out as captain was very special and wife Elsie and young son Brian were just two of a multitude of personal friends and relations squashed into the main grandstand to share his joy and watch the two teams being presented to H.R.H The Duke of Gloucester. Her Majesty Queen Elizabeth the Queen Mother was there to make the presentation of trophy and medals.

So it was that Finney, apparently at the pinnacle of his career, led North End out down the famous tunnel to emerge in brilliant sunshine before 100,000 ecstatic supporters. The teams were as follows:

Preston North End: Thompson, Cunningham, Walton, Docherty, Marston, Forbes, Finney, Foster, Wayman, Baxter and Morrison.

West Bromwich Albion:Sanders, Kennedy, Millard, Dudley,
Dugdale, Barlow, Griffin, Ryan, Allen,
Nicholls and Lee.

Len Millard, an enthusiastic defender, made an early psychological
breakthrough with a couple of timely tackles on Finney. Then, on
twenty minutes, the Lancastrians were rocked back on their heels as
Albion went ahead through an opportunity unintentionally started by
a deflected clearance from Willie Cunningham – as George
Thompson advanced from his line the ball was squared across goal by
winger George Lee and Allen accepted the easiest of opportunities.

North End's response was immediate. Indeed, it took less than a
minute for Tommy Docherty to swing over a centre into the jaws of the
Albion penalty area for Angus Morrison to leap high and equalise
with a strong header.

Finney, meanwhile, was getting little change out of Millard and
North End found it increasingly difficult to justify pushing the ball out
towards him. It took almost an hour before the crowd caught a glimpse
of the magic as Finney skipped his way down the touchline. As Albion
hesitated, expecting an offside verdict against Charlie Wayman, the
Preston striker ran on unchallenged to collect a Jimmy Baxter pass
and rounded the Albion keeper before scoring with ice-cool aplomb.
North End were ahead.

Wayman's delight was obvious, partially due to the fact that his goal
meant that he had scored at every stage of that year's knockout
competition. Many onlookers reckoned that Wayman had strayed a
couple of yards offside but any thought that Lady Luck was settling
down on the side of the men from Deepdale soon disappeared.

Midway through the second half Albion drew level courtesy of a
highly debatable penalty when Docherty was alleged to have pulled
down Nicholls. Allen stepped up to take the spot kick. Thompson got
his fingertips to the shot but the ball still crept in by the base of a post.

Suddenly playing with a rush of enthusiasm and spirit, Albion put
their opponents under intense pressure and always looked the more
likely winners. So it was to prove, although Thompson was forced to
shoulder much of the responsibility for the winning goal three minutes
from time. Griffin foxed Walton and then hit a cross-cum-shot which
Thompson, diving too early, completely misjudged and the ball ran
along the line before nestling in the back of the net.

North End's disappointment was collective but no one felt the
failure more than Finney. By his standards his own performance had
been poor, very poor; lethargic and lacking in spark.

The inquests started immediately. *The Daily Telegraph* said, 'When
Finney found himself locked out by numbers he should have upset

Albion's plan by doing some unorthodox wandering, Matthews style.'
The Daily Mail agreed, 'Finney showed that he is not yet a Matthews.
He frequently does not know when intricacies should stop.' *The Daily
Herald* was even harder: 'Preston should forget all about it and try
again next year . . . with a new captain. So far as Finney is concerned I
think this would be a pleasure.'

Harsh verdicts, indeed, but Finney has never once attempted to clear
himself of blame. If this was, as everyone insisted, his worst ever
performance, then no one knew better than the man himself.

After dwelling many moments during the past thirty-five years on
the matter, Tom now concludes:

'To play in a Cup Final at Wembley Stadium is accepted as one
of the most exciting and memorable experiences in any footballer's life. I remember feeling especially pleased for our
manager, Scott Symon, a charismatic figure in his first season at
North End. Symon didn't go out of his way to court publicity and
was often accused of being abrupt with the Press. Football was
his only concern but he was very much a players' man who put
the contentment of his team before all else.

'I was desperate to do well for him, for the club, for myself and
for all my family and friends present at the game. But I let them
down with a performance I have always wanted to erase from my
memory.

'A player's life is turned upside down by the events leading up
to a Cup Final and the chaos in my home was indescribable. The
telephone never stopped ringing and hundreds of people who
were total strangers to me got in touch in the hope of obtaining a
ticket. As a local boy, I felt obliged to satisfy as much of that
demand as possible but my allocation of tickets was woefully
inadequate. Unlike today when the players involved are whisked
away and protected from all the hype, I was always on call,
scurrying around all over town to try and do a favour here and a
favour there.

'On top of that came all the media attention, the interviews, the
photographs, the sheer intrusion by the world's Press into one's
privacy. By the time we were all pulled together for the trip down
to London I felt completely drained.

'Even in the dressing room before the game things were not the
same. Usually before any big occasion I would get an attack of
the butterflies. I was sometimes incapable of signing an
autograph because of a fit of hand shaking but, in normal
circumstances, all that tension and anxiety would disappear the
moment we stepped out onto the pitch. This time, though, it was

different. I didn't feel particularly tense and there were no butterflies in my stomach. Exhaustion had taken its toll and even after the game had started there was no zip in my play.

'My legs felt heavy and I was running around like I had a sandbag across my shoulders. All of this is not meant in any way to devalue the performance of Millard, who had a fine match.

'I can only draw the conclusion that the lack of proper and careful preparation cost me on the big day. But, whatever the reason, May 1st 1954 will always remain my worst performance. I could do little right on the day when I wanted everything to go better than ever before.'

Finney's ghastly experience was perhaps best summed up by watching Manchester City goalkeeper Bert Trautmann whose opinion appeared in the columns of a national newspaper:

'I felt sorry for many of the losing players, but most of all for Tom Finney. This was to be a great day for the star who had graced Wembley so many times and was a hot favourite for a winner's medal. But he never put a foot right. He fell over the ball, misplaced passes and shot shockingly. He had, in short, a footballer's nightmare.'

Chapter Seven

With England at the peak

BOBBY Charlton, Billy Wright, Bobby Moore, Peter Shilton – and a handful of other illustrious stars from English soccer's hall of fame – can all claim to have won more caps. Charlton and Jimmy Greaves also scored more goals for their country. But no one can boast an international playing record that quite matches up to that of Tom Finney. His seventy-six appearances at the highest level – the only man of his generation to wear three different numbers in an England forward line – produced thirty goals. More than anything else, however, it was the collective success of the team during the Finney era which surpassed even his own personal achievements. It was a time, after all, when the national selectors had, in Matthews and Finney, almost an embarrassment of talent to choose from.

When Finney made his debut, against Northern Ireland in Belfast on September 28th 1946 – the first full international after the Second World War – England won 7-2. He marked that first appearance with a goal and Wilf Mannion, with a little help from the right wing, got a hat-trick. When he played his last England international, against Russia at Wembley on October 22nd 1958, just after the World Cup in Sweden, England again enjoyed a five-goal victory margin, triumphant by 5-0. Finney didn't figure among the scorers but Johnny Haynes, this time with a little help from the left wing, also chalked up a hat-trick.

During that twelve-year span, England were involved in 101 internationals. Of the seventy-six games which included the Preston star, England recorded fifty-one wins. He played on the losing side just a dozen times; another twelve ended in a draw and one, against Argentina in Buenos Aires on May 17th 1953, was abandoned after twenty-three minutes with the scoreline blank.

Finney played against twenty-three different national sides and his globe-trotting took in some twenty-one countries. His full record reads: Played 76, Won 51, Drawn 12, Lost 12, Abandoned 1, For 227, Against 102.

Of his thirty goals, three came from the penalty spot and he also had the misfortune to fluff one other spot-kick chance. He took part in twenty-nine Home Internationals (scoring ten goals), eleven World Cup ties (scoring twice) and thirty-six friendlies (scoring eighteen). His most frequent opponents were Wales (eleven times) and the old enemy, Scotland (ten times) and, as for goal-scoring, he had a particular liking for the Portuguese, hitting the net half-a-dozen times against them. He scored four in a match once (against Portugal!) and hit a brace three times. Of his seventy-six caps, thirty came on domestic soil (sixteen at Wembley Stadium) and forty-six away.

But perhaps the most remarkable statistic of all is the one showing the fact that Finney did not sample the bitter taste of defeat for a remarkable two-and-a-half years! Not, in fact, until his fifteenth cap on April 9th 1949 when England went down 3-1 against the old enemy, Scotland. Incredibly, thirteen of those opening fourteen matches had ended in victory.

As for the positions he filled, he played as a right winger forty times, a left winger on thirty-three occasions and made three appearances as an out-and-out centre forward.

On his debut against the Irish the full England team read: Swift, Scott, Hardwick, Wright, Franklin, Henry Cockburn, Finney, Carter, Lawton, Mannion and Langton. For his farewell against the Russians the side went: Colin McDonald, Howe, Shaw, Clayton, Wright, Slater, Douglas, Charlton, Lofthouse, Haynes and Finney.

Flowing football and goals galore were the hallmarks of the England displays during what was a truly fabulous era . . . 10-0 v Portugal, 8-2 v the Netherlands, 9-2, 7-2 and 6-2 v Northern Ireland, 5-0 v Belgium, 5-0 v Russia and 5-1 v Denmark.

Occasionally the country suffered a defeat, the heaviest being a 7-1 education handed out by the legendary Hungarians in Budapest. Tom also had the misfortune to be involved when the USA recorded a single-goal success in Belo Horizonte on June 29th 1950.

B ut for Finney, who had actually pulled on an England jersey even before making a full League appearance for Preston North End due to selection for national soccer service during the war years, it all really started on that Belfast afternoon against Northern Ireland.

At the start of the 1946-47 season he was involved in a full England trial, winning selection for a short tour of Ireland. He was included initially to provide cover for Stanley Matthews but an injury to the established star gave him his big break. He took it, you might say, with both feet and played an impressive part in a convincing team effort.

Resumption of international competition after an enforced lapse of seven years drew a huge crowd in Belfast. Well over 60,000 spectators thronged the ground and swarmed over the fences. Loudspeakers announced that if any people remained on the running track by kick-off time the game would not begin. It made little difference until a further instruction stated that anyone not in the enclosure or terraced areas after a further three minutes would be removed from the ground. Order was quickly restored but the kick-off still had to be delayed for 15 minutes.

Mannion scored twice and Carter once to give England a 3-0 interval advantage and Finney dazzled the crowd with a 40-yard dribble which took him past virtually every member of the Irish defence only for Lawton to stab his eventual cross wide of the target. Finney's goal came on the hour and, within a minute, Mannion made it five to complete his hat-trick. Nearly all the interest in the game had disappeared by this stage and the main question centred around how many England would score. The Irish, players and spectators alike, were deflated. Lockhart gave the home fans something to cheer with two goals but, in between, were sandwiched further strikes from Langton and Lawton.

Finney's performance in this game was enough to spark off speculation about the future of Matthews himself – speculation which burst out into a full-scale blaze of controversy two days later at Dalymount Park, Dublin, when Finney scored the only goal as England beat the Republic in front of 32,000 partisan supporters.

England had snatched the glory in a game which had, in truth, been dominated by the hosts but all the headlines belonged to Finney. Two games, two wins and two goals . . . quite a baptism at top level! Finney had been selected for both at outside right and he remained the number-seven choice for the next fixture against Wales at Maine Road, Manchester. Again it ended in triumph, 3-0, and Finney reckoned that the inside-forward trio of Carter, Lawton and Mannion were unstoppable.

The Netherlands provided the next opposition and the rejuvenated Englishmen recorded a runaway 8-2 victory, with Lawton grabbing four, Carter two and Mannion and Finney one each.

By this time the Finney-Matthews debate, a topic commanding daily coverage in the national Press, reached boiling point. The advantage ebbed and flowed between the two as each turned in magnificent performances for both club and country. Thus, Finney was acclaimed for his Irish, Welsh and Dutch displays but the weight of support swung back in favour of the veteran when in a League game Preston, with Finney, lost 5-0 to Stoke, with Matthews.

For the next England game, against Scotland at Wembley on April 12 1947, Matthews, who had of course been a star before the war, was recalled at Finney's expense and the game ended 1-1, with Finney's Preston club mate Andy McLaren playing a starring role on his Scotland debut. As usual it was not considered satisfactory simply to share the spoils with the arch enemy and changes were made for the visit of France in May. Finney won a recall, ahead of his rival, and netted his fourth national goal as England cantered to a 3-0 success.

Finney had proved his worth and it came as little surprise when he won selection in a 16-strong party for a tour of Switzerland and Portugal.

Walter Winterbottom, the man in charge of the national side at that time, along with the selectors, was as puzzled by the Matthews-Finney issue as the spectators and media. They opted for Matthews against the Swiss but then pulled off a master-stroke for the clash with Portugal – the first soccer confrontation between the two countries – instead of Matthews *or* Finney, Winterbottom decided to play them both!

One of Finney's old acquaintances, Bob Kelly, who had spent several years on the Preston payroll, was a coach in Portugal at the time and he had gone on record to warn England of a stern test. Lisbon's National Stadium was awesome, with stands of white marble and turf specially imported from Cumberland, but England, thanks to Winterbottom's careful pre-match attention to detail, were well prepared . . . and how it showed.

In some respects it could be said that the manager's hand had been forced when Bobby Langton, the regular outside left, failed a fitness test. Finney was thrown the number eleven jersey and, as a natural left footer, had few problems adapting to the role. The combination of Matthews' guile and cunning on the right and Finney's speed and trickery on the left was a wonder to behold. In fact, the plan of playing the two great men together worked so well that it begged the question as to why it had never been tried before.

After 20 minutes England were four goals to the good and they went on to run Portgual a merry dance and finish winners by the staggering margin of 10-0. It became known as 'The Lisbon Story', as a forward line reading Matthews, Mortenson, Lawton, Mannion and Finney had a field day. Mortenson and Lawton grabbed four apiece and the two wingers made up the scoresheet. Mannion, despite missing out on the goal stakes, had a superb game and Finney maintains it was the finest footballing exhibition he was ever involved in.

The only performance to stand comparison was the 1948 meeting with Italy in Turin. Undisputed World Champions and described as a 'wonder team', the Italians had a side which, although ageing a little, was packed with talent. A crowd of 80,000 packed into the stadium to witness an 'execution' and England's cause was not helped by a kick-off temperature soaring towards 90 degrees.

Italy, determined to put on a show, opened up breathing fire and

England, confronted by a unique style of intricate close passing movements, looked likely to be hammered out of sight.

With professional discipline and a fair slice of good fortune, they weathered the early bombardment and eventually began breaking out on the occasional attack. Italy's pressure had brought no tangible reward but, by contrast, England made full use of their opportunities. Two first-half attacks produced two goals, from Mortenson and Lawton.

Italy responded with another spell of sustained attack before Finney took matters into his own hands. Telling passes forward, first from Mannion and then from Mortenson, brought him two goals in just three magical minutes as England scored a 4-0 triumph.

Aside from the 1966 World Cup victory, this period has a very good claim to being the highpoint of the English game. These were the days when Matthews and Finney master-minded success after success and the real winners were those privileged to witness the bonanza. Finney recalls 'The Lisbon Story' and the 'Triumph in Turin' with relish and affection:

'We had gone into the Portugal game hearing all sorts of rumours. They were emerging as a force in international soccer, their goalkeeper was reputed to be the best in the world and the Press maintained that the stadium alone would be enough to bring about our downfall.

'It didn't quite work out the way the experts had expected as we went 4-0 up and then gave them a football lesson. We had a beano. It was marvellous to be involved and the display in Turin wasn't all that far behind. Italy had an oldish side but what players they possessed!

'We found, though, that they allowed their tempers to get the better of them when we got our noses in front. As we celebrated our first goal they were arguing among themselves and when I looked across at Morty he just nodded and gave me a knowing wink. We knew we had them when the squabbling started and we never looked back.

'As far as outstanding individual efforts are concerned I remember a match against Belgium in Brussels; it was the game after the Lisbon massacre. We won 5-2 and Matthews was out of this world. That was the best game I saw him play. He had a part in every single goal and the poor Belgians didn't know whether to stand back and jockey him or dive straight in with a tackle. If every Belgian player had lined up in front of Stan I don't think they would have stopped him that day. His display had to be seen to be believed.

'I don't like to make sweeping judgements but of all the inside forwards I played alongside Mannion was the ideal. His style blended particularly well with mine and he had a marvellous football brain, using the ball to full effect and always making himself available for possession in telling positions.'

It is hardly surprising that Finney has a special soft spot for the luckless Portuguese as he had some of his most memorable moments at their expense . . . like the May afternoon back in Lisbon when England won 5-3 and he scored four! England were given a hard fight in the famous Marble Stadium in front of 70,000 observers but, as one continental soccer journalist reported, the game was a personal triumph for Finney:

'Finney's wonderful ball control bamboozled the defence so frequently that two substitutes were introduced to try and blot him out. The ploy failed. Finney scored a penalty four minutes into the game and then scored a second after Mortenson had increased the lead. The star winger added two more in the second half, another from the penalty spot, and constantly menaced the Portuguese defence. He was unstoppable.'

Tom himself recalls:

'What more pleasant flashback could there be in the life of a footballer than the following Monday morning in the million-aires' seaside playground of Estoril. The sun streamed through my bedroom window, the coffee was piping hot and the sports page boldly declared "Finney Dazzles – Scores Four!"

'We had been expected to coast to an easy win, with Portugal given no more than a 40-1 chance. On paper it was easy but in practice it proved anything but. They turned around a 3-0 deficit at half time to draw level at 3-3 within 20 minutes of the second half. Their precise tip-tap game tore our back line to ribbons. We got in front again and were hanging on for grim death when Morty was upended in the box and we won a penalty.

'Under the circumstances you have got to say that the Italian was a brave fellow and the crescendo of whistles which preceded my spot kick were deafening. As the jeering died away, I swear I heard some brave soul among a small English contingent shout "Come on, Tom, knock it in!". My legs went a little to jelly as I walked back but, thankfully, my kick was low and true and enough to clinch the game for us.

'Some people used to express surprise at the fact that I counted goal-scoring one of my duties. It was usually considered that a winger should be a provider, but I always worked on the theory that the man in the best position should accept the responsibility."

Tom's outstanding ability has always been matched by a truly phenomenal memory and he finds little difficulty in recalling precise moments of games and occasions 40 years ago. Pulversing the Portuguese and infuriating Italy provide his warmest team recollections but, as for the greatest single goal, the distinction falls to Stanley Mortenson back on November 19 1947 when England were enter-taining Sweden at Highbury:

'We were playing with a lot of confidence and panache, believing, I suppose, that we had become unbeatable, and had cruised to a 3-0 lead. Sweden, to their credit, refused to lie down and die and we got complacent. A couple of quick-fire goals put them back in the frame.

'It looked likely to be a nail-biting last quarter of an hour until Morty came up with a real gem. Seizing possession on the halfway line, he embarked on a run which took him past three defenders before anyone knew quite what was happening. Then, from around 25 yards, he hit a left-foot shot which flew past the goalkeeper like a rocket. It was sheer perfection and served a double purpose, for, as well as making the match safe, it also enabled Morty to complete his hat-trick.

'For personal satisfaction I remember getting a great thrill from scoring a fairly straightforward sort of goal against Scotland at Hampden Park in 1948 in a game which we won 2-0.

'Frank Swift played a long clearance and Tommy Lawton flicked on to Stan Pearson. No one had taken the ball under definite control but Pearson's touch put me in the clear. The Scottish defenders hesitated and I moved in to hit a rising ball which beat Ian Black at his far post. The move for the goal had taken in the complete length of Hampden Park without a single Scot getting a touch!'

After that game one Scottish follower submitted the following ode to his local newspaper:

'At Bannockburn, all Scotsmen know,
  We really laid the English low.
The reason for this victory sublime?
  I think I've tumbled to the cause.
We won because the battle was
  600 years before Tom Finney's time!'

Finney was involved in three World Cups, including England's debut in Brazil in 1950. Preparation for that campaign took in a short tour of the Continent and the build-up went excellently, with wins over Portugal and Begium. He was supreme in a 4-1 win over the Belgians on the 18th of May at the Olympic Stadium when, under the headline of 'Finney Reigns', one report stated:

'Finney, who had been asked to fill Jackie Milburn's role, was at his very best and had the crowd laughing in delight with his brilliant footwork. Although he did not score he had a foot in all the goals.

'Centre-forward Mermans gave Belgium the lead at half-time but in the second half England produced such a dazzling display of artistic football that goals from Mullen, Mortenson, Mannion and Bentley could easily have been doubled.

'The contrast was so marked as to suggest England in the first half were deliberately playing within themselves. The selectors were left in no doubt that Finney will be the key man in Brazil.'

England followed the Road to Rio assured of doing themselves proud, but the reception left them bewildered. Tom recalls:

'We knew that the Latin Americans were football crazy, but the anticipated frenzy was nothing compared to the reality.

'I can still see one small boy, only partially dressed, approaching us outside our hotel. He was bare-footed. Just imagine our reaction when he placed an orange on one instep before flicking it into the air and catching it on the other! He must have repeated the trick twenty times and we felt obliged to reward his brilliance with a few coins. It wasn't long before we became used to such stunning displays of ball control – in match situations!'

The orange boy's appeal was just the beginning for Finney and his colleagues. They visited stadiums housing up to 250,000 with moats and barbed wire separating participants from spectators, experienced pre-match firework displays and a whole host of other unusual attractions which demonstrated the intense interest, bordering on hysteria, which attended the games.

When the serious matter of playing football got under way, England opened up by beating Chile. They could not have imagined, however, just what lay in store a few days later . . . a 1-0 defeat at the hands of a team of no-hopers from the United States – the biggest embarrassment in England's international football history. Finney still squirms at the memory:

'The pitch at Belo Horizonte was in a right old state and if the fixture had been scheduled for 1989 they would never have allowed it to go ahead. That is not an excuse, just a factor contributing to our downfall. The game was supposed to be as good as a walkover for us. After all, the Americans were only part-timers and we were a highly-rated world force.

'Most of our opponents would have struggled to get a game in the Third Division but we failed to take any of the early chances that came our way and we also hit the woodwork at least twice. They had two speculative attempts at goal in 90 minutes and one happened to go in.

'We couldn't find an equaliser and I take no satisfaction whatever in being able to say that I took part in the soccer sensation of the century.'

The English Press slated the team and one account read:

'It was the worst performance ever by an English team; not a single player could be proud of his showing.

'The Americans held on stubbornly to the lead they gained in the 38th minute through a fine shot from Argentine-born centre-forward Gaetiens whose attempt slipped through a crowd of players and into the bottom corner with goalkeeper Williams unsighted.

'The English forward line frittered away chance after chance, blazing the ball high or wide and hesitating in front of goal when it looked easy to score.

'England had bad luck when Finney hit the upright with the goalkeeper beaten just four minutes before the all-important goal.

'There were scenes of wild enthusiasm from the 20,000 crowd when the end came. The Americans were carried from the field shoulder high and spectators all over the stadium set fire to papers on the concrete seats to celebrate the astounding success over England, the masters of football.'

England officials were dumbfounded by the defeat. Arthur Drewry, Football League President, declared, 'It is unbelievable'. Sir Stanley Rous, Secretary to the Football Association, reckoned that the Americans had been 'fitter, faster and better fighters', while manager Winterbottom added, 'The team played badly, especially the forwards, who were far too eager'.

The selectors decided, perhaps hastily after what was a one-off result, that sweeping changes must be made and out of a line-up reading Williams, Ramsey, Aston, Wright, Hughes, Dickinson, Finney,

Mannion, Bentley, Mortenson and Mullen, only two forwards, Mortenson and Finney, were allowed to keep their places.

'I know we had been poor, very poor, and we needed to win our next final group game against Spain in order to have any chance of qualifying for the later stages but I still maintain that the drastic action was unnecessary. It certainly didn't have the desired effect, for we lost by a single goal and the World Cup dream was left in tatters.'

England returned home with plenty to prove and successive victories over Wales and Northern Ireland the following autumn went some way to restore lost pride.

The months leading up to the 1954 World Cup in Switzerland brought two notable moments and, eight years on, the Finney-Matthews controversy was still causing headaches for the game's administrators.

On October 21 1953 England entertained a Rest of Europe XI in a full-scale international at Wembley Stadium. Finney had played a starring role in a previous win over Wales but the selectors, never far from controversy, caused a widespread groan the length and breadth of Preston by picking Blackpool's Matthews to the exclusion of Finney. *Lancashire Evening Post* sportswriter Walter Pilkington, in an extremely forthright article, said,

'The issue has been more discussed in this corner of Lancashire than anywhere else, owing to the players' local associations and long-standing rivalry. It has always been friendly enough between the two players but that is more than can be said for the countless arguments that have raged since the selectors delighted one camp by their decision and outraged another.

'The controversy many times has been tinged with bitterness which, to my way of thinking, is unfair to both. Each has given England long and distinguished service; their sportsmanship, supreme skill as entertainers and match winners and model conduct on and off the field of play have put them among England's greatest ambassadors of sport.

'They vary so much in style, manner and approach that it is wrong really to compare them at all. But there will always be comparisons, odious or not, as long as football is discussed, simply because circumstances drew their paths so closely together that frequently one criss-crossed the other.

'The Preston winger's supporters have long had the field almost to themselves, so they must not complain because it is now the turn of those who similarly idolise Matthews to crow with satisfaction.

'Yet I, for one, never thought that we should ever have a repetition of that stormy period seven years ago when the young Finney first ousted Matthews and was himself twice quickly deposed by the older player, finally for the selectors to please everybody by putting both of them in the team.

'It is a great pity that the selectors, having made up their minds to recall Matthews, the 38-year-old Peter Pan of football, have not taken the same course they adopted six-and-a-half years ago and put Finney on the left wing for this forthcoming grandiose affair.

'Therefore, I declare that Finney's exclusion from the national team for this showpiece fixture is scandalous, especially in view of his reputation abroad. His artistry and vast resource have made him a world-renowned football figure who has never once let his side down. This is a fine way of rewarding his achievements just a few weeks after our national representatives were enthusiastically extolling his virtues.

'But now he has to go, not, ironically, because he touched the depths but through figuring in a 4-1 win!

'Finney is alleged to be too individualistic. That is rich, considering that he has been replaced by one of the greatest individualists the game has known. Look at his record. Up to now we have won only two of the seven games he has missed; winning 34 of the 48 [he has played in].

'If he is wise and not too blasé to hope for further caps, he will vary his game more to please his "masters" and adapt himself more fully to the style of play required by his manager instead of endeavouring through his own skills to try and turn a game around.'

Pilkington was not alone in his support of Finney. Fleet Street offered similar backing and reckoned it grossly unfair that Finney should have so often been asked to play outside left for England when he had been playing outside right for his club. At the time Finney himself, in absolutely typical fashion, good-naturedly played the matter down, being quoted as saying, 'I suppose it is difficult to swap and change in such a way, especially when the left-wing role is for matches of the highest importance. It can be a bit puzzling but, at the end of the day, I must say that I would play in goal for England if they asked me to!'

He was still on the sidelines when the Hungarians came and conquered a month after the Rest of Eupore game had finished all square at 4-4. He took a seat in the Wembley stands to sample a performance regarded as one of the finest in international history as England were overwhelmed 6-3. He delighted at the masterly skills of Puskas, Kocsis and Hidegkuti; a combination of individual flair and tactical sophistication that was irresistible.

The general view was, and indeed still is, that no team has since managed to reach the standards set by those Hungarians. Finney stands in agreement to this very day.

'They were almost too good for words, brilliant both individually and collectively. Their brand of football was revolutionary and I will never forget the thrill of being present to see it for myself. To be frank, I came away from Wembley wondering to myself what we had been doing all those years. Yes the Hungarians were just so much better in technique it was untrue.'

In the World Cup, England were grouped with the hosts and Belgium in what was considered an easy section. Matthews and Finney both played in the opener with Belgium but even their double threat failed to bring anything better than a 4-4 draw, with Ivor Broadis and Nat Lofthouse scoring two apiece. England were left to reflect on some unforced errors in defence, which allowed a 3-1 lead to evaporate in the final fifteen minutes.

Matthews was ruled out of the Switzerland game in Berne through injury, but England were in determined mood to chalk up a 2-0 win. A place in the quarter-finals saw England paired with the World Cup holders Uruguay and goalkeeper Gil Merrick chose the game to have a nightmare, as England, despite goals from Finney and Lofthouse, crashed out 4-2. Finney was disappointed, especially with his own form:

'The Switzerland tournament passed me by somewhat. I never produced my best form. In fact I was so in and out in the group matches that I was quite shocked to be retained for the Uruguay game.

'Even in the lead up to the Finals we had not been able to gather what might be called a settled squad. Apart from one or two people who could be considered automatic, basically every other position was up for grabs. Any man who put together a couple of impressive displays on the trot was very much in with a chance of making a regular place for himself.

'I felt a degree of sympathy for poor old Merrick. The Birmingham keeper became the scapegoat and he was hunted unmercifully in the Press. Their main objective appeared to be to ensure that he was banished from the international arena. The media won, for Merrick never played for his country again but it was crazy to lay all the blame at his door. Goalkeepers have always been sitting targets, for one mistake by a man in a green jersey can be so fatal. It made me glad that I was a forward.'

After the World Cup in the mid '50s Finney suffered most of his injury problems and had to miss the England tour to France, Spain and Portugal. His absence was a blow and, even with Matthews in the side, England drew one and lost two of their friendly fixtures.

I n the October, against Denmark in Copenhagen, he returned . . . and normal service was immediately resumed. Twin strikers Lofthouse and Don Revie, later to enter a brilliant career in management with Leeds before assuming control of the national side, revelled in the service provided by Finney as Denmark were crushed 5-1. Finney played in the following four internationals and England stayed unbeaten.

In the first of those four games, however, against Wales in Cardiff, he was again asked to play outside left to accommodate Matthews. He was also far from 100 per cent fit with a mixture of shoulder, back and groin injuries causing aggravation.

Some reckoned that Finney's form suffered through his switch to the left but he was happy enough to soldier on in the team's best interest. The swapping and changing didn't end there and in 1956, for successive Wembley dates with Wales and Yugoslavia, he reverted to centre forward. As it did for Preston, the plan worked like a dream. Both games were won quite handsomely, 3-1 and 3-0, but even then the selectors would not allow him to settle.

At this time many pundits were arguing that Finney should be a fixture, a 'must' anywhere along the forward line. The main cry was for England to play Finney at inside right and so pair him up with Matthews. The mixture of Finney's swerve and Matthew's shimmy working in tandem seemed the perfect cocktail but no one in a position of power took heed. Throughout the run-in to the 1958 World Cup in Sweden another England manager of the future, Bobby Robson, had found a place in the team. Matthews had made his exit, following a 4-1 win in Denmark, and his place had gone to a tricky little ball-player from Blackburn Rovers, Bryan Douglas.

Bobby Charlton was also starting to emerge as star quality and a re-shaped team was to rely heavily on the inspirational qualities of established men like Billy Wright and Finney.

England's form was patchy and it was with uncertainty that they embarked on the World Cup programme. For Finney the competition was over after just one match. Once again injury proved his most difficult opponent. In the opening 2-2 draw with Russia in Gothenburg – an appearance he marked with a penalty goal scored against the giant goalkeeper Yashin – a combination of crunching tackles did considerable damage to his right knee and caused him a painful, sleepless night.

The following morning he needed a full five minutes to hobble a journey of about eight yards from bedroom to bathroom, and a descent down two flights of hotel stairs for breakfast brought excruciating pain. Manager Winterbottom and trainer Harold Shepherdson insisted on a visit to a local hospital and it soon became clear that England would be faced with carrying on without the services of their best and most influential performer.

'I underwent a fitness test as the staff did everything possible to get me fit for a crucial meeting with Brazil but the examination showed me incapable of running at any sort of speed and every time I placed my right foot on the ground I suffered a sharp pain.

'I was left to watch the game from the stands and the team did remarkably well to force a goal-less draw. The Brazilians were coming through as the most naturally gifted footballers on earth and it was very much a defensive effort on our part to keep them out. Included in their side was a 17-year old inside forward called Pele – and was he something special!'

England went on to score another draw against Austria before bowing out of the contest following a single-goal defeat against the Russians. Once again the team, management and officials came in for a slating in the media. England had competed in three World Cups and failed to make much impression in any.

The following October there were two more international friendlies, against Northern Ireland in Belfast and Russia (again!) at Wembley. Finney was back in business on the left flank and scored one of the goals which forced a 3-3 draw with the Irish, Charlton getting the other two. Finney's strike, his thirtieth for England, made him the country's leading marksman.

The game against Russia on October 22 was Finney's seventy-sixth cap . . . and his last. A career dogged by fitness problems was starting to take a toll and that season, 1958-59, he managed to take part in only sixteen League games for his club. It was the beginning of the end.

He sparkled in that final international appearance as England ran up a 5-0 win. Clayton was the star performer, though Haynes hit a hat-trick and Charlton and Lofthouse completed the rout. With his goal Nat Lofthouse equalled Finney's record of thirty international goals.

It was entirely appropriate that Finney should say farewell on the back of such a resounding 5-0 victory and fitting that the fixture should take place at the home of English football.

Interestingly, in the match programme, costing one shilling, journalist Sam Leitch looked ahead to the 1962 World Cup and discussed what was likely to happen in the build-up years. He reckoned that, 'of the national squad only a handful, including the 34-year-old Billy Wright and 36-year-old Tom Finney, cannot be seriously considered for the next World Cup series. But these two legendary performers must retain their places until the day when there are better men for the job and *not* before.'

Playing so often and so well for his country was undoubtedly the highlight of his soccer career.

'When I look back at those games I cannot fail to thank my lucky stars for being fortunate enough to figure in a glorious era. So many great players graced the stage between 1946 and 1958 it was really wonderful to be involved.

'Financial reward didn't come into it and I would have paid the administrators to play me. There is no feeling quite like walking out of the Wembley tunnel wearing your England shirt. For any English footballer it is the ultimate.'

Chapter Eight

A manager's dream

S IR WALTER WINTERBOTTOM can offer 76 good reasons
for considering Tom Finney a world-class footballer. For
Winterbottom was the man at the England helm for each and
every appearance which Finney made in the country's colours.
Indeed, the two men began their international careers side by side,
featuring as manager and player respectively in the first England
fixture after the Second World War. They stayed together throughout
twelve glorious years until Finney bowed out of the international arena
in 1958. Winterbottom remained in charge until 1963 to complete the
longest ever reign for an England manager.

The much-acclaimed Winterbottom was just 32 when he took on
England's top soccer position after a serious illness had brought his
own playing career to a premature close. Now 76 and living in
Cranleigh, Surrey, he remembers well those illustrious days when
Finney, Matthews, Mannion *et al* were at the peak of their profession.
It has been said that of all the outstanding players he supervised and
nurtured, Finney was his personal favourite. He has never denied the
claim.

'For a start I don't believe that you can single out individuals or
compare players from different eras. It's an impossible task, not
to mention an unfair one. But that doesn't mean to say that I
didn't have a soft spot for Tommy Finney. Of course I did . . .
and so had every other manager, player, journalist and spectator.
Everyone loved Tommy because he managed to combine his
phenomenal skills to the most delightful of personalities. He was
a gentleman footballer.

'A darting player with immensely powerful leg muscles, his
forte was to get round full backs both ways, inside and outside.
He was highly skilled and a great technician who put a lot of
thought into his game.

'His vision was quite superb and he could relate to the needs of
the other players in the side. Equally comfortable all along the
forward line I believe he could have also found great fame as a

wing half.

'He had the ability to create openings when there just didn't appear to be any and added something special to every single match. He also had an in-built determination which was not always properly recognised or appreciated. I recall one particular clash with Scotland back in April 1951 when Wilf Mannion suffered a nasty facial injury after just a few minutes and had to come off the field. There were no substitutes and we had to soldier on for almost an entire game one man down. Although the game was at Wembley the Scots were out in force and they were baying for our blood. The rivalry was so intense the Scots didn't look with sympathy on Mannion's injury; they just saw it as giving them a better chance of victory. It looked grim but Finney turned in a virtuoso performance. We were really up against it but Tommy tried to do the work of two men, fetching and carrying and refusing to allow our rhythm to be destroyed.

'I can see him now, laying on a goal for Harold Hassall and then scoring an absolute beauty himself near the end. We eventually lost the game 3-2 but, for me, it typified Tommy's spirit. He always had the right attitude, irrespective of conditions or situations, but when the chips were truly down he would try and try and then try a little bit harder still.

'The complete team man, I could never imagine an England team without him in it in those days.'

Such a statement suggests that under Winterbottom's sole control Finney would have won even more caps. For two decades after the war, however, England relied not just on the manager's view but on the various opinions of a selection committee. Some would contest that such a system undermined the manager's position and devalued his view. There were certainly many who thought that Winterbottom was more than capable of picking the team without assistance.

Winterbottom held great respect from within the game and was rated by the footballers themselves as a manager of charm and integrity with a shrewd sense of values. Hailing from Oldham, he was a Lancastrian like Finney and it soon became apparent that he was destined to become a sporting scholar and a leader of men. Despite being an Oldham Athletic fan he was snapped up as a footballer of promise by Manchester United before the war intervened. He saw service in the RAF, reaching the rank of Wing Commander in charge of Physical Training.

It was no surprise that after seeing his playing days cut short he should emerge as a 'star' off the field. A perfectionist in all things, the coaching manuals he wrote became best-sellers overseas and his methods won support from managers the world over. His systems were universally recognised as the best and he was rated as a supreme judge of opposition teams.

As Director of Coaching to the Football Association (managing the England team was only part of his duties) he was the perfect choice. When running the England show, he did not have to shine as a coach, for all the players under his control were outstanding performers in their own right. What was required was for someone to blend and harness such individual skills into an all-round team effort. And good judges reckon that no one has ever done that better than Winterbottom. Did it frustrate him, then, to have to pick the team by committee?

'There were advantages and disadvantages to the committee system. At the outset there were nine members but it soon became apparent that such a high number was basically unworkable and we whittled it down to half a dozen.

'The procedure could be clumsy but it usually generated healthy debate and meant that those responsible for suggesting possible team members did at least get out and cover many matches themselves.

'I didn't find it a particular hardship and, when we lost, everyone blamed a body of selectors instead of dropping all the blame at the door of one man. In that respect I was sheltered from a lot of criticism but, having said that, there just wasn't the same pressure in those days. Today's England manager has a difficult and often thankless job. He carries the can for everything where in my time it was shared out.'

Sir Walter insists that no satisfactory comparison can be drawn between the styles of merits of soccer then and now.

'I split my job between managing the national side and running the FA's coaching scheme and after the war we all returned to football with renewed enthusiasm and vigour. As an island, we believed in those days that our game was the best and I had great difficulty convincing players, managers and clubs that there was a whole football world over the waters growing up and growing up fast.

'We only played friendlies and the qualification for making the World Cup Finals was to win the Home Internationals. There were no floodlights, less strenuous training programmes and little opportunity to get players together. The whole attitude was more relaxed. In some respects you could say we didn't treat things seriously enough and that we were under-prepared for

World Cup football, which probably explains why our form in three successive Finals, 1950, 1954 and 1958, was decidedly ordinary by and large.

'Demands are greater now, far greater. The Press has managed to convince the public that anything less than victory is a national disaster. We were allowed more time, more breathing space, and that enabled us to plan ahead. I remember setting up the idea of England youth internationals with Sir Stanley Rous . . . and then forming the under-23 set up.

'European countries looked to us as leaders and we gave the Netherlands their first international in England, at Huddersfield, in November 1946. The Dutch hierarchy had been pestering for a fixture for some time, insisting that they felt confident of providing stern opposition. We won 8-2, Tommy Lawton got four and Finney scored one and made most of the others!

'It was a real thrashing but I can remember a Dutch official coming up to me afterwards and, with a tone of apology in his voice, saying: "Don't worry, Walter, we will learn from this and improve". And did they improve!

'We had so many great individuals and it was a matter of physically and mentally mixing them into a winning formula. You can pick the best players in every position but not necessarily create the best team.'

But what made Finney extra special?

'Every match he played in for England was memorable but the 10-0 win in Portugal in 1947 was extraordinary. Our flag had been trampled underfoot by a surprise defeat in Switzerland, a team who had themselves been beaten by Portugal. Their defence, particularly their goalkeeper, had won rave reviews and we were given to understand that a sound beating was on the cards. By half-time we were five up and after changing the ball twice they then changed the goalkeeper!

'Finney was in exquisite form and he was brilliant again in our 4-0 win over Italy in Turin a year later – a clash still called the football match of the century. In those days, Italy played a brand of football I had never seen before, based completely around individual skill and showmanship. It was a joy to watch but on that day they couldn't live with us and I recall Tommy scoring twice.

'The Italians took defeat badly. The day after the newspaper stories were surrounded by thick black print lines to suggest mourning. The Italian soccer President was dismissed on the strength of that result, even though Italy had not lost an

international for two years!
'The Italians couldn't stop marvelling over Finney. He was
their type of player . . . he was everyone's type of player.'

I f winning selection for your country amounts to the greatest
achievement a footballer can enjoy then being picked for a
representative fixture for the League in which you play must run it a
close second. Such an honour – a place in the Football League XI –
was bestowed upon Tom Finney no fewer than 17 times in a decade
stretching from 1948 through to 1958.

Surprisingly, this important facet of his career is relatively unknown
and rarely discussed. Yet that decade produced some vintage football.
Moreover, the system of representative games itself was an excellent
idea. Not only were players from around the country thrown together
and allowed to develop their individual skills in a competitive but
friendly atmosphere, but spectators in the regions could go along to
witness some truly first-rate soccer without having to travel all the way
to Wembley.

To illustrate this point, it is interesting to note that Tom began his
representative career right at home at Deepdale. Finney was chosen to
play on his own home ground against the League of Ireland on the
14th of April 1948, just over a week after his 26th birthday. Also
included was another North Ender, full-back Joe Walton, and a crowd
of 35,000 packed the terraces and stands to see the locally inspired
English XI run out 4-0 winners.

League matches of this type were often used as a way of testing
players on the brink of international soccer and were therefore treated
with care and great seriousness by both participants and administrators.

Tom's next sortie came at Ibrox Park in front of a huge and partisan
crowd of 90,000 on March 23rd the following year, when he scored and
helped create a couple of goals for Stanley Mortenson in a 3-0 success
over the Scottish League. Again, he was not allowed to feel lonely, for
Preston's 'flying machine', Bobby Langton, played on the opposite
wing.

In 1950, the year he scored a hat-trick for Preston in a friendly with
Dundee, Finney collected a hat-trick of representative appearances: at
Molineux against the League of Ireland; at Bloomfield Road against
the Irish League and at Ibrox against the Scottish League. The first two
ended in emphatic victories, 7-0 and 6-3, with Finney finding the net
against the League of Ireland, but the final fixture ended in a single-
goal reverse.

By the time of the next fixture, back facing the League of Ireland at

Goodison Park, Langton was still Finney's opposite flankman, although the two were no longer club colleagues. Langton had moved away from Preston to begin a new career at Bolton. Finney was at his most magical in a resounding 9-1 triumph. Although he figured on the scoresheet just once, Tommy Thompson profited most and helped himself to four.

Goals from Nat Lofthouse and Finney secured victory over the Scots on December 3rd 1951 and three months later he got two in a 9-0 win over the Irish, a game played at Windsor Park, Belfast. Lofthouse, who regularly admitted that he felt he could do no wrong with Finney by his side, got a treble.

But there was even better to come the following September when the Lion of Vienna – Nat Lofthouse – made full use of the stream of chances laid on by his Lancashire co-star to find the net six times in a 7-1 win over the same luckless opponents. It is interesting to note that the other goal came from Alf Ramsey, then an accomplished full back, who was later to receive universal acclaim as the master-mind manager behind England's 1966 World Cup triumph.

The second of only three defeats Finney endured at this level came via a 1-0 reverse at Ibrox against the Scots, but the Irish, not for the first time, were the team who were made to pay; crushed 5-0 at Windsor Park with Lofthouse revelling in the freedom to strike yet another hat-trick.

Another England manager of the future, Don Revie, then of Manchester City, got three when Finney and Stanley Matthews plotted a 6-0 win over the League of Ireland at Dalymount Park on September 22nd 1954, just a few months after Finney's personal nightmare in that ill-fated FA Cup Final against West Bromwich Albion.

Finney found the net again in a 4-2 win over the Scottish League at Hillsborough and was outstanding in a 5-1 success over the League of Ireland at Goodison in his 1955 appearances. He did not figure at all in 1956 and played only once the following year, when the Scots collected a 3-2 win back at Ibrox. Then came selection for what was to be his seventeenth and last representative match, again against the Scots at St James Park, Newcastle, on the 26th of March 1958.

Along with Bryan Douglas of Blackburn Rovers, Finney was too hot to handle and a 4-1 winning margin could easily have been doubled. The attendance of 48,800 witnessed a football feast but all the inter-League games produced high entertainment and the supporters, usually numbering more than 70,000 for clashes north of the border, rarely left disappointed.

'The League matches were very special occasions. They often provided a sort of unofficial cap for players who never quite

made the full international scene and I enjoyed them thoroughly.
'In England the games were played on League grounds and
gave those who couldn't travel to Wembley the chance to see the
cream in action on their doorstep. It is a shame that the idea has
died away and I think today's game would benefit if representative matches were re-introduced.'

All in all Finney played on the winning side fourteen times out of
seventeen, losing the other three and scoring seven goals. During his
spell as a 'rep', the Football League scored an astonishing total of
seventy-five goals and conceded just fifteen. Staggering statistics,
indeed.

Chapter Nine

Finney *versus* Matthews
- The Great Debate

HATEVER comes to pass in football circles over the next twenty years, one aspect of football folklore will still stimulate argument and discussion in stadiums and in pubs and clubs right across the nation. The question was asked at the time and has continued to be asked since. It involves the two soccer legends of that era – Tom Finney on the one hand and Stanley Matthews on the other. It poses, quite simply, who was the better player.

Inevitably, almost everyone has aired a view on the matter, some offering sensible, well constructed logic or a balanced view based on first-hand experience, others being unable to shake off the blinkers of prejudice.

As we have seen, the two wingers were available for selection for England for a lengthy period just after the war, much of the time contending for the same right-wing position. First Finney and then Matthews was chosen at the expense of the other. It produced a situation perfectly suited to stimulate heated debate. Media hype was directly responsible for throwing the two men into a soccer boxing ring. Since then the 'contest' has been unfairly refereed by newspaper editors. The journalists of Fleet Street had a field day as two of the greatest English footballers ever were simultaneously tormenting defenders of all nationalities. Sometimes playing in tandem, but usually separately, the two men inevitably found themselves at the centre of controversial and animated discussion about their relative playing merits.

While this may have begun in innocent fashion, newspapers fuelled the great debate on a daily basis to such an extent that, eventually, the football watching public was brainwashed into believing that the two stars were constantly at each other's throats.

The truth, however, was very different – the two men in fact shared a mutual respect and a close friendship. Indeed, Stan has gone on record describing Tom as 'England's greatest ever footballer'. Tom has reciprocated.

Sound neutral judges have tried to assess one man against the other but have consistently failed to draw definite results. Comparison has invariably proved immensely difficult, if not impossible.

To begin with, their respective styles were so different. Finney was a close dribbler, a player of twists and turns, displaying sudden, blinding spurts of speed and with the benefit of a now-you-see-him-now-you-don't quality which left full backs for dead. He also had a formidable record of creating and accepting goalscoring chances.

Matthews had the highest possible level of ball skill and the ability to dominate an entire defence – or simply reduce his marker to a jibbering wreck. He was a feinter, a swerver, a player capable of beating four or five opponents on the touchline before checking back to beat them all over again. Both were soccer superstars, players of extraordinary talent. If Finney was the Galloping Ghost then Matthews was the Silent Scientist.

As for answering the point of the question, in Preston, as you might expect, there has never been the slightest doubt. And, even in Matthews country – Stoke and Blackpool – many have cast their votes in favour of Finney. In the higher echelons of football, opinion is split and no one appears to want the responsibility of the casting vote. The question, it seems, will for ever stay unresolved.

Finney is often amused by so-called well informed opinion, but he comprehensively refutes ill-founded rumours suggesting any kind of friction or animosity between the former wingers. To squash such speculation and get to the truth, Tom states:

'There was never any animosity between Stan and I. By the time I broke into the England scene he was a recognised international of the highest calibre. He was brilliant, a pleasure both to play alongside and to watch. We both had more space and time than the modern-day players but he would still have been a massive star today.

'Privately I got to know Stan well, better than most. In fact, we roomed together quite regularly. In his playing days he was a modest, quiet, unassuming fellow, often preferring to read than to socialise.

'He had a fantastic love of football, completely enveloping himself in the game. He would chat away for hours about matches, goals and opponents and his verbal assessments on the strengths and weaknesses of full backs bordered on the phenomenal. Yet away from the privacy of a hotel bedroom he might not utter a dozen words in an afternoon. Some people reckoned he was aloof and standoffish but his reserved nature was always born out of shyness.

'His preparation was second to none, an excellent trainer and keep-fit fanatic. A man for the big occasion, he could turn games upside down through mesmerising trickery on the right wing.

'I can quite honestly say that of all the times we talked at great length I can never recall either of us mentioning the inquest into our respective merits as players. We both knew that a fued did not exist. Stan found it all rather distasteful and unnecessary – and so did I.

'Stan was a peerless player, an ageless genius who could turn on the magic at the drop of a hat. If I had been picking an England team at that time I would have started by putting the name of Matthews against the number-seven shirt and worried about the other positions later. He had amazing ability and was a credit to football. If I could have been born again as any other player then I would undoubtedly have chosen to be Stanley Matthews.'

A statement which must represent the ultimate accolade. Finney lost touch with his old friend when Matthews emigrated, first to Malta and then on to Canada, but they have since met up at various soccer occasions. Those meetings are always warm and friendly, with the conversation inevitably turning the clock back to their playing days.

I t is desperately difficult to know how to begin separating the two. In coming to a general conclusion, two approaches have been adopted. First, we will look briefly at a statistical survey of the two players' careers at club level and in the all-important national arena. Secondly, and more significantly, we will examine the opinions of five other England footballers who, having played with both men, are in the best position to act as a sort of informal 'jury' to adjudicate on the matter.

Let us begin by looking at the statistics for the England team.

Matthews: England appearances: 84 (30 pre-war), 54 caps. International goals: 3. Passes or 'assists' leading directly to a goal (post-war period only): 23.
Finney: England appearances: 76 (all post-war), 76 caps. Goals: 30. Passes or 'assists': 44.

All Matthews' games were as an out-and-out right winger and, including war-time, he played at international level for twenty-three years – from 1934 to 1957. His first appearance against Wales in Cardiff (September 29, 1934) produced a 4-0 win. His last, against Denmark in Copenhagen (May 15, 1957) ended in another triumph, 4-1.

Finney, as we have seen, played in no fewer than three different positions – left wing, right wing and centre forward – and his England spell lasted twelve years, from 1946 to 1958. His first appearance, the opening international after the war, against Ireland in Belfast (September 28, 1946) saw him run out a winner 7-2 and his last, against Russia at Wembley (October 22 1958), also produced a five-goal winning margin, 5-0.

Given the media talk about animosity, it is surprising to note that the two men figured on the same England side eighteen times and, out of those games, only five were lost. The men who gained most from having such gifted performers on the flanks were Stan Mortenson and Tommy Lawton. In those eighteen afore-mentioned internationals, Morty got twelve goals and Lawton nine.

In club terms no one has enjoyed a longer career than Matthews, who played in the Football League until he was fifty. Born in Hanley in the February of 1915 – seven years earlier than Finney – he joined Stoke City on the office staff at £1 a week.

He made several appearances as an amateur before his League debut arrived on March 19th, 1932, at Bury, some fourteen years before Tom began playing competitively for North End. In the years up to the Second World War, Matthews made 237 appearances and scored forty-seven goals. In 1946 he chalked up a further twenty-three games (and four goals) before moving to Blackpool. For the Seasiders he played in no fewer than 379 League games and scored seventeen times. He moved back to Stoke in 1961 (after Tom had retired!) and ran up a final fifty-nine appearances and three more goals before hanging up his boots for the last time. In 1963, he scored the goal which clinched promotion for Stoke and became the oldest player to figure on a League scoresheet, aged 48. In the same year, he joined Finney and Danny Blanchflower as the only men to win the coveted Footballer of the Year award twice. Two years later he was knighted.

When one compares the two men's League careers, one finds that, as in the international arena, Matthews played far longer than Tom but that he scored or 'made' far fewer goals. Matthews played 698 League games compared to Tom's 433 for North End. For Stoke and Blackpool, Stan scored 71 goals, compared to Tom's 187 for Preston. Thus, Matthews got one goal each 9.83 games, while Tom managed a goal once every 2.31 games, a strike rate four times better than Stan's.

In the Cup, similarly, Finney out-scored Matthews heavily, hitting twenty-three goals in forty Cup-ties (a goal every 1.74 games), compared to Stan's eight goals in sixty outings (one every 7.5 games).

Statistically, therefore, it emerges clearly that Finney was by far the more prolific performer. In general terms, it would also appear that he

46. *Finney bore the brunt of some cruel challenges in and around the penalty area, with some defenders taking it upon themselves to stop him at any cost. One example, in a game against Wales at Villa Park, is shown here. Despite some terrible tackling, however, Tom never retaliated.*

47. *The England line-up against Northern Ireland at Windsor Park, Belfast in the first full international after the war. Back: Laurie Scott, Neil Franklin, Frank Swift, Billy Wright, Henry Cockburn. Front: Finney, Raich Carter, George Hardwick, Wilf Mannion, Tommy Lawton and Bobby Langton.*

48. *Again on the right for England, this time in the 1950s.*

49. With Jackie Milburn on England duty against Portugal at Goodison Park, 1950.

50. On tour with England in Portugal on the steps of the hotel. On the front row are Wilf Mannion, Jackie Milburn, Tom Finney, Billy Wright and Stan Mortenson.

51. *Cartoon strip of the famous Derby County/Preston clash which many consider to have been the finest game they ever saw at Deepdale.*

52. *A ballet-style pose as Tom scores for North End in a 3-1 win over Everton at home in 1957.*

53. Shall we dance? Another full back bites the dust . . . .

54. A diving header strike by Finney against Ipswich in 1954.

55. *Skipping past Blackburn Rovers goalkeeper, Harry Leyland, on his way to a goal in North End's 4-1 win at Ewood Park, October 3, 1959.*

56. *Playing centre forward this time, Finney sets up a goal for himself against Newcastle at Deepdale on 16 January, 1960, just three months before he retired. Ironically, it was in this season that he topped North End's scoring list.*

Above: 57. The fateful day, the 1954 Cup Final. Here, Tom introduces Preston's line-up to the Queen Mother before the kick-off.

Left: 58. On the way there. Here Tom is helping North End to a 6-1 5th round victory at Deepdale on the way to Wembley on February 20, 1954.

59. *Finney and Albion captain, Len
Millard, toss for choice of ends in a game to
turn so sour for the Preston star.*

60. *A special souvenir poster to mark the 1954 Cup Final.*

61. **Right:** *One of the 100,000 Cup Final tickets which were sold for that eventful game.*

62. **Below:** *On the steps of Preston Town Hall, Tom gives a speech after the team returns home.*

63. *Jimmy Armfield, who played 568 games with Blackpool, for many years directly behind Stanley Matthews. He also played alongside Finney for England.*

64. *Ivor Broadis played inside forward for England and played with both Matthews and Finney in that position. He used to share a room with Finney on trips abroad.*

65. *Ronnie Clayton of Blackburn Rovers and England. He too played alongside both Matthews and Finney in the same team and is well qualified to comment on their respective skills.*

66. *Tommy Thompson of Stoke, North End and England. Thompson spent a season and a half with Matthews at Stoke and had several very successful seasons with Finney at North End. Not only that, but he also played with them both in one game, sharing a forward line with them both at Wembley against Scotland in 1957. For these reasons, he was selected to occupy the overall seat of judgement on 'The Great Debate'. See page 151.*

67. *Nat Lofthouse of Bolton Wanderers and England.*

68. *Putting the lie to the constant talk about friction and animosity, Finney and Matthews are seen here as linesman and referee respectively at a special challenge match in Manchester organised by* The Daily Express.

69. *Stanley Matthews, pictured here at Blackpool in 1960, had a remarkable career with Stoke, Blackpool and England. He has gone on record as saying that Tom Finney was England's greatest ever player. Tom has reciprocated.*

70. *Walter Winterbottom, the long-lived and highly successful post-war England manager, who is so full of praise for Tom both as a player and a man.*

71. *Stanley Matthews leading out the opposition on September 26, 1960, for Tom's testimonial game held in front of 30,000 fans at Deepdale.*

was also more versatile in the positions in which he could play. The statistical evidence is detailed and reasonably straightforward but it does not tell the whole story and we must rely on the judgements and expertise of those who saw both men play.

The fairest and most democratic way of reaching any verdict is by way of a 'trial' and, for the purpose of reaching a positive decision, a jury of five ex-England stars has been assembled to adjudicate on the matter.

It was difficult to decide who to include on the 'jury'. There are many well-placed people who have offered their opinions in the great debate. For example, ex-North End player, Tommy Docherty, has written on this very subject:

'In case [there are any doubts] in the minds of non-Finney fans, I repeat clearly and categorically: Tom Finney of Preston North End was the greatest footballer in the world.

'I know that Matt Busby agreed with that assessment, too . . .

'And if you want my views on another controversial comparison, I'll add that Finney was out in front of Stanley Matthews as a player, too. Give Stan one hundred per cent as an entertainer, but for pure football ability give me Finney every time.

'What is more, I think most of the men who have played against the two will agree with that assessment. That is why I sometimes lie awake at nights trying to work out what makes international selectors tick.

'I think of the number of times Finney has *not* been in the England team and I shudder and reach for the sleeping pills.

'. . . he was the perfect player. He had no weaknesses . . .

'His ball control was uncanny, his reading of the game superlative. His passing was pin-point in its accuracy. He could shoot hard with either foot and was a wonderful header of the ball.

'. . . at centre forward he reached even greater heights. With him tucked away on the right, we were sometimes inclined to play on him too much. At centre forward he not only gave the attack balance, but we got better results just cashing in on the sheer panic he caused.'

Others, such as Matt Busby and Sir Walter Winterbottom, have also gone on record to say that they felt Tom to be the better player. However, it was decided to consult only those who actually played alongside both Finney and Matthews and these men were not qualified in this regard.

The jury in this celebrated case of Finney *versus* Matthews reads: Nat Lofthouse, Jimmy Armfield, Ivor Broadis, Ronnie Clayton and

Tommy Thompson. The last member of that illustrious panel, Thompson, takes the role of judge for reasons which will become apparent later.

W hen it comes to the hardest job in professional soccer – hitting the back of the net – no one quite matches up to Lofthouse. In thirty-three appearances, for England the former Bolton Wanderers star scored thirty goals . . . an enviable international strike rate. 'The Lion of Vienna', a nickname attached to Lofthouse after a memorable scoring feat in the Austrian capital in 1952, is quick to place the thanks for his success at the feet of Matthews and Finney. On balance, however, while retaining great admiration for Matthews, Lofthouse insists that Finney was always his number one. He rates Finney, not only the better of the two wingers, but goes as far as to say that, for him, Finney was the greatest footballer ever to don a pair of shin pads.

Lofthouse's career ran parallel to Finney's. Both were men who always played for the same club, who played for England in the same era and who maintained close contact with their respective clubs after retirement. Once Bolton's manager, Lofthouse – who celebrated fifty years at Burnden Park this year to win a testimonial – has long been Wanderers' President, a post Finney has held for years at Deepdale.

A straight-talking Lancastrian, Lofthouse is candid in his assessment:

'Two totally different players, despite sharing a common brilliance on the ball. Stan was an individualist whereas Tom was the ultimate team man. Of the twenty-three goals I scored for England, twenty-two came when Finney was in the side, leaving me with a better than one-per-game average. Do I need to supply any more proof?

'There was a wonderful cameraderie among the England players at that time and I was lucky enough to play centre forward with those two on the flanks. It would have been hard for me to have failed. But Finney was extra special. He was a great who could make other lesser mortals rise to standards they never thought possible. My favourite memory obviously relates to the Austrian game in '52. Tommy supplied the pass which allowed me to run through and score the winner. But there was nothing particularly unusual about that . . . Tommy supplied the passes for almost every goal I scored at that level!

'Finney had the lot and all through his career I can never recall seeing him have an off day. He wasn't capable of having a bad 'un. Everyone at Bolton held him in high regard. With respect to the other players in his team we never feared Preston but, my, did we fear Finney.

'Our left back, Tommy Banks, once came off the field after taking a roasting, sat down in the dressing room looking completely knackered and eventually lifted his head towards me and said "That fellow Finney is a superman – we humans can't cope with him!" The greatest ever; yes, I put him ahead of Matthews.'

J uror number two is Jimmy Armfield. Like Finney and Lofthouse, Armfield was a one-club man, totalling 568 games with Blackpool between 1954 and '71. An accomplished, classy full-back, he was recognised by England forty-three times. Few people appreciated the magic of Matthews more than the quiet, pipe-smoking Armfield, who played directly behind the maestro during seven sparkling seasons at Bloomfield Road. He saw Matthews at first hand, game after game, week in and week out. And Armfield, now a national radio broadcaster and *Daily Express* sports columnist, is not afraid to admit that he was a regular paying customer at Deepdale – 'just to watch Finney' – when the fixture list so allowed. He sums up the merits of the two men thus:

'Stan was the greatest example of a footballer – an ultra professional who denied himself many of the standard pleasures of a young man's life. He was a non-smoker and a non-drinker who stayed in when others went out socialising. He kept to a strict diet and went running down on the Blackpool sands every morning. When I broke into the first team he was well in his 30s but you would never have known. His fitness was astounding and, even then, he could run full backs into the ground.

'Finney was more versatile and certainly better in the air. He had two excellent feet, whereas Matthews was a number seven, full stop. Finney was more physical in his approach, too, although Matthews was not the soft touch that many liked to make out.

'People claim that Finney was a better team man but I don't hold to that view. There was no bigger thrill for any young footballer than to walk out on to a pitch for a League game right behind Stanley Matthews. That lifted you to a new level.

'Matthews had his critics; they said he was hard to handle, a loner and generally difficult. I was his team-mate and I never found him like that. Sure, he could be critical of me and he demanded the highest standards. But what has ever been wrong with that? I found him a big help and a sound bloke.

'Finney was different both as a player and as a man. He was

Preston through and through and a quite brilliant artist. In the modern era he would have been a sensation. While Matthews would have globetrotted for a big-money deal to somewhere like Barcelona or Juventus, Tom would probably have stayed loyal to North End. I doubt whether you would have persuaded him to move much further than Liverpool or Manchester.

'I am regularly asked to comment on the greatest English footballers I've seen and three really stand out. Finney and Matthews – and you have to say them in the same breath – and Bobby Charlton. All three had many things in common; great skill, great fitness, the capacity to play on for a long, long time and the ability to entertain people. Also, their behaviour was impeccable. They never questioned a refereeing decision, although they perhaps looked across at the official a time or two with a knowing look as if to say "flippin' heck, ref, you slipped up there".

'Everyone had the greatest possible respect for Finney and there was a lot of admiration for him in Blackpool. He was better thought of at Bloomfield Road than Matthews was at Deepdale. When I played against Tom I never had instructions to go out and floor him; the manager always tried to devise a way of combating his threat through skill. It rarely worked, but no-one could have gone out to deliberately try and harm or hurt Tom. He didn't bring that particular instinct out in anyone.

'The derby games between Preston and Blackpool were unbelievable occasions in those days. I once remember playing at Deepdale (and we actually won there more than we beat them at our place!) and we were leading 3-2 when Charlie Wayman burst through and flicked the ball over our goalkeeper George Farm. I raced back and pushed the ball over the bar with my hand. A penalty was duly awarded and who should step up to take it but Finney. I remember thinking that was just my luck. His shot was saved by George but the ball deflected against a post and bounced straight out to where Tom had followed through and he couldn't believe it as he slid the ball into the opposite corner. The game ended 3-3 and in the dressing room after I said it was sheer fate that the ball should drop at Finney's feet in that way. One of the lads shouted across that the bloody ball always fell at Finney's feet at Deepdale!

'My father was a big Finney fan. More than that, he loved him. I can remember going with dad and paying at the turnstile on many a midweek game at Deepdale. We would stand in the Paddock and do little else but marvel at Tom's skill.

'Playing in his benefit match was one of the highlights of my career. I was 24 at the time and think I told just about everyone in Blackpool that I had been invited to take part in Tom Finney's testimonial. It was such a thrill and I was an international by then!

'Without wishing to dodge the issue, I would find it difficult to separate Tom and Stan. This is football we are talking about, a 'team' game, not one of the loner sports like tennis and golf where it is relatively easy to make comparisons. I must say, though, that as great as Tom was, no one provided football spectators with more entertainment than Matthews He was the ultimate entertainer who could fill stadiums the world over. I can remember going to places like Australia and America where football was just starting to take root, but people came out to watch because they had heard of Stanley Matthews. No one else, and I must include Finney here, has ever held that sort of magnetism.'

Ivor Broadis won fourteen caps for England between 1952 and 1954 and enjoyed a fine career with stopovers at Carlisle (twice), Sunderland, Manchester City and Newcastle. He scored eight international goals as an inside forward. Recently retired as a sports journalist in Cumbria, Broadis used to be a regular room-mate of Finney on the England trips abroad.

Like the other members of the 'jury', he too played on the international stage with both the famous flankmen. Again, like the others, Broadis finds it difficult to compare the two:

'Both had great natural talent, but the biggest difference for me was that Tom was always ready to take a pass or deliver one. He was very aware and conscious of the need to involve colleagues in better positions. With Stan, it was a matter of getting the ball to him and then forgetting all about it until he was ready to bring you back in to the game. The way he retained possession for such long spells was extraordinary, but Stan rarely made a first-time pass.

'So you might say it was easier and more satisfying to play with Finney. He lifted people and was always available to take what we used to term the "get-out" ball. He could take the pressure off. Besides, all my favourite England memories involve and concern Tom. I recall one particular clash with Scotland at Hampden when, as usual, we had taken a terrible pre-match slating in the Scottish newspapers. The hacks had got in to watch our training session where Tom was trying out some new-style up-to-the-minute shorter shorts. All the stories took the mickey, sarcastically announcing in bold type that the "new-look" Finney was not likely to cause many problems. We went out there, strolled to a 4-2 win and Tom absolutely crucified their defence! He was brilliant but, then again, he made a habit of saving some of his real top notch displays for the Scots. Although those games were like sporting wars, the Scottish fans always appreciated skill, whether it came from a Scotsman, an Englishman or a Chinaman. They took Finney to their hearts, although I am not quite so sure about the Scottish full backs!

'Every generation produces one complete player. In my view Georgie Best was the darling of his era and Finney was definitely the bees knees in the '50s. He had two great feet and it must have been most disconcerting for full backs to watch him play on the right wing using his left foot and vice versa. He could head the ball, too, although I have always maintained that football should be played along the floor and that if God had intended it to be an aerial game he would have left holes in our foreheads for studs. Finney had the lot.

'The style of that era – long, baggy shorts – has since prompted a great deal of fun and laughter. The mere appearance of '50s stars sometimes provokes the opinion that the likes of Finney and Matthews would never have lasted in the modern game. That is nonsense. Both men would have been heroes nowadays. I also believe that Tom could have played on for several more seasons if Preston had nursed him with a little more compassion. He took a lot of knocks and regularly played when he wasn't fully fit.

'Stan would have to be runner up to Tom in my book. I don't think that any praise for Finney as a footballer and as a man could ever be too great.'

Ronnie Clayton captained England many times during a glittering career with Blackburn Rovers. He played thirty-five times for his country and, although twelve years younger even than Finney, he turned out alongside both men at international level. Also honoured at under-23, B and League level, Clayton shared the England stage with Finney sixteen times and with Matthews eight.

'In many ways it is a little unfair to pass judgement because there was very very little to choose between the top two players of my lifetime. If I was selecting the greatest right winger of all time, then I would plump for Stan; in that particular position, with all his guile and trickery, he had no equal. He could beat two defenders with just a wiggle of his hips and invariably managed to get a telling centre across the face of goal.

'But there can be no doubt that, taken all round, Tom was number one. I saw more of him than Matthews, being a proud Prestonian and getting plenty of chance to watch him from the Deepdale terraces. He was a God at Preston and little did I know as a kid drooling over his skill that one day I would feature in the same England side.

'He was the ultimate schoolboy hero for my generation and the aspect of Finney which always put him on a pedestal for me was the way he tolerated some hard physical punishment without losing his rag. His disciplinary record has never been matched. He never fouled, never retaliated and never swore. And all that despite being the subject of some crunching tackles in those days. The way he would just get back up on to his feet and run into position without so much as a passing glance for the player who had fouled him was quite amazing.

'When I played against him for Rovers we always considered North End a top-class side. But, to be honest, the main reason was Finney. When he was missing it was as though Preston had fielded a side four men short! He was the master craftsman and a gentleman into the bargain. I dare say there will never ever be anyone to touch him.'

The credentials which allow Tommy Thompson to occupy the overall seat of judgement are irrefutable. Thompson, himself an international with England, also had the unique privilege of playing in the same team as Finney at Preston and spending a season and a half turning out alongside Matthews at Stoke. Remarkably, he also figured in an international appearance sharing a forward line with them both. So he played with Finney and Matthews individually and collectively.

Five years separated Thompson's two England caps. He was included for the 1951, 1-1 draw with Wales in Cardiff but then had to wait until the April 1957 Wembley victory over Sotland for his second international call up. The line-up that day read Alan Hodgkinson, Jeff Hall, Byrne, Clayton, Wright, Edwards, Matthews, Thompson, Finney, Derek Kevan and Grainger.

Thompson featured in a Football League representative eleven which defeated the League of Ireland 8-1 at Goodison Park. Finney was playing and Thompson remembers it well. He should – he got a hat-trick! This consistent inside forward began his career at Newcastle and went on to enjoy success with Aston Villa, Preston, Stoke and Barrow, scoring 224 goals in 442 League outings. At Deepdale, supported by Finney, he found the back of the net 117 times in 188 games; with Matthews at the Victoria Ground he made the scoresheet eighteen times in forty-two games.

Thompson is therefore well placed to act as 'judge'. Emphasising that both Finney and Matthews were world-class performers, Thompson concludes:

'My most successful spell was with Tom at Deepdale. Those were great days and it was a privilege to share the same dressing room. Although Tom will always be remembered as a winger, I always thought that he was at his very best at centre forward. In fact, as a winger he was one of the best centre forwards I ever saw!

'When I arrived at Stoke, Stan was nearing the end, well into his forties. I knew of him and had seen him perform but to play next to him was an unforgetable experience. He was a genius.

'I have always held them both in the highest regard as athletes, entertainers, teammates and men. They were similar in many ways, sharing a common confidence in their own ability, and yet, somehow, they were completely different.

'I shall never forget that Wembley international with Scotland in 1957. Stan was at outside right, I was inside right and Tom was centre forward. What a sandwich that was, and what an honour for me.

'I hear a lot of rubbish talked about players from our era struggling to make the same sort of impact in the modern game. I concede that today's players have a better level of all-round fitness, but few would be able to match the speed of Stan and Tom over the first ten yards.

'Believe me, they would both be huge stars in any team, in any country, at any time, in any era. As far as sticking my neck out and picking the greatest then I would risk being banned from the Potteries and say that Finney would shade it. Quite simply, he was the better "all round" player.'

England lost both Finney and Matthews within the space of 18 months and many reckoned the national game never properly recovered from what was a shattering double blow.

Not surprisingly, perhaps, it has been impossible to come to a definite conclusion as to who was the better player. Just as when the two men were actually playing, there are different views and different assessments. Statistically, Finney undoubtedly comes out on top because he was consistently more successful both at scoring goals and creating goal-scoring chances for others. Also, as we have seen, he was generally reckoned to be the more complete player, extremely adaptable and able more easily to play in any position across the forward line, left, right or centre.

To set against that, Matthews played superlatively well for so long – despite losing his 'best' years to the war – and the longevity of his survival at the highest level seems almost incredible today. The skill and charisma of Matthews cannot be doubted.

The 'judge and jury' in the case of Finney v Matthews did eventually make a choice. Lofthouse reckoned that Finney was the better of the two, as did Ivor Broadis, Ronnie Clayton and Tommy Thompson. Only Jimmy Armfield has reservations about this judgement, returning a split verdict which concluded that, although Finney was undoubtedly more versatile, Matthews had more 'star' quality and was better to watch.

But what emerged much more clearly from their deliberations were the facts that both men were right at the top of their profession; that no one else could quite compete on the same level; that both men would still have been great stars if they had been playing in the modern game; and, finally, that, as Tom said right at the beginning, any question of rivalry or animosity between the two men was thoroughly misplaced.

Perhaps it is time to lay the great debate to rest – though you can be fairly sure that it will rage on well into the next century.

Chapter Ten

Pride of Preston – North End, 1954-1960

J AMES Scotland Symon – the man Tom Finney rates as the most astute and possibly the best Preston manager of his playing experience – never took charge of another game after that 1954 Cup Final choker. Six weeks after striving to console his team, Symon, only one season at the Deepdale helm, moved on to the enormous challenge provided by mighty Glasgow Rangers. Many of the North End squad were rocked by his departure and none more so than Finney.

Symon had won a fine reputation even prior to his short foray into the world of the English League through his achievements in the comparative backwater of East Fife. A dour, determined Scot, he held respect and was considered a man of deeds rather then words. An excellent sportsman in his own right, he had played football for his country and also gained selection on the international cricket field.

He had worked a minor miracle at East Fife before accepting the Preston post, where he continued to preach a gospel which would be admired and applauded by all the purists; academic football full of drive, style without any futile elaboration, art harnessed to a purpose.

Symon did not stay at Deepdale long enough to break records but he certainly made a lasting impression, particularly on Finney.

'He was a brilliant tactician and had that happy knack of getting his players performing to a consistently high level. He was a first-class manager. In a section of the Press he was considered awkward but for the players he was a sincere and honest boss. His time at Deepdale was all too short but I never played under anyone with a better football brain.'

Symon departed back north of the border on June 15 1954 and in the six weeks it took North End's Board to unearth a successor, old reliable Will Scott bridged the gap. Another famous football figure, Frank Hill, was eventually given the full-time appointment but his stay was destined to be uncomfortable and unsuccessful and he lasted a matter of twenty-two months before resigning.

However, Hill it was who took charge when North End kicked off the 1954-55 season with fire in their bellies, anxious to erase from memory the pain and anguish of Wembley. Four days into the season they had gone a long way down the road to achieving that objective when a 5-0 home victory over Manchester City was swiftly followed by a 5-2 success at Cardiff. Against City, Charlie Wayman chalked up a hat-trick while Finney, starring at outside right, got on the scoresheet only once in the romp at Ninian Park.

A single-goal reverse at Everton threatened to spoil the revival but in the very next fixture Cardiff were hammered 7-1 and Finney was simply unstoppable. Hardly surprising, then, that North End found themselves leading the First Division table. That early form proved impossible to sustain, however, especially when Finney, the inspiration, grew increasingly injury prone, succumbing mainly to thigh strains and leg muscle problems but also to an attack of fibrositis. Indeed his fitness problems also kept him out of the international limelight and he featured in only two thirds of the League programme.

Home attendances continued to hover around 30,000 and the Boxing Day Deepdale date with Burnley – a 1-0 defeat – was witnessed by 38,515, only a few thousands below the all-time Deepdale record. North End only managed to finish fourteenth that year, mainly due to an indifferent home record, but did well on a short tour of Scotland in May. Then, a few weeks later, Finney was globetrotting again . . . this time on a personal engagement out in Rhodesia.

During the closing stages of the domestic season Finney's involvement had been minimal, with the public accepting North End's reason that the star turn was being plagued by a 'troublesome injury'.

No one outside the club had any idea, however, just how serious Finney's fitness question had grown. Indeed, Tom firmly believed that his playing days were numbered. He had developed backache which eventually spread down into his legs and caused him fierce pain, especially when he attempted any sudden movement or burst of speed.

'It was a nightmare. I couldn't find any comfort and felt like an old man. Apart from the sheer physical strain, I also began to get mentally depressed. I spent several weeks worrying over my future until one day Elsie said I should consider packing the game in.

'Her theory that the backache wouldn't get a chance to ease if I continued playing was, of course, quite correct. But, with Preston fighting for First Division survival, I felt obliged to put the club first. In my only appearance for England I had a poor game and was on the verge of putting Elsie's advice into practice before I suddenly realised that the only torture which could possibly be worse was the thought of actually retiring from the game.

'I carried on playing as best I could and I realise now that it was a grave mistake. People would say that North End needed me, even if only at half pace, and I fell in line with that school of thought.

'I have always been the world's worst for dodging a problem. The fact was that Preston were desperate and they needed me to turn out. I was swayed and soft-headed when I needed to be strong for my own personal well being.

'And, yes, in answer to the statement that has been aired so often over the years, I can categorically say that I often pulled on the white shirt of PNE when I was far from fully fit.

'After the Easter programme I realised I just could not carry on. If anything, I was becoming more of a hindrance than a help and even walking from the car park to the ground had become a test of endurance.

'I told the manager and the club officials and they made a hospital appointment. That was another nerve-racking experience and I remember sitting in the waiting room wondering whether the doctors would end my career.'

The specialist carried out a selection of X-rays of Finney's lower back and it became clear that, fortunately, there was going to be no major long-term cause for concern, although he was prescribed with a special corset for support. A damaged sciatic nerve lay at the root of the trouble and, amazingly, he was at first advised to train and exercise 'through the pain barrier'. However, further examination prompted the doctors to tell Tom to keep off the playing field until the following season, though he was given their consent to take up a coaching post he had been offered in Rhodesia.

Along with Elsie and the two young children, Brian and Barbara, he flew out to the northern end of the country, first based in Livingstone before working through to Ndola. His invitation had come through the Northern Rhodesian Football Association and he found the position most rewarding:

'The hospitality was marvellous and I was amazed at the local people's enthusiasm for football and expert knowledge of the English game. They were attentive pupils and although I wasn't supposed to accept cash for the visit the people presented me with a cheque for £100 to mark my efforts in a special challenge match. The Rhodesian FA had taken care of all expenses for my family and the trip was so successful that I accepted another invitation to stop off on the homeward journey for a short stay in Kenya where I won another £200 cheque for figuring in two challenge matches.'

F inney's back was feeling much better. Continued exercise and a warm climate proved very beneficial, and when Tom returned to Preston the 1955-56 campaign was just two weeks away. Striker Tommy Thompson, later to become a close friend, had been captured during the summer – stating from the outset that he had agreed to sign purely for the chance to play in the same forward line as Finney.

Thompson's debut was stunning. He got a brace of goals and Finney added another – his 100th for Preston – as North End roared to a 4-0 victory over Everton at Goodison Park.

The Finney-Thompson partnership was to prove an outstanding highlight and the former Aston Villa frontrunner made hay by finding the net in all of his opening four outings. Although Finney's back was presenting no problems, he was constantly hampered, first by a gashed knee, then a twisted shoulder and finally an operation for varicose veins.

Again he played when not quite fully fit but his form stayed at a remarkable level despite an overall down turn in team performances. Also, this was a time when Finney was regularly forced to withstand extremely physical treatment from the opposition. One soccer pundit estimated that, on average, Finney was foul-tackled around twenty times in a game . . . one every four-and-a-half-minutes!

Nevertheless, this was a glorious time for Tom. He was a sportswriter's dream and again the national Press heaped praise on top of accolades. Just a small selection of their eulogies will suffice to indicate the overall tone of their writings:

After a 2-2 draw with Charlton in September:

'Brilliant Charlton keeper Sam Bartram earned his die a point, but he couldn't deny Finney who scored a remarkable goal. He sprinted 20 yards, swerving past two defenders before somehow shooting the ball between Bartram and an upright. Even more fantastic was the acute body swerve necessary before he shot, for he had almost run behind the goal!'

After a 3-0 victory at Birmingham in the same month:

'This was a triumph for Finney. Cool and crisp, he looked every inch the best player in the land. His masterly touches ran Birmingham ragged and had his colleagues shown more steadiness they could have rattled up a cricket score.'

After a 2-0 win over Wolves in December:

'Finney was as dangerous as ever and no defence can cope when he is in this mood. Even Billy Wright was forced to concede that fact afterwards.'

After a 4-0 victory over Spurs at White Hart Lane in March:

'Quiet, modest and a pale poacher. In action Finney was pure dynamite wrapped in velvet. Unequalled ability and intelligence enabled him to run the show from first kick to last and he even chipped in with a couple of goals for himself.'

After a 2-1 home win over Portsmouth in the same month:

'Finney shone like a light in a darkened room and the brilliance of his dribble which produced the winning goal had to be seen to be believed.'

I n spite of Finney's individual glory Preston failed to respond as a unit and found themselves deep in relegation trouble when February saw them lose four games in a row. March, however, opened in a new light . . . Six days into the month Tom and his colleagues were party to an historic soccer moment – London's first floodlit match against Arsenal at Highbury. National newspaperman George Harley saw it like this:

'The League want to limit floodlit football and the Players' Union want more pay for it. The public? They just want more and more of it!

'On a chilly evening involving two teams well down the table 35,000 people turned out to watch. A fortnight ago only 16,000 watched Arsenal entertain Everton. Don't black out night-time soccer . . . it's a must for the future.'

Preston lost and relegation worries deepened markedly but Finney was not prepared to accept such a fate and he scored four times in five games to earn wins over Portsmouth, Spurs and Chelsea and draws against Blackpool and Sunderland.

Yet another injury – this time suffered in winning his 60th England cap against Scotland at Hampden Park – put him back on the sidelines and, surprise surprise, Preston slipped back into losing habits to miss demotion in the end by the narrowest of margins. A final placing of nineteenth meant they were only one point above safety. Hill's reign as manager had done little to improve playing matters and, within a month of the season closing, he left.

In truth he had never been accepted by the supporters after selling goal-hungry Charlie Wayman to Middlesbrough. Wayman had been a terrace favourite and grabbed 106 goals in 157 matches – a striking record no one has ever bettered at Deepdale. Wayman left under a tide of protest and claimed that North End had shown him the door stating: 'North End gave me short shrift after I had wanted to end my career at Deepdale. The scales were weighted against me and I left convinced that there was little reward for loyalty. I was given the impression by the management that I had overstayed my usefulness.'

Supporters were incensed by Wayman's departure and public feeling ran so deep that Hill was forced to use the newspapers as a vehicle of reply, stating: 'We did not kick out Charlie Wayman but thought that as he was nearing 34 he and his wife would have appreciated the opportunity to return to the north east where they originated. We believe in being fair to our players and believe that we have been fair to Wayman both during his stay at Deepdale and over his transfer.'

Nevertheless, Wayman's transfer and the poor form of the team were undoubtedly the main causes of Hill's downfall. Cliff Britton took over at Deepdale on August 30 1956 – four games into a new season, all of which had resulted in defeat.

During that torrid start, however, came a flash of inspiration from a sporting photographer which produced a picture that has become something of a Tom Finney trademark. At a waterlogged Stamford Bridge on August 25 a 1-0 defeat is now best remembered for a picture of Finney in spectacular action known as 'The Splash' and featured on the front cover of this book.

B ritton's ability to organise, coupled with Finney's brilliance, soon brought an upturn in fortunes and the most significant moment arrived just prior to the new manager's arrival. Tom was asked to play at centre forward . . . a decision which not only meant that he had occupied every forward position for Preston North End but one which provided a new springboard to his career.

And many good judges insist that the following three seasons – leading up to retirement – saw him produce his best football ever. Britton has consistently been applauded for the switch but the man responsible for moving Fnney into the middle was actually one-time manager and trainer Jimmy Milne. Finney explains that, after a third successive defeat at Chelsea, Milne approached him with his master plan.

'He had asked me to move to centre forward for the last ten minutes at Chelsea but on the way home he convinced me that a spell at centre forward might just do the trick. When I agreed he seemed delighted and said he would put the business before his directors. We were struggling at the foot of the table without a single point and getting fairly desperate. I thought it was a panic measure to swop me over but I have always believed that as an employee you should endeavour to satisfy your employer.

'At several inches under six feet and on the slight side I knew I didn't hold any of the physical advantages normally associated with big strikers. It was a gamble for both club and myself . . . but what did we have to lose?'

Britton, one of football's most famous names who had given sterling service in spells with Everton and Burnley and won England honours at right half, won a contract worth £2,000 a year. Nowadays an average Third Division boss could expect to command at least ten times that sum. He had walked out on Everton, a club valued at £500,000, with more than two years of his contract to run around six months prior to the Preston approach. Disenchanted, he had declared himself 'finished with the game', but Preston had flattered him with a substantial offer and the promise of a long contract and complete control of team selection.

While his first game, against champions United, ended in narrow defeat, he was suitably encouraged and positively drooled over the success of Finney in a number-nine shirt . . . a move that had originally brought howls of derision. Britton didn't show his face in the dressing room before, during or after the game at Old Trafford, explaining that he wanted to see the players perform before holding a meeting.

'He was quick to praise us on our performance when we eventually met up the following week. He said we would soon get the right results if we continued to show that sort of form and gave us a vote of confidence by keeping an unchanged line-up for the next match.'

It proved to be a master-stroke, for Preston responded in the best possible way with a 6-0 thrashing of Cardiff City, a result which was to completely transform their season from despair into delight. It was Preston's biggest win for two years and a display from Finney to rank alongside his best. North End were five goals to the good by half-time and left the field to a standing ovation from a delirious crowd of 22,102.

His display was perhaps best summed up by the following newspaper article written by Steve Richards:

'I don't go much on the old timer's line – you should have seen Gallacher, you should have seen Dean, you should have seen Camsell, they *were* centre forwards.

But I admit that if, and when, I reach 60 [in 1989], I will tell the lads on the park . . . you should have seen Tom Finney when I saw him against Cardiff at Preston one day . . . now there *was* a centre forward for you.

'Maybe the days of this great England winger at centre forward are numbered. Preston's new manager Britton will doubtless revert him back to the wing when he can find another centre forward.

'But please don't rush it Cliff, don't rob the soccer millions of an imperishable pleasure.

'Finney frightened Cardiff's defence into silly dizziness. He dribbled like Matthews, feinted like Docherty, raided and plotted like Carter and distributed like James.

Cardiff were caught "napping" before half-time. Finney made two of the five, scored another and converted a late penalty to end the massacre at six. Cardiff centre half, Danny Malloy, looked shell shocked long before the end and could only offer, "I'll dream about the guy".'

Any doubts about trying Finney in that central position vanished within those ninety pulsating minutes. The weaving and winding, the elusive skill and the great imagination he showed had proved that one does not need the physique of a bulldozer to be a centre forward. It is worth noting that Tom had celebrated his 34th birthday, a time when most strikers are looking to take a break from the rough and tumble. But he relished the challenge provided by the brawny central defenders and played with the verve of a teenager out to make an impression.

The second month of the campaign became known as 'Golden September', as Preston picked up eleven points out of a maximum of fourteen, scoring seventeen goals in the seven games. Finney's first eight matches as a number nine brought him seven goals. After the crushing of Cardiff came the first win at Highbury for thirty-two years and journalist David Williams reported:

'They came to see Tom Finney, the centre forward and stayed to applaud Finney finesse. It was worth watching Finney every single time he went within ten yards of the ball.

'My sympathy went out to Bill Dodgin for he wasn't up against the stereo-type leader but a near complete forward line wrapped up in one man. Despite wretched rain-sodden conditions, he was truly majestic.'

Finney's performances were setting football agog and the headlines began to call for him to be selected for England in his new position.

One magazine commented that he would give a five-star show . . . even if he was selected as the goalkeeper!

The next international opportunity was a mid-November Wembley date with Wales but, prior to that, the selectors decided to include Finney at number nine in a Football Association clash with the Army at Maine Road. He lived up to expectations and managed a couple of goals, including a header, in a 7-3 victory.

The selectors were suitably impressed and he played centre forward against the Welsh with Stanley Matthews on the right flank. The combination worked perfectly and Finney found the net in a 3-1 win.

An injury forced him to miss the next Preston fixture but his club form remained outstanding right throughout the season and North End, seemingly destined for relegation at the beginning of the season, finished the campaign third, beaten to the runners-up spot by Spurs on goal difference. A total of twenty-three victories brought fifty-six points, a record for the club in the First Division.

Finney grabbed twenty-three goals (striking partner Thompson topped the list with twenty-six) – including his 150th, against Portsmouth at Deepdale on February 2 1957 when North End had triumphed 7-1. National journalist Bill Fryer said:

> 'With no trepidation I say that Preston's eminent recruit to the position, Tom Finney, gave the greatest centre forward show I ever did see and he scored only one of the seven.
>
> 'Preston did everything twice as quickly as Pompey. Finney looked a stronger, faster, fitter, trickier, brainer bamboozler than he ever was before. And, boy oh boy, is that some bamboozling.
>
> 'With a Pompey defender breathing down his neck he did one trick that some showmen would give £500 a week for an option on. A sort of about-turn with his feet and an "as you were" with the rest of his body and there he was . . . gone, ball and all!'

Finney even eclipsed some of the great traditional centre forwards of his day, notably when he overshadowed the Gentle Giant John Charles on an occasion when Preston beat Leeds 3-0.

North End were rated dark horses for the FA Cup but after crushing Sheffield Wednesday 5-1 in a second replay and Bristol Rovers 4-1 they came a fifth-round cropper in another replay with Arsenal. The Highbury crowd of 61,501 saw the Gunners win by the odd goal in three.

But, apart from that disappointment, the club was able to reflect on a season of success and the entertainment provided by their new-found centre forward.

Britton had played a major part, too, although his strict code of conduct, including no alcohol on away trips, did little to increase his popularity among many of the playing staff. Such a ruling never worried Tom for whom drink has held little attraction and he recalls his first season at centre forward with great joy.

'Few people have ever been aware of the fact that Cliff Britton devised a special team plan to accommodate my style in the middle. I was not simply switched there without careful preparation and it was not simply by chance that everything clicked so well.

'We worked hard at the system, for the manager believed that a bad team with method was better than a good team without method. The other players fitted in supremely well and I could not have blossomed without their assistance.

'I stole the headlines but it was a collective effort and the change did my form a power of good. I was chosen to lead the England line within a matter of weeks and I relished the new opportunities thrown my way through a change in position.

'I was often asked if I had copied the retreating style of that brilliant Hungarian, Nandor Higegkuti, but I didn't set out to imitate anyone. I was always conscious of the need to keep "free" to seek out open spaces and go searching for the ball. You should never tie yourself down in a game as fluid as soccer.

'I would sometimes take up the most ridiculous positions, way back deep in my own half or out on the flanks, just with the intention of putting the onus on the centre half. He had to decide whether to follow me and leave the middle wide open or stay in his territory and leave me unmarked. Unbounded possibilities opened up and I enjoyed the extra thinking time I received. It became a battle of wits as much as a battle of physical strength.

'I found that I got no more bumps and bruises than I had as a winger. By and large I found that defenders played it fair and square. I got to know when to expect a crunching challenge and was, for the most part, nippy enough to get out of the way.'

Finney was given additional responsibility at the start of the 1957-58 campaign – his twenty-first at the club. He was awarded the captaincy, a post he had held around the time of the 1954 FA Cup Final, in succession to full-back Joe Walton.

I f North End followers had been satisfied with their team's efforts the previous season they had many more thrills in store, for Preston were to enjoy arguably their finest campaign of the Finney era – finishing runners-up to League champions Wolverhampton Wanderers.

They collected a club record fifty-nine points, scored a hundred goals for only the second time in history, recorded eight 'doubles', had the best home record in the land and Thompson grabbed thirty-four strikes, just three short of Ted Harper's all-time high of thirty-seven recorded in season 1932-33. It was, in every sense, a magnificent all-round showing from a team now established among the world's greatest line-ups.

Having said all that, it started in disappointing fashion, with successive defeats at Nottingham Forest and Burnley. Indeed, North End lost four of their opening half-dozen fixtures. But the line-up which started was to stay more or less unchanged throughout and, when they clicked, few could live with them. That team, in essence, read: Else, Cunningham, Walton, Docherty, Dunn, O'Farrell, Dagger, Thompson, Finney, Baxter and Taylor, although there were to be telling contributions from the likes of Derek Mayers and Dennis Hatsell.

Deepdale had become a fortress and no team relished a visit. An eventual home defeat by the champions on December 7 was in fact the first time Preston had lost on home soil in thirty games – fifteen months. Finney, it must be noted, missed that particular encounter with a groin strain.

Finney and Thompson were rarely off the scoresheet and the former added twenty-six to his partner's thirty-four – a dynamic duo. By the middle of November Preston were looking as though they were very much in the running for the Championship, although Finney blotted his copybook at home to Manchester United by missing a last-minute penalty in what ended as a 1-1 draw. His spot kick accuracy was again called into question against Leicester on March 29 1958 . . . this time he missed two. Fortunately, his mistakes were not crucial, as North End ran out 4-1 victors anyway.

Earlier that month North End had beaten Leeds United 3-0 and Finney had laid claim to another wonderful goal. It came in the sixteenth minute and followed an oblique pass forward by Baxter which Finney anticipated to perfection and took in his stride. Moving to his left of goal he was nearly brought down in the penalty area by Jack Charlton who turned in desperation as a last resort. If Finney had fallen he would undoubtedly have won a penalty but, as it was, he somehow managed to rescue his balance and shoot before the advancing keeper could intervene. He pulled his drive across the face of goal on to the far post from the foot of which the ball rebounded into the net.

Finney also claimed another goal later in the game and his efforts were recorded the following Monday night by *Lancashire Evening Post* correspondent Walter Pilkington:

'There were many present who remembered Finney's debut against Leeds in August 1946 and the great goal he scored soon after the start. Now they saw two similarly dazzling self-inspired efforts and nothing finer will ever be seen at Deepdale than his rapid acceptance of the two chances that yielded him further success.

'Great is the football glory of Finney, the artificer and designer who can so magically turn his tormenting skill into the finished product bearing the master stamp.'

Even better was to come – the outstanding display of that season was on February 1 when North End rattled Birmingham to the tune of 8-0 with a performance that still makes conversation in the pubs and clubs of the Lancashire town and, doubtless, in similar venues in the Midlands!

The Blues were mastered and then pulverised as Preston put together their biggest win of the century. Those present refuted suggestions that Birmingham were a sorry spectacle, little more than a rabble. More accurately, the visitors did their utmost to contain opponents who would, in such form, have lacerated, lambasted and overwhelmed any club side in England, if not the world.

Preston scored four times in the last 20 minutes, three coming in the space of 180 seconds, and Finney, who got two, shared the limelight with Thompson and Sammy Taylor, each of whom had two. Both Finney's strikes came in the first 12 minutes and he remembers the game well:

'I really thought that this was going to be the day when I finally claimed my elusive hat-trick for Preston. With 78 minutes to go I had only one goal to get, but it wasn't to be. I remember hitting the woodwork twice and their goalkeeper making a couple of fine saves but I just could not find that third finishing strike.

'The team was brilliant and it was as good a club effort as I was ever involved in.'

Regretably, only 21,373, one of the season's smallest attendances, were there to see the rout. It was a display which prompted one journalist, James Alfred, to report:

'Calling Old Trafford and Molineux . . . forget those hopes of a double, for you haven't got a chance. On this evidence Preston will be champions and if you don't believe it have a word with a Birmingham defender!

'They had ex-England goalkeeper Merrick to thank that the score wasn't fantastically doubled. He punched shots around both posts and dived at the feet of rampaging Preston forwards to save at least a dozen situations when his outer defence had cracked.

'Finney was superb, his body swerves and dribbles mesmerising. His second goal will be talked about for years.'

Unfortunately, of course, Alfred was wrong in his forecast and the reason for Preston missing out on the title probably lay in the fact that they failed to take a single point off Wolves. Finney missed the first game through injury and then was absent for the return at Molineux in April because of international commitments. He was busy helping England to a 4-0 win over Scotland at Hampden Park on an occasion when that other Deepdale inspiration, Tommy Docherty, was also away, captaining the opposing Scots.

Without the internationals, Preston failed to produce anything like top form and went down 2-0. The defeat enabled Wolves to clinch the Championship with two matches to spare, although North End did bounce back to finish on a high note with wins against Bolton Wanderers, 4-0, and Arsenal, 3-0.

The clash with Blackpool, a morning kick off on Easter Monday, had brought more than 31,000 through the Deepdale turnstiles despite the fact that Preston were without Finney and the Seasiders minus Matthews, both suffering with illness.

For a reason which was never properly explained, Preston decided to use Finney as an orthodox left winger for the FA Cup third-round tie at home to Bolton. Replaced at centre forward by Hatsell, Finney was ineffective and North End lost 3-0. Finney's performance was little better than his ill-fated Cup Final game in 1954 and he was immediately restored to centre forward.

It must be stressed that while the Preston-versus-Wolves Championship fight had caught the public's imagination, the English League was overshadowed by the events at Munich Airport on February 9th when the game was dealt a terrible blow. On that miserable day Manchester United FC became headline news right across the world. On board an aeroplane which crashed were seventeen United players, four club officials and nine football journalists in addition to several other passengers.

Eight of the players lost their lives, one reporter survived and the death toll also included the United trainer, secretary and coach, a travel agent, a supporter, co-pilot and steward. For days, legendary manager Matt Busby lay critically ill in hospital, although he went on to make a complete physical recovery.

Tom was working on a plumbing assignment at a foundry in Radcliffe when the news broke. He recalls:

'It took several minutes to sink in; at first I thought there had been some mistake. The Busby Babes obliterated in a plane crash? It just couldn't be right.

Tragically, it was right, and so many of the people who perished were close friends of mine; Duncan Edwards, Roger Byrne and Tommy Taylor were all England colleagues. In football terms

United were being heralded as the team of the future, the side that was certain to dominate the domestic game for five years or more.

'I was able to offer some positive help by assisting United officials to sign a player as they tried desperately to re-build their team. United's caretaker chief Jimmy Murphy had contacted me to see if I would meet him at a Manchester hotel for a special appointment. I had already promised my services to a local event but, under the circumstances, backed down after getting another player to deputise.

'I met up with Jimmy who told me that he was having quite a job trying to persuade Aston Villa wing half Stan Crowther to sign on the dotted line. Jimmy asked if I would, as a neutral, have a word with the lad.

'I got the distinct impression that Stan was a little overawed by the prospect of having to replace Edwards but nevertheless he finally agreed and I like to think I played a small part in helping to re-build United's future.

'There can't have been many occasions when a player contracted up to a club has been asked to sell the merits of a rival club to a prospective new signing!'

At the conclusion of season 1957-58, North End went on a tour of South Africa and their excellent form continued unabated with a record boasting seven wins from nine matches.

North End opened the following season aiming to go one better, with Finney back on the wing as the management attempted to accommodate the emerging force of Hatsell at centre forward. The new number-nine choice responded with three goals in the first two outings and the team lost only once, at home to Leeds, in the opening nine fixtures. Finney was still getting his quota of goals and by the end of September they stood top of the First Division table.

Despite consistent success, Preston were still considered to be something of a one-man team and, although Finney fought long and hard to squash such suggestions, the events of the campaign's second half certainly fuelled the argument.

A serious groin injury, suffered in a Christmas meeting with Blackpool, was to prove a turning point and, as we shall see, probably marked the beginning of the end for the star.

He only managed to figure in one more game that season and in his absence North End struggled and struggled. Form in the FA Cup was sound enough, even without Finney, as Preston reached the fifth round but in the League it went from bad to worse and eventually they had to settle for a place in mid-table, having lost more games than they had won.

Finney fought a career-long fight against injury and, by his retirement, had been forced to sit out more than a hundred North End matches. Intensive treatment in the summer enabled him to be fit and ready for the dawn of season 1959-60, Finney's last.

He was put back in partnership with Thompson but also figured several times as a winger. Early team form was scratchy but things came together in sensational style in the late autumn with a run of seven straight victories, the pick of which being a 3-0 win over Arsenal at Highbury when former Deepdale half back, Docherty, broke his left ankle.

Preston were scoring goals for fun and it wasn't until the first week of December, at home to Everton, that they failed to find a goal from somewhere. They responded when Finney scored twice to earn a point against Sheffield Wednesday but then, just prior to Christmas, came a game in a thousand with Chelsea winning 5-4 at Deepdale. North End, at the head of the table, were demoralised by the cunning of Jimmy Greaves who scored all Chelsea's goals – the best individual striking rate ever recorded against the Deepdale club.

North End never properly recovered and, in crashing 4-0 in front of 50,990 spectators at Everton, the forward line was described as pathetic, not an adjective often used about the Finney-Thompson link. They didn't manage a victory for more than two months until they defeated Blackburn Rovers 5-3.

It was to prove only a one-match revival and despite four Finney goals in three games at the start of April and a good show in the FA Cup, which ended in round six against the Second Division opposition of Aston Villa, the season was dying on its feet. Injuries, not only to Finney, were starting to take a toll and in one game against Nottingham Forest they were forced to field six reserves; Cunningham, Milne, Dunn, Thompson, Finney and Taylor were all absent.

Some of the home attendances had dropped to as low as 15,000, although Preston still managed to finish in a respectable ninth position and Finney topped the scoring charts with 17. But as the season drew to a dreary close, the club and the town was rocked by the news everyone had dreaded for so long. Tom Finney was the subject in question and Deepdale was never to recover from the bombshell.

Chapter Eleven

All over bar the shouting

HE 30th of April 1960 was a day of gloom, despondency and tears for thousands of football followers nationwide, especially for those flying the flag for Preston North End. For at 4.45 p.m. that particular afternoon the curtain fell on Tom Finney's professional soccer career.

The feeling of grief was universal. For many it really was as though a close relative had passed on. In effect, Tom was a key member of a large but close-knit family and they might as well have tied a giant black armband around the circumference of the town itself.

Football is a game of feelings and no single individual has ever stirred up emotions quite like Finney. But even he couldn't defeat time and he had to come to terms with the fact that his legs could no longer guarantee to ride the tackles and weave the magic which had enthralled spectators for two gruelling decades.

Tommy Docherty wrote, just after Tom's retirement that 'in Preston Finney was a god. The fans up there built a legend around him. Nobody had ever been as good as Tom; probably nobody ever would be. It was not that Finney incited a small section of the community to hysteria, as so often happens in a town team, but that he generated a warm certainty [not an opinion, mind you, but a certainty] in that part of the world that he was the greatest. And I agreed with them – completely and whole-heartedly.'

Yet Tom's reputation in the town of Preston is based on far more than his football. Even today his very presence at the opening of a charity garden fete warrants a report in the local paper. Tom's unassuming nature and down-to-earth charm continue to make him respected and admired wherever he goes. But never before or since has the town's emotion been shown so clearly and unambiguously as on the day of his final game for North End.

The announcement of his retirement was not entirely a surprise but it still came as a shock. The immediate cause for Tom's decision was a groin strain which he had carried for some time and which had become increasingly troublesome. Around the previous Christmas period he aggravated the injury in a local derby game with Blackpool.

it caused internal bleeding and led to a 12-week stint on the sidelines.

Doctors involved themselves with various and extensive examinations but Tom, approaching his 38th birthday, was not to receive encouraging news. 'Hang up your boots' was the essential point of the medical opinion.

As with so many other decisions in his life, Tom was well prepared for the moment. Over the last few seasons he had been giving the matter serious thought. He rarely suffered hardship through lack of careful preparation but, when it finally came, the doctors' recommendation still caused his stomach to turn full sommersault. The end was in sight; the experts offered no real alternative and Tom knew deep down that he would be taking a ridiculous and unnecessary risk to ignore the advice.

Quite rightly he first elected to inform his employer and sent the following letter to Preston North End chairman, Nat Buck:

'Dear Mr Buck,

'I find this letter difficult to write but it is only a reflection of the problems that have confronted me in arriving at one of the major decisions in my life.

'I have decided to retire from football, at least in the active sense, as from the end of this current season. I have given a lot of thought to this problem. I have discussed it with my wife and family and my business associates and I have had quite a few sleepless nights before making up my mind.

'I came straight into North End's first team more than 20 years ago. I have remained in it ever since and want to go out while still in good health, physical condition and playing ability. I do not want to either drift out due to deterioration arising from increasing age or the ever-present possibility of serious injury which could have a lasting effect on my future fitness.

'As you know I had a lot of trouble with my groin injury last season which fortunately has not as yet recurred. Nevertheless, I have had one or two twinges of pain which remind me that the possibility of a recurrence is still there and reinforced my desire not to tempt providence any further.

'Football has provided me with a long, happy and enjoyable career not without its material benefits. It has allowed me to travel all over the world and to meet people from all walks of life who, apart from football, I should never have had the opportunity of knowing. I want to go out with these memories and recollections untarnished.

'I should like in this letter to say thank you to you, your predecessor Mr Jim Taylor, your directors and all who have assisted in the management of the club in the 21 years I have been associated with it.

'Thank you for your help and assistance throughout that period and the happy relationship which has always existed between us.

'Comment is frequently made in the Press about a player remaining loyal to one club throughout his career, but in so far as it takes two to make a bargain, a relationship such as ours is reciprocal.

'It reflects loyalty on the part of the directorate and management to me and it is for this that I most want to express my appreciation.

'There is one other point on which I should like to comment. It may be a presumption on my part to imagine that efforts may be made to bring about a change in my decision but I would prefer that this should not be done and that my decision should be treated as irrevocable.

'As I said earlier in this letter, it has not been easy to contemplate retirement. It has taken me a long time to make up my mind. I have vacillated quite a lot and do not want to go through a similar period of indecision again.

'Finally, although retiring in the active sense I would not like to think that I was severing my connection with football, the game that has given me so much enjoyment and to which I owe so much.

'Nor would I like to think that my association with my one and only club was coming to an end. If, therefore, I can continue to serve the interests of the club in any capacity whatsoever I shall be only too happy to do so.'

Yours very sincerely,
Tom Finney.

When Mr Buck received the letter a Board meeting was duly called and, as requested, Tom's decision was honoured, without pressure being inflicted. Indeed, within a couple of days, Tom received the following reply from his chairman:

'Dear Tom,

'Thank you for your letter which I read to my colleagues at our meeting tonight.

'My directors were naturally deeply shocked to learn of your desire to retire from the game at the end of the season.

'At the same time they cannot but agree with the sentiments expressed in your letter and fully appreciate the decision you have taken.

'I will be writing to you more fully in the near future but in the meantime the Board accept with the deepest possible regrets your decision to leave the game you have graced for so many years.

'They desire to place on record on behalf of Preston North End their sincere appreciation of your unremitting efforts on the club's behalf for so many years and your unsurpassed contribution to the game of football, not only in this country but throughout the world.

'Kindest regards and every good wish for the future.'

Yours sincerely,

Nat Buck (Chairman).

Having gone through the right and proper channel, Tom then made his decision public and announced that the last game of that First Division season would be his swan song. The news brought an outcry from thousands of distressed Prestonians. The Board might have respected his wish but the public was not prepared to go down without a fight. He came under considerable pressure from widespread sources but, in truth, he was never really in a position seriously or sensibly to re-think. The situation was, in part at least, out of his control.

W hat made Tom Finney such a special player? In tangible terms, his Deepdale career had failed to produce a sideboard crammed with medals and trophies. For many seasons Preston were English soccer's 'nearly' men, always challenging but rarely coming through on top. In the early 1950s, for example, there was a runners-up slot in Division One and then, a year later, an FA Cup Final defeat at Wembley. Nor did Tom ever score a hat-trick for his club.

Despite this, Finney's place of supremacy in the Preston hall of fame is assured. The crowd hushed and then cheered madly whenever he had the ball; he could turn full backs inside out; he could make the most competent defender look slow, stolid and dim-witted. He had supreme balance and control.

Finney was a part of nearly every worthwhile attacking movement and he had a foot in most of Preston's goals. He would sometimes collect the ball near the half-way line before skipping past his marker to pull back an inch-perfect centre right into the path of an expectant colleague. But he was rated equally dangerous when cutting in across the front of a defence with the intention of making for goal himself. This capacity was particularly noticeable when he was playing at centre forward.

Because Finney could do all this at such high speed and without losing control for a split second, he was almost impossible to challenge. Many a full back would run alongside before either being left behind in his wake or through diving in with a poorly timed tackle.

Finney was creative with set-pieces. He was entrusted with penalties for both North End and England. In play, he was equally impressive either by making a typical jinking run down the flank or by cutting inside. He was versatile, adaptable and immensely imaginative. The opposition simply could not afford to take their eyes off him; this alone left them vulnerable to attack. He would stalk the wing, drawing defenders out of position, and then run rings round them. Many a full back would return to the dressing room despairing of how anyone could stop him. On a good day, probably no one in the world could.

He was a master of crossing the ball back from the bye-line to create chance after chance for his fellow forwards who would crowd into the box eagerly awaiting the ball. It is noteworthy and significant that these men are the ones who still speak most highly of him today.

His talent for spotting and exploiting opportunities, for selecting the gap which made defences most vulnerable, brought him the absolute respect of all who opposed him.

He had blinding acceleration over the first ten to fifteen yards which he used to great effect as, even when cramped for space, he would swoop past his marker with a sudden, lightning-fast move, often working the ball with his 'wrong' foot. In truth, of course, he did not have a 'wrong' foot, equally at ease on left, right, centre or in the air (several action photographs testify to the incredible height and strength he could achieve in the penalty box). Many said that he had powerful legs but a light upper body, thus making for exceptional stability and tremendous manoeuvrability.

Outstanding, absolute footballing skill, therefore, is what makes Tom Finney immortal. But behind all the speed and the flair, the imagination and the sheer mastery of his game, there was a player who never fouled or spoke back, who was never booked or sent off and who earned and deserved the respect of all those who knew him, both within the game and outside it.

Luton Town provided the opposition on what was to be a most memorable finale. The average Deepdale crowd that season had fallen to around 15,000, but this day was so different that 27,000 turned up to wave a fond farewell.

Under the chairmanship of Mr Buck the North End Board of the time comprised J. H. Ingham, H. Cartmell, W. Cross, A. Harrison, W. Mercer, R. Robinson, W. Shorrock and Dr. A. R. Wood. In the club's official programme for Finney's farewell (then selling for 3d), the directors printed the following editorial:

'This afternoon marks a sad occasion in the affairs of Preston North End Football Club when we acknowledge one of this country's most illustrious soccer sons. Tom Finney has graced the football scene in all parts of the world for many a long day, to the lasting credit of his club, his town and his nationality. . . . the game is the poorer for his retirement. For us at Deepdale the loss is emotionally personal, in this we echo the affectionate sentiments of every North End supporter. It is with deep regret that we must abide by his decision to retire after his years of sterling service and unrivalled example both on and off the field. We wish to place on record our deep and abiding appreciation and heartfelt thanks for Tom's invaluable contribution and devotion to the welfare of this football club.

Both sets of players lined up in a train of honour and the crowd, in which grown men visibly fought back the tears, sang a moving version of 'Auld Lang Syne' before bursting into a raucous rendition of 'He's A Jolly Good Fellow!' Directors and management officials stood together, shoulder to shoulder on the touchline, to offer their own salute.

The Preston team on an emotion-charged occasion read: Else, Wilson, Walton, John Fullham, Dunn, Smith, Finney, Milne, Alston, Dave Sneddon and Taylor. For Luton, the selected players were: Baynham, Dunn, Daniel, Morton, Kelly, Brown, Bingham, Turner, McBride, Cummins and Tracey.

The game itself never reached the standard everyone had hoped or expected it would. A hard surface proved to be the master and Tom, clearly far from 100 per cent match fit, was able to supply only a few of the touches which had graced the playing fields of England for so long. A capricious ball seemed determined not to run kindly for him and Luton's Alan Daniel, a full back just half his age, played the maestro with great verve and intelligence. And Daniel, it must be added, was part of a Luton team already doomed to relegation to Division Two.

North End took the lead on 35 minutes from Alec Alston and, then, Finney – playing on the right wing by public demand – set up the chance Jim Smith gleefully accepted soon after the interval to wrap up the points.

Tom was disappointed by his own contribution to the entertainment. Nevertheless, he was a team-man through and through, always conscious of the need to marry his own individual brilliance to the best collective interest and he was happy to go out on a winning note. But he would have dearly loved to have given a better account of himself.

He did manage to turn on the style in the final 20 minutes, with some vintage wing play which set up a stream of goal chances. Yet he showed he was only human when, late in the game, he slipped two defenders like a phantom to home in on goal. The crowd held its breath and the goal gaped wide and inviting. This was surely it, the moment everyone had anticipated, but Finney hesitated for one fateful second and fluffed his great opportunity.

When he was quizzed on the incident afterwards and asked how on earth he had failed to score Tom offered more of a reason that an excuse. 'Don Bradman was out for a duck in his last Test Match at The Oval because he said he couldn't see the ball for tears in his eyes. Well, that's the way I felt for the whole of the game.'

Tom was choked and his voice trembled when he stood high on a rostrum after the final whistle to address multitudes of his disciples. His speech from a microphone out on the pitch afterwards went like this:

'I hardly know what to say. It is such a sad, sad day for me. I would like to thank you all for the wonderful support I have enjoyed during my time here. Also for the many marvellous tributes paid to me in letters from all over England. I would like to thank the North End directors and my colleagues for making it such a wonderful time while I have been at Deepdale. It is sad but today is a day I will remember for ever and thank you all for making it so grand.'

Indifferent, spasmodic and below par he might well have been on his last League afternoon but, to be honest, the fans had hardly noticed. They had turned up not to see Tom play but simply to see him, wish him well and join in a mutual appreciation.

It was not so much Preston North End and Luton Town that day, more a case of Deepdale United. Town-centre shops and stores were decked out in a blue and white tribute and the cheering which greeted his arrival on to the hallowed turf lasted for several minutes.

Tom never regretted his decision to quit, often reflecting with the benefit of hindsight that he probably got the timing just about right. It had not been in any way a snap decision and it would have bordered on tragic had his reputation and image been damaged by a stubborn reluctance to accept the simple inevitability of the passing of time. There are those who say that, had North End not relied so heavily on the great man over so many seasons and nursed him along rather more than they did when he was not fully fit, Finney might have been able to continue for several more years. Be that as it may, injury and age catch up with every player and Tom, for one, refuses to speculate on what might have been.

Tom Finney will go down on record as having played in 433 League matches and 40 Cup ties for Preston. He wore the England colours seventy-six times and scored thirty goals. He also found the net 187 times for North End during League appearances and added twenty-three in the Cup, seven more in seventeen inter-league games and a further two in four FA matches – a grand total in first-class football of 570 appearances and 249 goals – undoubtedly a record and a ratio of goals-per-game to rank alongside the very best.

One of the privileged 27,000 to witness his last match was Walter Horam, a one-time goalkeeper on the North End books who had never quite made the grade, but a man who was later to carve out fame in the field of comedy. Wandering Walter had taken his place in the Paddock as usual and it soon became apparent that he was alongside two southern gentlemen.

'I take it you are from Luton,' Walter enquired.

'No. Actually, we are Arsenal supporters,' came the response.

'But Arsenal have a match today. Why aren't you with them,' Walter persisted.

'Well, we heard last night that Tom Finney was due to play his last match today, so we caught the first train from Luton this morning. There is only one place to be today if you love football and that's here at Deepdale!'

In that reply the Arsenal supporters had voiced the feelings of football fans nationwide.

Regretably, it must be recorded that many North End fans also 'retired' on April 30th, 1960. Like their hero, they too decided to quit at the top. For them there was no worthwhile football life after Tom Finney.

72. *Tom rushes between defenders to make an attack on goal.*

73. *Arsenal keeper, Jack Kelsey, denies Finney this diving header as the Gunners win 1-0 at Preston on 24 February 1954. Bobby Foster is the North Ender looking on.*

74. *Missing a penalty against Liverpool goalkeeper Charlie Ashcroft on 23 August 1952.*

75. *In the fog. Vision was restricted to 50 yards during this First Division match against Wolves at Deepdale on 22 November 1947. Billy Wright blocks a Finney shot.*

76. Tom's Footballer of the Year Trophy, awarded in 1954 (and 1957) by the Football Writer's Association.

77. Stretching and exercising.

78. *Challenged to a spot of limbo dancing at the Preston Odeon. Tom has always been in high demand in his home town to make guest appearances, open church fetes and such like. He has always tried to oblige.*

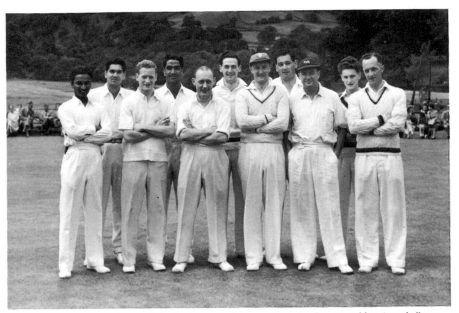

79. *The less well known Finney. Right-hand batsman, left-arm off-spin bowler, pictured here in a challenge match at Ambleside Cricket Club in the Lake District in July 1957.*

80. *And, again, the Tom Finney XI, this time at the West Cliff Cricket Ground in Preston.*

81. *Meeting the Queen Mother at St. Oswald's Youth Club, Preston. Tom is admired by many in the town for his involvement with the local community.*

82. *A souvenir photograph showing Tom in a typical pose.*

83. *A slightly older but remarkably similar shot. As in all these photographs, the stands and terraces are packed to capacity.*

84. *In the week leading up to his last Football League game on 30 April 1960, Tom gives a full interview to the national television network.*

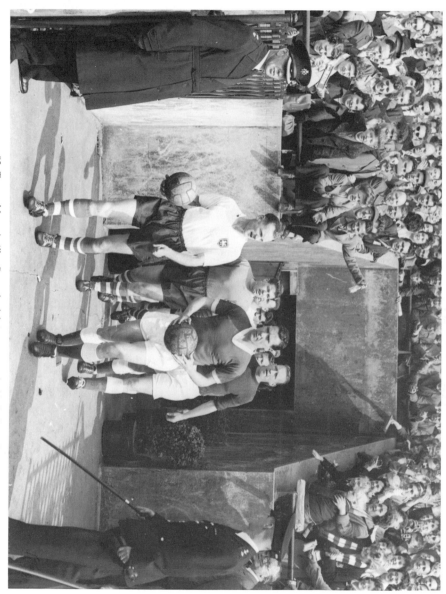

85. Tom and Luton's Allan Brown lead their teams out for his final match.

86. *Arms linked and singing 'Auld Lang Syne', Tom's Preston team-mates join in the farewells.*

87. *A packed Deepdale stadium applaud Finney.*

88. *Police hold back the fans at the final whistle as the Press photographers gather and Tom takes a place of honour at the tunnel.*

89. *Tom's voice cracks as he fights back the tears. He delivers a short 'thank you' speech to a crowd double the normal size.*

90. *Preston gave their hero a glorious send-off. This town-centre barber's shop was typical of the sort of elaborate displays on show.*

91. *All over bar the shouting. Tom, changed and ready for home, hangs his boots in the Deepdale dressing room . . . the end of a 14-year playing career with his home-town club.*

92. *Finney rises above Everton's Alex Parker to score a header in his own testimonial match at Deepdale.*

93. *Presentation night at Earleston Town Hall soon after his retirement in 1960. Tom is pictured with Nat Lofthouse (left) and Dennis Viollet.*

94. *Right out of the blue came an offer to play in the European Cup. Irish club, Distillery, signs Tom up for their clash with Benfica. He is pictured here with Distillery manager, George Eastham.*

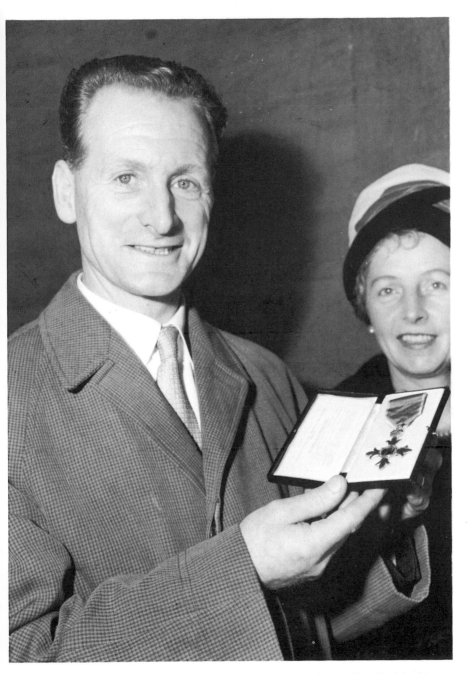

95. *Tom Finney O.B.E., 1961. Many in Preston feel that he should have been honoured by a knighthood by now. Perhaps next time around!*

96. *Testimonial matches dominated the diary long after official retirement and here he gets stripped for action alongside three other former Deepdale favourites: left to right, Frank O'Farrell, Tommy Docherty and Willie Cunningham.*

97. *The hair's a little thinner and the middle a little thicker but Tom could still weave the magic and pull in the crowds at local benefit matches.*

98. *Preston Sportsmen's Guild Re-union, 1952. Preston Guild is held once every twenty years and this re-union brought together some famous names from the town's sporting past. Back row: Alfred Frankland (Manager, Preston Ladies' FC), Charles Webb (the host), Joe McCall (former North End and England centre half) and Tom Finney. Front row: Bob Holmes (Preston North End 'Invincibles'), Bill Brown (ex-North End), Jas. I. Taylor (President and former Chairman of North End), J. B. Edwards (ex-Preston North End) and Percy Smith (ex-Preston North End and Blackburn Rovers).*

99. *Tom and Elsie at home.*

100. With a young Brian and an even younger Barbara.

101. And another family shot, this time playing records in the front room of their home.

102. With son Brian.

103. Explaining the rudiments of the game at an early age.

104. A marvellous picture taken for the media at Deepdale.

105. *Wearing a number-seven jersey, Brian sends one flying past his goalkeeping dad.*

106. *A little older this time, and Brian is shown how it should be done.*

107. *And he watches as the maestro shows him how to work the ball out of a tight spot.*

108. *During the summer of 1955, Tom, Elsie and the children touch down after a soccer coaching trip to Rhodesia and Kenya.*

109. *Tom stars with Brian on a TV commercial for Shredded Wheat. Could he eat three, we ask?*

110. With daughter Barbara shortly after announcing his retirement in 1960.

111. *Tom and Bobby Charlton pass on some hints on how it used to be done to England internationals Dave Watson and Trevor Steven before a memorial match held at Deepdale on behalf of the late Mick Baxter, ex-North End centre half and community officer.*

112. *A line-up of legends. Tom is sandwiched between Joe Mercer and Sir Matt Busby at a sportsman's dinner.*

113. No place like home. Tom and Elsie relax in the sweeping bay window which fronts their delightful house in ,Fulwood, Preston.

114. Outside the Royal Preston Hospital. Tom spent nearly four years as Chairman of Preston Health Authority.

115. Retracing old steps. Tom calls in at Deepdale Modern School, his first place of learning, and soon gets involved in a kick-about.

116. Place of honour . . . Tom singles out his own entry in a special 'hall of fame' mural which runs across the back of the main Pavilion Stand at Deepdale.

117. *Tom was a 'This is Your Life' victim in the autumn of 1988.*

118. *He has also received honorary degrees from Lancaster University and Lancashire Polytechnic.*

119. *Cheers! . . . Tom pulls the first pint at the 'Tom Finney' public house in Penwortham, near Preston.*

120. Tom is made a Freeman of the Borough of Preston, pictured here with Mayor, Dennis Kehoe, and senior councillors at a special ceremony in the Town Hall.

121. And back where it all began. Tom is still a regular spectator at Deepdale and can be seen there at most home games. He still hopes and believes that North End can make it back to the First Division.

Chapter Twelve

Night of nostalgia

A LTHOUGH that emotion-charged spring afternoon marked his last competitive appearance for Preston North End, Finney and his disciples still had another great occasion to look forward to. Common practice for many years within the professional game has decreed that long-serving players should benefit from a testimonial game. No footballer was ever more loyal, or gave his club more than Finney gave to Preston and his reward took the shape of a testimonial match on Monday September 26th 1960. It turned out to be a marvellous, star-spangled night which people in Preston remember to this day. Rarely, if ever, has so much soccer talent gathered within the confines of one stadium.

An augmented North End XI took on the 'Invited All-Stars' and every opponent was a household name Trautmann. (Manchester City), Parker (Everton and Scotland), Armfield (Blackpool and England), Shankly (Preston and Scotland), Franklin (Stoke and England), Wright (Wolves and England), Matthews (Blackpool and England), Mortenson (Blackpool and England), Lofthouse (Bolton and England), Mannion (Middlesbrough and England), Liddell (Liverpool and Scotland) . . . a footballing who's who of the 1950s.

The biggest crowd seen at Deepdale in months, a staggering 33,157, went along to watch a galaxy of stars playing together in an atmosphere redolent of nostalgia and good humour. At Tom's final League game, the overwhelming feeling had been one of sadness; at his testimonial it was different. People were saying farewell to the great man but they were enjoying themselves as well.

The match ended in a 9-4 win for North End and Finney scored twice. But this was a night when such facts paled into insignificance. The result, although obviously pleasing from Tom's viewpoint, hardly mattered. It was an event more than a football match and an opportunity for the Press reporters to wax lyrical. Local newspaper correspondent, John Taylor, saw it like this in the following night's edition of the *Lancashire Evening Post:*

'Football's international supremacy that once belonged to our hardy race of islanders came flooding back to this country, to Preston, last night. It was seen in only fleeting glances, disguised by greying hairs, or lack of them, or middle-aged corpulence, but here were the men of England, particularly, and Scotland, who made in their day this very greatness.

'Perhaps the younger men will forgive little mention for they are having their day. This was the night for the men of yesteryear, a night of sentiment and old-world charm. No fouls, no pressure for two points. Some courtesy though . . . "Will you come past me, Robert, on the right or on the left?" or "Thank you very much, William. By your leave. I'm taking the touchline route at speed".

'It was an evening of memories of past achievements of personalities who will live on in the game.

'Shankly, at 47, hands still flicking backwards, the oldest man afield, passing with deadly accuracy. He stayed on to the very end, as did all the veterans who might have been forgiven had they graciously retired for substitutes long before the 90th minute.

'Matthews, at 45, revelling in the occasion, charming the crowd. He brought his own magical trickery to Prestonians' own doorstep and dispelled doubts that "it is still there". In which class do you dare to put him? Among the eight or so old gentlemen whose night this was, or among the youngsters who looked so promising?

'Golden-haired Mannion recalling ball control and passing of a golden era. Such deft touches were these. Bobby Langton, surprisingly agile, would have missed the game but for Mitchell's unfitness, and thereby made the spectacle the poorer . . .

'Whenever this match is recalled Finney will be remembered for a late injury in a career scourged with hurts and with which he often played with distinction. His generous presentation of a goal to Thompson, the inside forward's first of three, when he could have scored himself, was typical. It would have given him a personal hat-trick, a distinction which never accompanied his name in league records.

'This may have been football in exhibition style with the brake on, but one was left wondering how much has been lost to the game by the fanatical worship of the god Speed.

'The goals went thus:

'9 mins: Liddell cross beats Dunn in the air, waiting Lofthouse scores.

'25 mins: Langton lays on equaliser for Douglas.

'29 mins: Composure of Finney at its best. A delightful pass by

McIlroy and the host lobs over Trautmann's head.

'35 mins: A great 20-yard drive from McIlroy which went in off a post.

'39 mins: Finney again. A pass from McIlroy, Trautmann advanced only to be sent the wrong way and ball tapped into empty net.

'42 mins: A great goal by Lofthouse, a hard shot from an acute angle which beat Else by sheer speed.

'Half-time: PNE XI 4, All-Stars 2.

'51 mins: Thompson's first, a present from Finney.

'55 mins: Shankly own goal after being harassed by McIlroy.

'74 mins: A Douglas centre and Thompson shot home from close range.

'75 mins: Douglas manoeuvred Thompson his third.

'79 mins: That fine run by Langton and Trautmann beaten.

'80 mins: Lofthouse completes his hat-trick.

'85 mins: Parker centre for Mortenson to sidefoot through and ensure Blackpool Town Council were "mentioned in the minutes"!'

Tom had actually been in some doubt for his own big night because of a knee injury which he sustained in playing in Billy Liddell's testimonial the previous week. Ligaments had suffered considerable damage and he was not only in pain but below match fitness. His appearance was touch and go until the last moment but turn out he did and all was well.

He wanted it to be a game for the 'old brigade' and was overwhelmed at the response of his former team-mates and opponents and staggered by the turn-out on the terraces and in the stands.

'It was my first appearance at Deepdale since my retirement and I was determined to be there, injury or no injury. It was a wonderful occasion and we had a ball, before, during and after the match, reminiscing over old times.

'The money was very much appreciated at the time. It was a fortune in many eyes and we decided to invest in a new house, moving from Regent Drive up to a big detached house on Black Bull Lane. I would hazard a guess that my handshake would have multiplied ten-fold by today.'

Tom's favourite story relating to his benefit match concerns a telephone call a few days prior to the game with one William Shankly.

'I had made my mind up that my old North End pal, Andy Beattie, who was such a stalwart for the club, would run the line on the big night and that Shanks, well into his 40s, could run the other.

'When I rang him to explain my intentions he nearly blew a gasket. 'Look here son', he said, 'Run the line, you must be bloody joking – I am playing and that's the end of it!'

'I put the telephone down and just laughed aloud to myself. Shanks never changed. There he was at 40-odd, keen as mustard, totally indignant and making your decisions for you. What a fellow!'

Chapter Thirteen

The Gentleman Footballer

I N an uncertain world one thing remains sure . . . there will never ever be another Tom Finney. Those who saw him play were so fortunate, so privileged.' That is the statement of Jimmy McIlroy, a Finney contemporary who was to Burnley and Northern Ireland what Finney was to Preston North End and England. A player of delightful skill and the subject of a similar sort of public adulation, he was king of Turf Moor while Finney was the darling of Deepdale. Such a parallel of comparison causes McIlroy a certain degree of embarrassment for, again like Finney, he is a man of humility. The very mention of Finney's name, even today, sends him dreaming about a host of golden memories.

There was an obvious twinge of nostalgia and a twinkle in the Irish eyes as Jimmy, now a Lancashire sports journalist, sighed, sat back and reminisced on days of old.

'I can confess that Tommy Finney was my hero; the most complete of footballers, capable of giving a world-class performance in every position on the park. It used to fascinate me to watch his balance and uncanny turn of speed.

'He would run up the line chased by two or three defenders – the full back had usually been left somewhere near the half-way line sitting on his backside! – and somehow manage to keep his body between the ball and the opposition. And he could go from first gear up to overdrive in the blink of an eyelid.

'I remember once taking a girlfriend to Deepdale for a night match when Preston were playing Leicester. We took our places in the stand and there must have been 35,000 people in the ground. Finney was on the wing and Preston had clearly been told to get the ball over to him as quickly and as often as possible.

'When he took up possession there was a sudden deathly silence as everyone waited to see what would happen next. With every stride Tommy took forward, the noise level increased until as he either cut inside for a shot or headed straight for the bye-line the roar had reached crescendo point. He didn't put a foot wrong all night and my girlfriend had never experienced anything like that atmosphere or seen football played that way. Come to think of it neither had I.'

McIlroy played 439 games for Burnley, scoring 116 goals. He had spells at Stoke and Oldham and totalled fifty-five international caps. He also has a vivid recollection of first seeing his hero in action.

'I was a 14-year-old schoolboy from a tiny Irish village called Lumbegwhen when I got the chance to attend a Northern Ireland international against England at Windsor Park. I remember standing behind the goals looking on with great sympathy at our goalkeeper, Tommy Breen. What chance did he have against an England forward line that had Finney and Stanley Matthews dancing down the wings and an all-time great inside trio of Raich Carter, Tommy Lawton and Wilf Mannion?

'Finney was brilliant that day and I was lucky enough to play alongside him in Billy Liddell's testimonial many years later at Anfield. It was then that I discovered a new side to his character.

'Players treat such matches with a certain amount of caution by and large, but I can still see Tommy racing through to contest a 50-50 ball as if his very livelihood depended on it. He injured himself but what made the incident remarkable was the fact that he was prepared to be so committed and his own testimonial game at Preston was less then a week away!

'Finney was a God to the football folk of Preston in those days – and still is. As a footballer he was a one off, an original. To judge a footballing superstar you must take many factors into account and top of that list is longevity. George Best was tremendous but only for a relatively short period. Tommy and Matthews did it for years, season in and season out, without the standard falling for one moment. I once attended a sports forum in Preston and was asked to choose between Tom and Stan. My answer still stands today . . . Finney. In a world eleven he should be everyone's first choice.

But how can McIlroy be so confident that England will never produce a modern-day equivalent?

'Wingers have all but disappeared. The only way they will return is if a country wins the World Cup with a star player on either flank. Young players don't want to be exposed out on the wing; they want to be involved in the thick of the action from first kick to last. Every position used to be specialist but nowadays only goalkeeping falls into its own category.

'Times have changed dramatically. When we were young we developed our soccer skills on street corners, under lamp posts and with a tennis ball. There were often as many as thirty lads involved and you had to be good to keep possession. It enabled you to get a feel for the ball, a touch that you cannot properly master in today's over-technical world.

'By the same token, if such coaching had gone on in the '30s we might well have been denied the utter joy of Finney.'

And finally, with just a hint of Irish logic, Jimmy added: 'As a right winger converted from a left footer, he was the best centre forward I have ever seen!'

J IMMY McIlroy was not alone is holding such opinions about Tom. Indeed, if one were to gather together everyone involved with the game who have recorded their immense regard and respect for Finney, you could fill, not just Deepdale, but Wembley – twice over. To list them all would be impossible and selecting the few to include in this chapter has been difficult enough. Opponents and playing colleagues alike have emphasised, not just Tom's enormous playing ability but also his great affability, his sound and even temperament and his high level of professional commitment. The term 'gentleman footballer' perhaps best typifies the attitude of all those with whom he came into contact at all levels of the game.

One such was an old North End centre half, Tom Smith, who was well placed to remember the early days when a fresh-faced young Finney would tease, torment and terrorise opposing full backs.

As a defender – and Preston FA Cup Final winning captain in 1938 and 1941 – Smith was a good judge of forwards, ever thankful that he never had to confront Finney out on the competitive field. 'Those given the job of marking Finney had my sympathy', laughed Tom, now approaching his 80th birthday.

Smith, an uncompromising centre half, was fortunate enough to lift the Cup at Wembley, every professional's dream, when North End defeated Huddersfield 1-0 in '38 thanks to a George Mutch penalty. 'The whole thing was a blur, for so much happens on Cup Final day. It was unreal and, although I can recall receiving the Cup from the King, I never even noticed the Queen standing by him!'

Smith, capped several times by Scotland, joined the paid Deepdale ranks in 1936, arriving at a fee of £4,000 from Kilmarnock. He was a first-team regular in his first season, before being dropped for the Cup Final defeat against Sunderland. 'On Wembley day I was playing in the reserves at Bolton. Sick? You might call it that! The next year when I skippered the side I insisted that the reserves match be postponed so that everyone could come down to London and watch the game.'

Like so many others of his generation, Smith's career never really recovered after the war but he did write himself into the record books by captaining the side which won the Inter-Allies Cup in 1942, thus becoming the only player ever to receive silverware from both King and Queen. Although his career saw many highlights, all his favourite memories revolve around Finney.

'Memories live longer than years and no one who saw Tom will ever forget him. He will never die.

'I remember Tom and Andy McLaren, two Deepdale youngsters, coming into the side bursting with enthusiasm and telling us seasoned pros how the game ought to be played. Cheeky buggers, both! I can see Finney as though it were yesterday standing on the bench in the dressing room chatting with the manager Will Scott. He talked with great self-confidence and good sense and it made me realise that Tom knew, within himself, that he was a crack player. Not in a big headed way, just in a manner born out of personal belief.

'Bill Shankly once had a quiet word or two in his ear during the interval of a game in which Tom had made a complete fool of an established international full back. I think Shanks felt for the poor guy, understood what he must have gone through, and he went over to Tom and told him to tone things down.

'Finney was so gifted and once he had the ball his eyes would light up with sheer devilment. He enjoyed himself, you know, and how defenders suffered. He never had an equal; he was a supernatural. As a forward he was outstanding and he could defend when he had to.

'That is why he always had the edge on the likes of Matthews. Stan would stand out on the flank and wait for the ball to come and then perform miracles. Finney was far too impatient to hang about; he came looking for the ball. He was, in every footballing respect, the finished article.'

One illuminating incident took place a few years ago when Tommy Docherty was resident on the merry-go-round called soccer management. He had just witnessed a spectacular debut by a young English footballer – the young lad in question had set the game alight and dazzled the crowd with a virtuoso display.

Afterwards the Doc, never short of a word or two, was hounded by the Press for an expert and considered opinion on the debutant.

Doc offered: 'Oh, he looks a good 'un, all right. In fact I would go as far as to say that he is better than Tom Finney.'

The conference was thrown into stunned silence, with journalists staring open-mouthed at Docherty. Eventually one of the scribes pulled himself together and inquired, 'We're quoting here, Doc. Better than Tom Finney . . . are you serious?'

'Oh aye, he's better than Finney, but you are forgetting one thing, gentlemen', replied the Doc. 'Tom Finney is nearly 60 now!'

Not for the first time Docherty had earned himself the last laugh. Joking apart, however, Docherty's admiration for his old colleague knows no bounds. In his book, *Soccer from the Shoulder*, first published back in 1960 Docherty devotes a full chapter to 'Finney the Magnificent'. In it the Doc states:

'Tom Finney was the greatest footballer in the world. Di Stefano and Puskas were not good enough to have laced Finney's boots. And he was way out in front of Stanley Matthews too. Stan got one hundred per cent for marks as an entertainer, but for pure football ability give me Finney every time. Such was Finney's brilliance that I never knew anyone subdue him for the full duration of a match. In short he was a football dream.'

A host of other personalities, colleagues, team-mates, family and friends provide the evidence, if such were needed, that Tom's appeal was universal.

Of course, one would expect his family to speak highly of him. Thus, his father Alf, so important in his childhood and early career, was able to say, 'Tom has been a credit to his family and a fine son. Football enchanted him from an early age and, as a boy, he always thought that his mission in life was to play football. I always tried to advise him to play good football and he made me very proud by doing just that.'

Further support and encouragement had come to the young lad from teachers and other adult acquaintances. Foremost among these, perhaps, was Bill Tuson, Tom's former schoolmaster and later Preston's Chief Education Officer, who said of Tom, 'There was never a nicer boy at school. He was a natural footballer and Preston should also always remember the many many hours he has given to good causes.'

Tom's England colleagues provide some of the most ringing tributes to his warmth of character as well as his playing abilities. Old rivals and playing partners like Nat Lofthouse are fulsome in their praise: 'The greatest footballer I ever saw. I am proud to call him my pal. He was the complete player. He could make goals and score them, dribble, tackle, head the ball and play on either wing or at centre forward. And, on top of that, he was the most unassuming sportsman I ever knew.'

Sir Stanley Rous offered, 'The sight of Finney gliding ghost-like down the wing, riding one tackle after another, not just beating a defence but demoralising and demolishing it – the most glorious sight in soccer' and Eddie Hapgood was so impressed with Tom's skill that, after the very first time they played against each other, he said 'He is an outside right who does all his dribbling with his left foot. What can you do with a fellow like that?'

Right at the beginning of his England career the Manchester United assistant manager Jimmy Murphy said, 'Finney did more for the morale of the troops than any pep-talking General could have mustered. I realised then that I was seeing a player who would dominate English football for years to come', while after he had played his final game Stanley Matthews was the first to mourn the loss, describing Tom as 'undoubtedly one of the greatest all-round players I played with or against. A great loss to football'. The Liverpool legend, Billy Liddell, said of him, 'A credit to the game – a quite brilliant player'.

Former Scotland international, George Young of Glasgow Rangers, once said, 'If I were to award a medal to the best winger I have opposed then Tom Finney would be my man. Finney is a genius. There is no other word that can do justice to this fair-haired young man whose serious face is of the type one would associate with a student. But, then again, he *is* a student – of football. It does not take him long to find the weak chinks in an opponent's armour. The remarkable thing about Finney is his ability when running up the wing to suddenly shift the ball from one foot to the other when you least expect it and chip over a perfect centre with his wrong foot. Tom does this on both wings to emphasise what a problem child he can be for full backs. There has been criticism of him for holding on to the ball for too long. I can state that he has never given me a better chance by doing this . . . !'

Sir Matt Busby once said of Tom: 'A true great in every possible respect. A most gifted footballer and an outstanding gentleman. His career was an object lesson to young players to follow both on and off the field of play.'

Not surprisingly, his Preston colleagues join in the praise with alacrity. Officials like Nat Buck could hardly believe that they had a player who so completely matched excellent football skills with such a professional character. Nat said that, 'the saying goes 'be a man and play the game'. Tom played the game and was a man'. And Cliff Britton, ex-North End manager, said, 'An all-time great who remained one of the boys. No club could possibly have had a better servant.'

A surprising number of Tom's team-mates are on record as saying that they decided to join North End simply, or largely, because Tom was there. Thus, the famous centre-forward, Charlie Wayman, said, 'I only joined Preston for one reason – Tom Finney. It was a privilege to play alongside the great man. My, was he something special'. And Joe Dunn, a defender, added that he 'joined Preston because [Finney] was there. The chance to change in the same dressing room as Tom, never mind play alongside him, was a chance I just couldn't miss.' Even the great Tommy Thompson admitted, 'There could be no better team-mate. Like many others at that time I signed for Preston just for the opportunity to play with him.'

Eddie Brown, another Preston centre forward, recalls that 'one morning at training I was put in a pair with Tom. We had to stand sixty yards apart and hit the ball to each other. My passes had Tom running all over the place but his landed in the same spot with such regularity that eventually the patch of grass where the ball bounced turned brown! He was unbelievable.'

One player with North End reserves, the Preston comedian, Wandering Walter, tells the following true story: 'I had become a regular in the North End reserves and was beginning to fancy myself as a star goalkeeper. Thinking about such matters one day as I set off for a match, I shouted up to the wife, "By the way, dear, tonight you will go to bed with the PNE player of the year!" "Really?", she replied, "So tell me, Walter, what time is Tom Finney due to come round?!" '

On a more serious note, Willie Cunningham said, 'We were lucky enough to have the best player of all time in our side. We used to smack the ball up to Tom when we fancied a ten-minute rest and left it up to him. He was phenomenal.' And Ken Horton, the inside forward, describes how 'we would get the ball out wide to Tom and then run into the penalty box and wait for the cross to come over. It nearly always did and we just sidefooted it home. He was a genius. The best player ever by a mile.'

Goalkeeper George Thompson insists, 'Forget whatever else anyone might say, Finney was something extra special and the undisputed king among footballers.'

Even Harry Anders, for so long Tom's understudy at North End, reckons that Tom was 'the best player of them all', despite the fact that whenever Tom was unfit to play and Anders' name 'was announced over the tannoy before a game there would be booing all around the ground'.

Much more has been said in praise of Finney but these extracts can at least indicate the general feeling. And the millions who watched him from the terraces were his worshippers. To bring the curtain down, however, perhaps it is fitting to reflect on the comments made by a certain lady on the day he retired . . . his wife Elsie:

'Tom's decision to retire from football was the hardest decision of his life. But he is a man of his word and he will never play professionally again. He has lived for the game – I know.

'It is not all laughter and cheer for a footballer. I have seen Tom brought home with a fractured jaw; carried in concussed; seen him arrive here in agony with one injury or another.

'But the game has been his life. He enjoyed travels around the world he would never have known but for being a footballer.

'I am happy that he has finished in one piece, going out at the top after fourteen years. I had no part in the final decision but, I must say, that in so many ways I am glad that he has made it.'

Chapter Fourteen

Life after football

CONSIDERING the high esteem in which Finney was universally held, both as a player and as a great ambassador for all that was good in the game, it came as little surprise that he was much sought after to appear in testimonials, benefits and charity matches when the professional days were behind him. Like his England colleague, Stanley Matthews, he had a way of attracting people into football stadiums everywhere with a magnetic force which retirement did little to reduce.

Moreover, after the boots had been polished for the last time, there was widespread speculation, almost inevitably, over the possibility of Finney turning his attention to management. Even before the cheers had died down from his last farewell appearance against Luton, many clubs were rumoured to be on the point of making official approaches. Wrexham, for example, were reported to be ready to tempt him into their hot-seat at a manager-coach salary of £2,000 a year.

Such speculation prompted a near-universal chorus of advice, however, that Finney should never consider such a move. One influential and outspoken opponent was, ironically, the manager of PNE, Cliff Britton. Not renowned for keeping his opinions secret, but a well-respected figure in the game nonetheless, Britton left Tom in no doubt. He said that Finney simply wasn't cut out for the job; that, in truth, he did not really have the right temperament. Knowing Finney as he did, he reckoned that his former star player would be too likely to take his club worries home and suffer sleepless nights.

There were many others who shared Britton's view, not least Tom's father Alf and brother Joe. At the time Joe remarked:

'We have all been proud of Tom as a player, but I would do all I could to keep him out of management. He rose to such terrific heights as a player – that's the way he should always be remembered.

'Besides, we have built up a business together. I think Tom can do a great deal for football yet; but not as a manager. His professional days are over and I expect him to report in at our business premises at 8 o'clock, kitted out in his overalls!'

Alf offered much the same advice, adding, 'I think Tom would be courting trouble if he became a manager, but he can still do a lot for football. To be a successful manager you need the perfect set-up and a lot of luck.'

Tom was never frightened to follow the advice of those he respected – another throwback to the lessons and influence of his father during his formative years – and he quickly dismissed thoughts of management to concentrate all his efforts, firstly on his family and secondly his business venture.

He was simply not allowed to slip quietly into retirement, however, and the telephone developed a strange habit of disturbing the Finneys' tranquility. When he was 40, one such 'phone call came. He had not kicked a football seriously for two years when a caller from Ireland left him speechless.

George Eastham, then managing Irish outfit Distillery, was on the other end of the line and had rung up to plead with Tom to play in the European Cup – against Benfica!

To say that Tom was dropped on would be the sporting understatement of the century. He told Eastham that there was absolutely no chance. He was, after all, too old and out of practice. Such reasons represented little more than excuses in Eastham's eyes and the Distillery chief was not prepared to take no for an answer.

He took time out to journey over to Preston, turned up on Tom's doorstep, pleaded his case and, eventually, secured one of the most remarkable signings of all time. After non-stop persuasion Tom agreed but, with increasing business commitments, refused right from the outset to appear in the second leg over in Portugal.

'I remember the first leg being played on a quite dreadful night. The rain lashed down throughout and Benfica, then a crack side, included the legendary Eusebio.

'To be quite honest, I enjoyed the match and felt I did quite well. Distillery played me at centre forward and we drew 3-3. I didn't score. I kept to my decision on the second leg and Benfica won the return game 5-1.'

Distillery officials had been impressed by his fitness level but that was no surprise. On the one hand Finney had looked after his body during so many years as a professional athlete and he had glided through with few of what might be termed serious injuries: 'I once had a fractured jaw and my legs were often black and blue but, by and large, I did reasonably well to escape major problems. I was blessed with a very strong pair of legs, which meant I was never frightened of competing for the 50-50 balls.'

In retirement Tom took regular training sessions with the North End youngsters and joined in six-a-side matches. Finney's physical power proved invaluable when, quite frequently, the going got decidedly tough out on the park during his professional days.

'You got used to defenders trying to stop you any way they could. I can recall a few opponents trying to talk me off my game with threats and such like and I can remember being clattered from behind on umpteen occasions. To be truthful, it never really bothered me over much.

'People say that I have always been a placid sort of guy and I rarely lost my rag. As a kid, I had been taught that two wrongs never added up to a right and that simple schooling stood me in good stead.'

It also enabled Finney to play out his career without ever once having his name taken by a referee. Little wonder they called him the Gentleman Footballer.

Successful businessman, newspaper columnist, soccer administrator, globetrotter, magistrate, health authority chairman, prize-presenter, after-dinner speaker and still Preston's number one citizen . . . life has been far from dull for Tom Finney since he left the game nearly three decades ago.

Decorated with an OBE, he has also been honoured by being made a freeman of Preston Borough and President of his beloved North End. A pub in the Penwortham district of town carries his name. Finney's fame and public appeal holds no bounds and his diary remains crammed with appointments. Locally there has long been a widespread belief that he should have won a knighthood too. The New Year's honours list has consistently overlooked his claim but that has failed to prevent him being labelled 'Sir Tom'. Tom has always been a fans' man and his difficulty in declining offers and invitations has created a most public figure; a man in demand with no satisfactory escape or hiding place.

There can be little doubt that his loyalty to North End has contributed largely to his community appeal. He was regularly linked with transfer speculation but nothing ever materialised. Why?

'I remember being linked at different times with Manchester United and Newcastle, who I had turned out for in war-time football but, as far as I am aware, there was never a definite bid. It was little more than paper talk, although I must concede that there was always a chance that an offer or two did come in and, because the matter never got further than the Deepdale Boardroom, I may never have been told.

'Apart from the odd occasion, I was never unhappy at North End. One time was just after the war when they tried to cut me down to part-time earnings due to the fact that I was working part of the day as a plumber. I told them I wanted the full first-team rate or I wouldn't sign a contract and, after a couple of weeks of wrangling, the club backed down.

'People have often said that I could have moved on to a big club but Preston *was* a big club in those days; a First Division set-up with a first-class team. We went close to the League Championship more than once and reached the FA Cup Final. Furthermore, there wasn't much point in asking for a transfer on purely financial grounds because no club paid more than the maximum wage. My wage at Deepdale was enriched by a series of sponsorship deals. I marketed the Tom Finney Football Boot for a Northampton company called Raundes and also put my name to shinguards. Stanley Matthews was also in high demand at that time and was linked up with the Co-op.

'I also worked as a newspaper columnist, writing a weekly diary which was syndicated around the provincial Press and I appeared on a television commercial for Shredded Wheat. All the deals were handled personally – agents didn't exist until Jimmy Hill made a breakthrough some years later.'

Finney signed up for the *News of the World* soon after announcing his retirement and travelled the country covering the big matches for some fifteen years.

'I was always accompanied by a qualified reporter who would put my thoughts and opinions into firm copy. I enjoyed the work until one day I received a telephone call from the sports editor to say that the paper was under pressure because of my non-union contribution. He suggested that I should go down to London and take a six-month journalism course but the idea was out of the question because of my pressing business commitments – and I ended work for them.'

Tom's OBE arrived in 1961.

'I received the standard letter asking me whether I would be prepared to accept the honour. Obviously I was delighted and word came through that I had been officially recognised when I was out in the Far East managing a touring side on behalf of the Football Association. On returning home Elsie and the kids went along with me to Buckingham Palace for a ceremony conducted by The Queen.

'I was flattered to be made a Freeman of Preston in 1979 and also to be asked to lead out the England team in the 1982 Centenary match with Scotland.'

Tom has served as a magistrate for the last twenty years and is still very much involved, sitting on the bench at least once a week. Five years ago he agreed to take on the demanding role as Chairman of the Preston Health Authority.

'The offer came right out of the blue, as have many things that have happened in my life. I showed an immediate interest in what they said was a two-day-a-week post and, after sitting an interview, was appointed by the main government ministry. It was a challenging and rewarding job and I suppose a position of great responsibility. Our authority employs thousands.

'An emotive subject, it certainly gave me a better understanding of the intricate workings of a major public organisation. Good health is something to be treasured, for you don't have to look very far to see someone suffering.

'The chairmanship was more time consuming than I had first anticipated and after serving for four years I declined the chance to continue for a second term. It would have taken me into my seventies and I didn't feel that I could go on devoting so much of my life to the role.'

In the last year, Tom has also been honoured with a special guest spot at the prestigious Football Writers' annual dinner at London's Savoy Hotel; soccer trips to Canada and Australia, honorary degrees from Lancaster University and Lancashire Polytechnic and an appearance on the popular television show *This Is Your Life*. When the ITV researchers first approached Tom's wife Elsie on the possibility of making him a subject on the programme she refused, believing that it would cause him more embarrassment than pleasure. Daughter Barbara recalls:

'Mum said no initially but the television people persuaded her to chat the matter over with the family and we convinced her that she should agree. It was very difficult keeping the thing secret from dad and we all fell guilty of a few white lies along the way. They arranged for dad to go down to London on the pretence of him taking part in a television documentary on football. He knew absolutely nothing about the true reason for his trip. The family and friends travelled together on a coach and I will never forget dad's face when he was confronted by Michael Aspel and that famous red book. We all enjoyed it and everything went off well.'

Stanley Matthews, Omar Sharif and one of Finney's biggest fans, Conservative Minister Cecil Parkinson, all contributed to the show and there were guest appearances from many of his old Deepdale colleagues and ex-England internationals: Billy Wright, George Hardwick, Neil Franklin, Laurie Scott, Johnny Haynes, Wilf Mannion, Ivor Broadis and Ronnie Clayton.

Tom is not a religious man, but a great believer in what he calls 'practical Christianity':

> 'I don't attend church regularly, although I went often as a schoolboy. There was always at least one service and then Sunday School to attend on the Sabbath. But when football started to take off, Sunday was looked upon as our one complete family day of the week. I have great admiration for the true Christians – the people who get out into the community offering help, love and compassion where it is most needed.'

Tom spends part of his private social life with the occasional round of golf, travel and meals out with family and friends. Of all the major countries in the world India, Pakistan and Japan are the only places left for him to visit.

> 'I still call in at work every day despite the fact that I officially "retired" a couple of years ago and being in demand and attending functions is all very pleasant. But, quite truthfully, there is nothing I like more than coming home, taking off my tie, pulling on a pair of slippers and spending the evening with Elsie.'

In reality, Tom Finney's life has never really been his own and one story succinctly sums up his position as Preston's most wanted man. A recent telephone caller to his home of the last fifteen years on Newgate, Fulwood, Preston, invited Tom to be special guest at a local sporting function. A clash of dates led to a polite rejection but the caller was not to be easily discouraged.

'But Tom', he declared, 'we have 500 people booked in and we want you there as our star attraction. If you have something else planned for that night there is only one thing left for us to do . . . cancel. So tell me when you *can* come, Tom, and we will re-arrange the date . . .'

Get out of that one!

Chapter Fifteen

Finney United – family life

STANDING outside the Deepdale players' entrance, umbrella clutched tightly to shield against the pouring rain, patiently waiting for Tom Finney to emerge from within the inner sanctum. Such was a typical winter Saturday evening scene, not only for autograph hunters, but also for a dark-haired young woman in a raincoat . . . Elsie Finney!

For Elsie might well have been married to Preston's most famous star but North End, in common with many clubs in the '50s, failed to recognise such titles properly and offered sparse comfort and few privileges for 'the wives'. There was no special room, no social suite, no executive club . . . barely a cup of tea and a biscuit. They were provided with a seat in the stand, certainly, but little else.

When the game was over it was simply a matter of hanging around outside the ground for a long, long wait. It would not happen nowadays, of course, but soccer wives in the years following the war fared rather poorly. Elsie winces at the memory:

'Many is the time, afternoon or night, that I have stood in the rain waiting for Tom to appear. We couldn't get through the door for love nor money, not even to shelter from the wet. It was unfair but just seemed to be accepted as the norm. The wives would refuse point blank to put up with it now and quite rightly so. Women didn't stick up for themselves in those days and that was the sort of thing that happened as a result.'

Elsie Finney is not a football fan, a point which needs to be underlined in black felt tip. She never has been, not even when her husband was at his prime and everyone's all-conquering hero. Neither of her parents, Jim and Ruth Noblett, were in the slightest bit sports minded and Tom's fame or love affair with football has failed to leave any lasting impression on Elsie.

The first time she saw Tom play in a 'proper match' he wasn't even wearing the North End colours!

'He was playing as a guest for Newcastle United and I remember it vividly. It was during the early part of the war and I was working in munitions at English Electric, a month on days and then a month on nights by rotation.

'This particular weekend I came off the night shift at seven o'clock on the Saturday morning and ran to the railway station to meet Tom. We hadn't been engaged long and travelling up to Newcastle was quite an adventure. I can't recall the result or how Tom fared but I do remember a feeling of great embarrassment.

'Stan Seymour, then the big noise at Newcastle, had arranged overnight accommodation for us both in a hotel, but my mother wouldn't hear of such a thing and I had to come home, even though it meant arriving back in Preston at 3 o'clock on the Sunday morning. We did as we were told in those days!'

It was not until a few years after the birth of their second child, Barbara, that Elsie began attending Deepdale on a fairly regular basis. Her parents would babysit and Elsie became increasingly friendly with Mary Thompson, wife of the Preston and England striker, Tommy Thompson.

'I am not what you might call a football expert now, but I knew little or nothing about the game then. I went along only to watch Tom and, although it sounds a little silly and selfish, I hardly paid much attention to anyone else. Preston used to run socials and day trips for the players up to the Lake District or over to the seaside. The wives sometimes had the chance to go too and we always had plenty of fun.'

Despite her lack of expertise, Elsie was Tom's biggest critic: 'I knew when he had done well and when he hadn't and once told him that he had had a very good game . . . for the opposition. He was quite taken aback!'

Now 67, Elsie is a sprightly, lively woman with an easy manner and a warm and witty sense of humour, though she hasn't always found it easy to share the limelight:

'I used to have an inferiority complex, getting myself into a right old flap when invited to accompany Tom on an official "do". I was convinced that people were glancing across and thinking "what's so special about her?"

'I used to hold back and it irritated me because Tom has always mixed well even with complete strangers. Sometimes when an invitation arrived I would tell Tom to feel free to go along and then stay at home out of the way. I missed out on a few things through that lack of self confidence but it was my own fault.

'I can cope better now – although I still fall foul of the occasional fluster – but I have lost count of the number of times, especially when writing cheques, that people have looked up and said "Are you any relation to Tom Fin . . .?" It can make you scream at times.'

Elsie is the first to admit that she owes a debt of gratitude to football, without which she might never have had the opportunity or money to enjoy such a comfortable standard of living or see so much of the world. But it was by no means one long bed of roses, particularly in the early days:

'The aspect of football which used to rile me most revolved around the end-of-season trips. Tom could be away for as long as a fortnight, first with England and then with North End and it really took a chunk out of our summer.

'I couldn't drive and with two young children it seemed like an eternity, especially after having had to manage without Tom for much of the winter. I didn't like the situation one little bit and made my protests, but there was nothing I could do to change things around. I was lumbered and it was infuriating.'

With Tom committed to generating funds for his plumbing business money was tight early in the marriage.

'If anyone thinks we had it easy just because Tom was a footballer then they are wrong. It was hard going. We used to have tins into which we would drop coins to pay the weekly gas and electricity charges and all other such bills.

'We didn't have a car for several years and I remember us buying our first, a black Rover with a registration number of DCK 804. We sat in it and I can picture Tom's face as he turned across to me and said "My, my, Elsie, did you ever dream we would ever get one of these?" It was such a thrill.'

Soccer has granted the Finneys some golden moments. In 1955 Tom was invited over for a coaching spell in Rhodesia. Elsie and the kids went too. 'We had several weeks out there and a short stopover in Kenya on the way home. It was the first time I had ever been in an aeroplane and my mother was quite distraught at the prospect. She thought we would be gone for good!'

Then there was the visit to Buckingham Palace for Tom's OBE presentation from the Queen, Tom's award ceremony as a Freeman of the Preston Borough, an appearance on *This Is Your Life* and many glorious moments shared.

The worst experience for both Tom and Elsie came at the 1954 FA

Cup Final – his poorest performance, her biggest upset. Some thirty-five years on, the memory still brings pain:

'It is the only time I have stood there and wept at a football match. I knew Tom wanted to do so well, for a Cup Final is so special. He flopped on the day and I felt so very, very sorry for him.

'Really, too much was expected and the pressure even before the game was unbelievable. Everyone was so up tight.

'Tom looked so dejected at the end I just stood up there in the stand at Wembley and cried. Apart from that and the result, the actual experience of the Wembley weekend was wonderful. The players had gone down on the Tuesday and we, the wives, followed on by train on the Friday morning. We stayed at the Savoy Hotel and, as the captain's wife, I got special treatment, with a full suite of rooms for entertaining.

'We really were treated like Royalty and didn't return home until Monday. Preston did us proud and I know the treatment handed out to West Bromwich Albion was nowhere near as good – and they had won the Cup!'

The next time Tom and Elsie stayed at the Savoy was in 1988 when the Football Writers' Association threw a dinner in his honour.

Elsie insists that their marriage has provided her with great happiness:

'Essentially we have got on very well. We have had our rows and arguments but I refuse to believe any marriage doesn't and Tom can have a very stubborn streak. He will fight his corner and always kept a strict rein on the children although I was usually the one who clipped them around the ear when they mis-behaved.'

The Finney offspring both arrived in December – son, Brian, on the 15th 1947 and daughter, Barbara, on the 29th 1949. Mother, incidentally, split them by a week, with a date of birth of December 22, 1922. Brian spent his teenage years playing fly half for a local rugby union club and base guitar for a pop group. If nothing else those two facts underline that simply being a 'Finney' does not necessarily guarantee a glittering career in soccer! Brian did play the round ball game but never progressed beyond the amateur leagues operating in and around Preston. There was a good reason why he didn't follow in his father's footsteps – he just wasn't good enough!

'I was nowhere near the standard to even consider football as a profession', Brian confirms.

The game is in his blood, however, and he still shares his father's love for Preston North End, serving on Deepdale's Guild Club Committee. But if he failed to emulate his dad on the field, he certainly made the grade in business, starting, like Tom, as an apprentice plumber, eventually to work up through the ranks to his current position as managing director at the family business.

A self-confessed rebel during his teens, Brian was born in the town's now defunct Mount Street Hospital at a time when the Finneys had just moved to their first house on Victoria Road, Fulwood, next door to the then Deepdale chairman Jim Taylor. Brian attended Fulwood and Cadley County Primary School before being moved up to Lancaster 'Friends School' as a boarder. Five years there ended when his parents decided that his academic chances might be increased at Preston Polytechnic.

'I was never keen on school and it showed in my results. The sports side was great but classroom lessons proved little attraction.

'I was moved down to the Poly for my 'O' Levels but I fluffed those too and, at 16, I joined the business. Or, should I say, my dad decided that I should.'

Brian, soon to reach 42, was thrust into the spotlight soon after he learned to walk. He was, after all, Tom Finney's son and, as such, a marketable commodity. He starred with Barbara in a Shredded Wheat television commercial and would join his father at the opening of village fetes and such like. It was VIP treatment, toddler fashion, and he was soon in full appreciation of his father's standing in the soccer world. Trips to Deepdale were commonplace, although he recalls little prior to the aforementioned and fated 1954 Cup Final.

'I can't bring back much about the day but I do remember a funny incident a few weeks later when we were holidaying in Blackpool.

'We always went to the same bed and breakfast guest house owned by a couple called Dorothy and Alex, near the main railway track and a stone's throw from Bloomfield Road. Stanley Mortenson used to have a small newsagents shop just around the corner.

'That particular week one of the other guests was none other than Ray Barlow, a giant of a man, who had played for West Brom in the Final. I was more than a little peeved that he had the nerve to stay in the same place as us!'

Brian's early experiences of seeing his father in action came when he was often allowed to sneak on to the trainer's bench on the perimeter of the pitch. One Saturday he sat alongside Tommy Docherty's son,

Michael, and watched on in awe as North End trounced Birmingham City 8-0. 'What a treat that was. We were both about eight at the time and it was a day made in heaven for us. We also sat there when Chelsea came and won 5-4 and Jimmy Greaves had a field day for them.'

While all his school chums idolised his father, Brian's boyhood soccer hero was North End goalkeeper Jimmy Gooch. 'I fancied myself as a keeper but nothing materialised. I did play on the right wing at junior school but up at Lancaster there was no football and I got involved in rugby.'

He turned out for Vale of Lune and Fylde before reviving his soccer during a holiday job with a company with the unlikely name of Geest Bananas, situated down on Preston Docks. Later he played Sunday League soccer for The Trojans but two cartilage operations affected his fitness and he packed in at twenty-six. Did he never feel pressurised into becoming a footballer?

> 'Dad never pushed me. I used to train the odd time at Deepdale when George Barge was running the juniors but I was no great shakes. I played for fun and dad encouraged me at rugby and came to watch the games.
>
> 'He always allowed me to do my own thing at sport and I think he appreciated the awkward position I found myself in. Being Tom Finney's son and not being very good at football wasn't easy.
>
> 'I used to get involved in my share of scraps, mainly through football-related arguments and I got the occasional black eye after being provoked by lads who saw me as something of a target for their jokes.
>
> 'As a redhead I had a fiery temper and often got to fisticuffs over whether Stanley Matthews was better than my dad and daft things like that. I knew I shouldn't get involved but I just couldn't ignore it.
>
> 'Eventually experience taught me to turn a deaf ear but when people are making a nuisance of themselves that isn't always easy.'

Early life was strictly governed through the regimental discipline at boarding school: 'I was a bit of a rebel and needed checking both at school and at home. It calmed me down a lot and has stood me in good stead. When I joined a pop group we would play at local youth clubs and I can remember dad being far from pleased the first time I waltzed home in the early hours!'

It was at such a gig that Brian met up with Marlene, now his wife for the last twenty years: 'We were playing in a pub called the Leyland

Tiger and Marlene was there to help celebrate her friend's birthday. We got chatting and it developed from there.' The couple, who live in a smart detached house within a mile of Tom and Elsie, were married on August 6th 1969 and have two teenage children, Donna, nineteen and Paul, sixteen. Tom's grandson is no footballer either: 'He has two left feet, but he is a keen North Ender!', laughed Brian.

Like most schoolboys of his era Brian was never far away from soccer. He kept a scrapbook and collected autographs and the pictures out of cigarette packets.

'I was proud to be Tom Finney's son and cried on the day he played his last game against Luton in 1960. It was also very touching when North End staged his testimonial a few months later.

'To be candid I don't think I ever really appreciated just how great a player he was until he had finished and we looked at all the tributes that poured in.

'From my viewpoint the advantage was getting in to places for the chance to meet famous footballers; experiences other lads my age would have given their right arms for.

'Nat Lofthouse and Tommy Thompson were always big friends of the family, as was Harry Johnson. Dad has always got on well with Stan Mortenson too.'

Brian was in the crowd at many of Tom's international appearances for England at Wembley and Hampden Park and recalls, in particular, seeing his last England game against Russia in 1958.

But what was home life really like for the Finney clan?

'I suppose we were fairly typical. As a unit we were close but dad and I did have our moments. We rowed but enjoyed a good understanding. I never pestered him and he rarely interfered in my life. He was always there to give advice when I asked for it . . . and sometimes when I didn't!

'Barbara and I were never spoiled and he showed me no favours in business. I started right at the bottom and he didn't even grant me a crack at the office side until my early twenties.

'He has high principles and believes no one achieves anything without hard work.'

Some have said that Tom's success in business came about through his success at soccer – that, without his football name, the business would not have prospered. Brian refutes such opinion. 'He is a good businessman, hard but fair. He is supposed to be retired but he still comes in most days to do the pricing up. With my uncle Joe he started the company from scratch and we now employ 80 people. I have nothing but admiration for what he has achieved in life.'

Barbara was never interested in the slightest in football. Dad might have been the game's greatest but his daughter can count her days spent as a soccer spectator on the fingers of one hand. On match days in the late 'fifties, when Tom was busy delighting the fans at Deepdale, Barbara would choose against a seat in the stand, preferring instead to spend an afternoon with Aunty Mary just around the corner from the Preston stadium.

She explained: 'It is only quite recently that I have become fully aware of dad's fame and I now wish I had got involved more as a young girl. I clearly missed out on quite a lot.'

Now approaching forty and married with two young children, Lee (seven) and Lauren (four), Barbara, like her brother, was no academic mastermind, failing her eleven-plus before leaving Fulwood Secondary Modern at fifteen to attend the local commercial college to follow a secretarial career.

She worked for several years in the police service, as secretary to the chief superintendent, and it was there that she met up with her policeman husband, Jim Herbert.

'I saw dad play a couple of times but could never claim that I actually watched what was going on. It just passed me by and I remember being told off for talking through his testimonial match.

'I was never aware of his standing either in football or in the community until much later in life.

'Being his daughter probably helped at things like job interviews but it has always got to me a bit when people point at you and whisper to one another in supermarkets.'

Barbara's sporting passion has always revolved around horses.

'I can remember pestering and pestering dad to buy me a horse from being about nine or ten years old. He eventually gave in . . . when I was twenty-two! A horse called Kelly came up for sale at a local stables and dad agreed to splash out the necessary £250 under the condition that I looked after all foodstuffs and general upkeep.

'I have always enjoyed a good relationship with both my parents. Mum was always around and the home life centred around her but I leaned a lot towards dad as a young girl.

'He was strict but easy to talk to. He insisted that I be in at a given time and would always prefer to pick me up after parties. I often protested at this over-protection but it was usually a case of if he couldn't collect me then I couldn't go at all.

'He is a placid sort of fellow but he does have a temper which was never apparent on a football field. He holds strong views on most subjects and it has never been easy to change his mind.'

Barbara and Brian shared in the early 1950s' television stardom which fell Tom's way when the family was invited to promote a commercial for Shredded Wheat.

'My recollection of that day is a little vague but it was recorded in London and Brian and I made more than one error and the film crew had to run through the whole procedure several times before we got it right.

'I am very proud of my father and everything has achieved, though, throughout my life, I have regularly wondered whether people were being friendly because they liked me or because I am Tom Finney's daughter.'

236

Chapter Sixteen

For better or worse?

T
HE general standard of soccer in England is just as high
today as it was in the heady days of the 1950s . . . but the
spectacle is poorer."
    The first half of that statement, aired by Tom Finney today,
may come as a major surprise to the vast majority of football followers
who so frequently maintain that the contemporary domestic game is
grossly inferior to its predecessor.

Finney's opinions are forthright and his conclusions enlightening.
He concedes that the overall scene sadly lacks the high number of
individual stars who thrilled packed houses during the post-war boom
but he insists that in many other aspects the current state of play is not
only equal, but better.

Unlike many other players of his era, who turned their backs on
soccer when their own active part was over, Finney has kept close
contact. As a respected authority, an influential administrator and,
above all, a regular spectator, he talks from a well informed viewpoint
based on evidence collected over many years.

Comparing generations is as difficult in sport as it is in life itself and
few have managed to come to any very satisfactory conclusions. In
soccer the whole conception of the game has changed. As a man who
spent his boyhood on the terraces, his career out on the field and his
retirement in the stands, Tom Finney is well qualified to comment:

Finance

'Everything altered so dramatically after the abolition of the
maximum wage soon after my own retirement in the early '60s.
Clubs who had been used to paying players a top whack of £20-a-
week suddenly found themselves with a revolution to contend
with. Players stifled for so long under a system of restraint began
to speak out for themselves and make demands of their
employers.

'They became in charge of their own destinies and many clubs got into severe difficulties in attempting to pay out money they could ill afford. This keeping-up-with-the-Joneses theory proved a road to ruin for many clubs.

'The big city clubs, however, consistently gained strength. The likes of Liverpool, Manchester United, Spurs, Everton and Arsenal have continued to cream off the top individual talent because large attendances have put them in a position to pay huge transfer fees and wages.

'Some say that today's players are greedy but they will get no criticism from me for making what they can. I have always been an advocate of star pay for star play. It's a short career and I say good luck to any player who can persuade a club that he is worth £3,000-a-week.

'I also strongly and vehemently dispute the argument that a sliding-scale or varying wage structure is bad for team morale. Had Preston North End signed Stanley Matthews or Di Stefano during my time on the playing staff at Deepdale, I would have applauded and welcomed the move wholeheartedly. And I wouldn't have given a damn about his earnings. It would have been of little consequence for a start and none of my business for that matter.

'Pay is a private matter between a player and a club and the mistake often made these days is to make such matters public knowledge and fodder for the headline writers on the tabloid newspapers.

'The men on big money are also under considerable pressure. The microscope is consistently focused their way, much more is demanded from them and they have to produce the goods every time they take the field. There is, of course, nothing wrong with that and anyone getting super-high wages should accept the situation and get on with it.

'The old system of paying every player on the books much the same rate was terribly unfair. It would never have happened on the stage or in the movies. Many men made themselves public enemies when the fight was launched to give footballers a fairer deal, but today's stars have a lot to thank them for.

'Had the revolution come before the war then it might well have been I who had stood to benefit. On the other hand, had I played today then there is no way I would have had a guilty conscience about accepting a huge wage. To say anything less would be hypocritical of me.'

Fitness and Coaching

'We were just as quick and just as sharp in the '50s – no one has ever played successfully at top level without a high degree of physical fitness.

'Players trained equally hard; at Deepdale we had people like Tommy Docherty and Willie Cunningham who could run all day and then through the night as well.

'The game is faster now, no doubt about that, but speed often results in more mistakes being made and I think the product would benefit from being slowed down a touch. The secret is to harness pace with skill and intelligence. Being able to run fast has never been enough, for this is football we are discussing, not sprinting. Otherwise Arsenal might as well go out and sign Carl Lewis and expect him to come up with 30 goals in a season!

'Of the young modern players Brian Clough's son Nigel always strikes me as a lad with an astute soccer brain. He hasn't got blistering pace but can make up for that yard by mental awareness and antcipation.

'Preston used to have a couple of fellows called Bobby Beattie and Jimmy Baxter and they could read the game so well, with the ability to see an opening a split second before it actually happened.

'As far as coaching is concerned, I would rather see youngsters given the opportunity to mature the natural way. There are good and bad coaches and advantages and disadvantages to the idea, but I must say that some of the methods used these days disappoint and sadden me.

'I see many schoolboy matches and positively cringe when I hear teachers screaming orders from the touchline like "get rid of it" or "stop trying to dribble". I would much prefer to see the opposite approach whereby lads are encouraged to get a hold of the ball, pass it thoughtfully and basically develop their skills through touch and feel.

'No one tried to "coach" me as a young player. There were people around to offer advice and point out weaknesses and ways to improve, but I can't recall anyone ripping my head off for trying to beat a full back by skilful play!

'Winning at all costs has been to the detriment of the game. We always went out to win, don't get me wrong, but it was never considered the end of the world if we lost, as tends to be the case now. People went to watch for entertainment and were usually satisfied to see a good, flowing, open game and the best team win.

'Coaches should also realise that you cannot make a lad skilful – skill is a natural gift that cannot be implanted, no matter how long you stay behind at the training ground or how many manuals you care to read.

'Over-coaching, of the kind that I believe we have seen in the last decade, produces anonymous, manufactured players. Everything I did on a football field was born out of instinct and I could never have taught anyone how to do a body swerve.

'The game is very technical now and highly skilled and has produced some most effective teams. Liverpool, I feel sure, would have been a tremendous force in my day or any other era for that matter. They have managed to marry individual talent to a shrewd team system.

'I consider the standard of play exceptionally high, but, as a spectacle, today's game is not as good. This, I believe, is down to a reduced number of star players and to the big clubs gobbling up all the talent. All the top-notch men are with a handful of clubs whereas in the '50s every club housed a few individuals who were worthy of prising admission money from anyone's wage packet.'

Tactics and Technique

'I believe that technique has switched emphasis away from pure ball skills but that the teams are more tactically aware than they use to be.

'Liverpool's knack of flair and precision is a sort of footballing perfection, at times approaching the standards set by those amazing and legendary Hungarians three decades ago.

'It riles me to read and hear some of the absolute rubbish written and talked by some of those who fell foul of the game for one reason or another and I suppose I am out of step with many from my generation. But the basics of football remain the same and skilful individuals still hold the key.

'Some say, for instance, that formations (4-4-2, 4-3-3, 4-2-4 etc) have been a modern mistake, but formations are nothing new. We used to line up 2-3-5 and, at the end of the day, it was still eleven versus eleven, though, admittedly with a little more emphasis on attack.

'That system was based on a "pivot" idea, with the game revolving around the centre half. The key positions are the same, although inside forwards and half backs are now a collective breed – midfielders. Every team plays a minimum of two and up to five in this department and the general performance of the team unit usually hinges on who gets a grip in midfield. Billy Bremner and Johnny Giles did it with success for Leeds United and Bobby Charlton and Paddy Crerand were equally effective for Manchester United. The best examples today are Steve McMahon and Ray Houghton at Anfield. These are the telling combinations that can make a whole team tick.

'Defending nowadays often incorporates a sweeper – someone employed to mop up at the back – and this is where the game has probably changed most. Teams used to go out with the sole intention of scoring one more goal than their opponents. Now it is all about "closing people down" and "prevention".

'Tactically I am a purist and like to see the ball passed well and played through the midfield from defence and not simply walloped downfield. Such a hit-and-hope approach leaves me cold, although I can understand teams playing that way if their players are best suited to such a simplistic system. There is nothing wrong in playing to your strengths.

'The Continental style has always fascinated me and I have always harboured a desire to have tried my skills on the European circuit.

'Football by its very definition should be played on the floor and the absence of wingers is another sore point. I don't for one moment believe that a 2-3-5 formation will ever return – team coaches would consider it too much of a risk by introducing such blatant defensive vulnerability! – but there will always be a place for wingers.

'The game is condensed in far too tight an area now; players cannot breath and a winger is an ideal solution. Tactics are all about "shutting out" star players, but true greats cannot be erased in this way. People of the calibre of Matthews or Best would have brought any defensive system to its knees through skill and initiative. Any plan can be unlocked if you have the key.

'We knew all about tactics in our day. We talked about opponents and always had a plan of action. We practised corners and free kicks. We discussed strengths and weaknesses and even used blackboards and special table-top pitches with mini plastic footballers!

'There was man-to-man marking although, I must stress, that much much more is expected of a player these days in terms of workrate.

'My job was to get the better of the respective half back and full back and their roles were to stop me. The full back would wander alongside me and stand there if his team was attacking, for he was never expected to overlap or play an attacking part.

'How it has changed. I have even heard full backs judged on how many goals they score in a season. Even allowing for that, I would always be careful to pick a defender who could, first and foremost, defend.

'As a winger myself I know only too well that defences detest having to deal with the ball whipped back from the bye-line – a ploy not used half as much as it should be. Nearly all the truly great sides employ a winger – or wide-man as he has become labelled. John Barnes does the job ever so well for Liverpool and I am afraid that one of England's proudest moments cost us dearly in this regard. Winning the World Cup in 1966 with the "wingless wonders" was a tragedy for the wide boys. Perhaps it will take a Brazilian triumph in that competition to reverse the trend.

Training, managing, playing and watching

'A manager's role has taken on a whole new look in the last 15-20 years . . . and I wouldn't accept such a post under any circumstances. The pressure is ridiculous, with far too much importance placed on results. Everyone demands to be a winner and logic tells you that out of 92 Football League clubs who start the season only a handful can be successful. Does that make all the others failures?

'Whatever happened to the view that to finish around half-way in the table was to have had a fair season. Managers have been sacked for finishing just a few points adrift of a promotion or championship place. It really has gone plain crazy.

'On the whole, managers become managers much younger now and many seem obsessed with creating perfect physical specimens rather than exciting footballers. Training all revolves around circuits and weights and a ball can often be left feeling sorry for itself at the side of the pitch.

'What a contrast to the '50s! We would do a couple of gentle laps around the pitch, bob into the gym for a few minutes and then spend the bulk of the time playing six-a-side matches. That probably explains why PNE was always considered a good footballing side. The ball was our business and we saw a lot of it. I couldn't imagine Steve Davis practising without using a snooker ball. It wouldn't make sense, would it?

'I think players today can probably run further or for longer periods without flagging and defences are much better organised. We had to contend with a more physical approach, with slide tackles from side and behind being allowed, along with shoulder charging and general argy-bargy.

'I didn't mind the physical side of the game and I honestly believe that I would have found life more difficult now. Attacking has always been the hardest part of football and never harder than today.

'I get a great deal of pleasure from the memory bank, recalling the wonderful times with both club and country and one of my greatest wishes is to see the rise of Preston North End continue right through to the First Division. People might scoff at such a suggestion but my club is in better shape now than for some time. Although the scene is dominated by the big cities, there is still scope for the small town clubs to make a mark. Wimbledon are the perfect example and look at the modern achievements of the likes of Watford, Oxford, Millwall and Norwich.

'No one was hurt more than me back in 1986 when we had to apply for re-election to the Football League after finishing next to bottom in Division Four. The ground I remember holding regular crowds of 30,000 was sparsely populated by around 3,000 on one depressing Saturday afternoon after another.

'The pride went out of the window and North End became something of a joke . . . it didn't make me laugh. We have experienced ups and downs in the thirty years since I called it a day but have never seriously threatened to get back on the top rung.

'If the club was to go on first to win promotion to Division Two and then elevation to Division One I would be thrilled, particularly for the efforts of chairman Keith Leeming.

'Keith has done more then the majority are aware to keep the club alive . . . especially in a financial sense. He has kept the wolves from the door more than once and then had to sit in the directors' box and take abuse from spectators because the players weren't producing results. Few would have taken that criticism on the chin the way Keith did. They would have reacted by pulling the plug.

'It pleases me to see the way the club has put great emphasis on a sound youth policy – the only positive way forward for the likes of North End who are unable to compete in an inflated transfer market. I also believe the supporters identify with a home-reared talent. It certainly did me no harm.

'I still cling to the hope that one day I will walk down Lowthorpe Road on a Saturday afternoon, take my seat in the stand and witness the return of First Division soccer at Deepdale.'

Spectators

'Following football on the eve of the 1990s is so much different than it was in the 1950s. Then it was a form of escapism for men locked in mill or factory work for five-and-a-half days a week, without cars, without televisions and without much idea of how else to spend their leisure time. Football was to Saturday what morning service was to Sunday . . . a religion.

'Living standards are so different now in a fast-moving society where women, quite rightly, demand their space and opportunity and going around a supermarket is a family event.

'I am pleased to say that of the thousands and thousands who still find their main pleasure through watching professional soccer, the majority are true lovers of the game. But it sickens me when hooligans step in to spoil that freedom of fun and enjoyment. These people are mindless thugs who are simply using football as a convenient but unfortunate platform from which to bellow a frustration.

'Equally nauseating is the increase in foul language on the terraces. There has always been noise and cheering at soccer, but the chanting of obscene songs is most definitely a modern scar on the game. Sure, people would drop the occasional swear word in a heated moment but I have seen the culprits go out of their way to apologise to any woman standing within earshot.

'Many fans are extremely well versed in what football is all about but others simply turn up for matches and allow the events to wash over them. I have always maintained that it takes almost as much ability to watch soccer properly as it does to play it. A scout, for example, is just a well-informed spectator. Most fans go along to watch the performance of their team and cannot really appreciate a game as a whole with such a blinkered viewpoint.

'Others come away only satisfied if they have seen a hatful of goals, irrespective of the overall standard of play. I once said that I would rather watch two clever skilful teams contest a goal-less draw than see two kick-and-rush sides reach double figures, and I still stick by the argument.'

244

Chapter Seventeen

Finney's best ever eleven

IF YOU were to survey the opinions of players, managers, administrators, commentators and spectators right across the world of English Association Football then Tom Finney would unquestionably figure in 99.9% of this country's greatest all-time line-ups. For Finney, along with possibly Stanley Matthews, has an unrivalled reputation. The word is grossly over used in modern-day sporting jargon, but Finney was without the slightest doubt a true 'great' with an eternal place in the hall of fame.

But who, in a hypothetical situation, would Finney select as his 10 playing colleagues in his English all-star side? His freedom of choice has been restricted to men who have competed at full international level in the 44 years since the Second World War.

Given this task of acting as a make-believe manager with a vast and multi-talented squad at his disposal caused Tom umpteen headaches. His job was to find a balanced team framework under the old 2-3-5 formation. For the purpose of picking a true representative line-up the great man himself was pre-selected at outside left. He would have been too modest to select himself, but no such team could be considered complete without him. Over to Tom:

'England has been blessed with some outstanding goalkeepers throughout my life span. You need only to think of Bert Williams, Ted Ditchburn, Frank Swift, Gordon Banks and Peter Shilton. With good justification you could pick any of those but I must go for big Frank Swift.

'Frank was a giant, capable of picking the ball off the ground with one hand and then, quite effortlessly, tossing it half the length of the field and beyond. At well over six feet tall, he had a huge frame but was surprisingly agile, particularly quick at getting down to low shots, which is so often a weakness in big keepers.

'He was a master at reducing angles and anything in the six-yard box was his. When the ball came into that danger area it was bad news for anyone, opponent or colleague, who had the misfortune to be standing in his path.

'He had some rare old tussles with the likes of Trevor Ford and other robust centre forwards who could rough things up a bit and enjoyed the physical side. And Frank played in a era when bodily contact was part and parcel of the game and referees were slow to offer protection to the men in green jerseys. He also had a magnificent attitude and was a laugh-a-minute joker in the dressing room. Swiftie would be my number one every time.

'As a winger I am able to talk with a sound personal knowledge of many of the full backs who graced our national game between 1946 and 1958, but my selection at left back didn't start his career until I had retired . . . Ray Wilson. The other wide defender, at right back, would be Don Howe and I will give my detailed reasoning for those choices in a moment.

'But first let me just examine the competition Howe and Wilson had to overcome. In the reckoning one must include the likes of George Hardwick, Laurie Scott, Bill Eckersley, Jimmy Armfield, Johnny Aston, Alf Ramsey and Roger Byrne. All had sound defensive qualities and I can recall some particularly rousing tussles with Eckersley when we faced up to each other in the Preston-Blackburn derby matches at Deepdale and Ewood Park.

'Nevertheless, Howe was such a cultured full back who served West Bromwich Albion and Arsenal so well. He had an astute knowledge of the game and was so quick off the mark. Wilson was the most complete left back of the lot, with pace and good skills. He was the first to make over-lapping part of the full-back's art and he was outstanding in helping England take the 1966 World Cup.

'At right half were the likes of Ronnie Clayton, Bill Slater and Ken Barnes but, with all due respect to the others, Billy Wright had no equal. Billy was a model of consistency; a tenacious tackler who was incredibly strong in the air despite standing several inches under six feet. You could rely on Billy to turn in a sound defensive display every time he pulled on a pair of boots. The first man to win 100 caps for his country, he was an inspirational captain too.

'Perhaps the easiest position to fill is centre half for, in my book, no one has ever come anywhere near the standards set by Neil Franklin. He was a 'footballing' defender and a great tactician. Not a giant by any means, he was a player who always seemed to be one step ahead. His uncanny reading of the play allowed him to win possession through interception but he was also very strong in the tackle. An excellent player.

'At left half the choice basically rests between three: Jimmy Dickinson, Duncan Edwards and Bobby Moore. Dickinson was a little like Wright in that he was ultra dependable and we never really saw the best of Edwards whose career ended tragically in the Munich air disaster. He would surely have developed into a superstar but, all things considered, I would choose Moore.

'I remember meeting up with Bobby when he was just 17. Soon after my retirement I agreed to play-manage a Football Association squad on a 1961 tour of the Far East, Australia and New Zealand and he was a member of the party. It didn't take him long to make an impression – about ten minutes of his first appearance – and he went on to become a tremendous player, He always had so much time to play, was never hassled or hurried out of his easy stride and had a great temperament.

'Right wing is simple – Stanley Matthews, the ultimate entertainer and the greatest ball-player ever produced in this country. He was a man for the big occasion and had the killer instinct. If he sensed he had the beating of his marker (which was virtually every game he took part in) Stan would clinically run the poor fellow into the ground. People have claimed that he would "hide" if the going got tough or the game became physical but few were able to catch him in the first place, let alone clatter him!

'Picking the inside forwards is probably the hardest job of all. Choosing two from Raich Carter, Wilf Mannion, Ernie Taylor, Johnny Haynes, Ivor Broadis, Bobby Charlton, Jimmy Greaves, Alan Ball, Kevin Keegan, Bryan Robson, Peter Beardsley . . . well, it is nigh on impossible. Greaves was a phenomenal goal poacher – the best in history – and Charlton had power and grace as well as a flair for striking spectacular long-range shots. Haynes was a masterful passer of the ball and Carter had the knack of making the right move at precisely the right time. Robson, too, could expect a spot in most sides, but my choice goes the way of Keegan and Mannion.

'I have always respected Keegan both as a player and as a man. His ability was often under-rated, overshadowed perhaps by his workrate. Not a natural in the Matthews sense but a player who got 150% out of himself and became a credit to his profession. He did it right up there at the top and, unlike many other illustrious players, performed magnificently in the Continental game. Believe me, you don't win the European Footballer of the Year unless you are something very, very special.

'Mannion was my old sparring partner, colleague and roommate. A beautiful exponent of one-touch football, he would have enjoyed equal success today. He was the ultimate players' player, always reading your intentions and moving into position.

To lead the forward line and, therefore, to take on the main responsibility for scoring goals I would choose Tommy Lawton, under considerable pressure from Stanley Mortenson, Nat Lofthouse, Tommy Taylor, Jackie Milburn and Gary Lineker.

'Mortenson, Lofthouse, Taylor and Milburn all boasted outstanding scoring records and Lineker has impressed me because he scores goals in an age of mass defences. He can find a route to goal in the minimum amount of space and is a player who would have revelled in the free-flowing attack-minded game of the 'fifties.

'But Lawton was the best of the bunch. The greatest header of the ball – his headers had the power of shots – he had incredibly strong neck muscles and could hang in the air and wait for the cross to come over. For a big fellow he had good close control and was always there to aim for. The ideal target man, there has never been a better all-round number nine than Lawton.

'Although I have been saved the task of choosing an outside left I must make mention of Jimmy Mullen, Colin Grainger, Bobby Langton and John Barnes, the last member of that quartet being our most skilful and elegant performer right now. I love to see Barnes in full flow. Watching him ride tackles and breeze past defenders as if they were invisible is a delight and, along with Chris Waddle, he has the ability to make England a real world football force throughout the coming decade.' As for substitute, well Bobby Charlton gets my vote ahead of Bryan Robson.

'So my greatest all-time soccer line-up since 1945 reads as follows:

		Caps	Goals
1.	Frank Swift	19	—
2.	Don Howe	23	—
3.	Ray Wilson	63	—
4.	Billy Wright	105	3
5.	Neil Franklin	27	—
6.	Bobby Moore	108	2
7.	Stanley Matthews	54	11
8.	Kevin Keegan	63	21
9.	Tommy Lawton	23	22
10.	Wilf Mannion	26	11
11.	Tom Finney	76	30
Sub.	Bobby Charlton	106	49

248

Conclusion

The parting shot

FOOTBALL was a way of life for thousands of people in post-war England. Millions of Britons followed the fortunes of their own local teams and marvelled at the high level of play and sportsmanship which was so regularly on offer. Few sports have held the attention of so many for so long. What other sport can regularly attract 40,000 spectators out on a wet and windy Wednesday evening to stand (not sit down, mind) and watch? For workers across the length and breadth of England, and nowhere more so than in the industrial centres of the North, Saturday afternoon *was* football.

Preston North End was a club which had a tremendous following. For a town of 100,000 inhabitants, it regularly boasted 30,000 spectators on a Saturday. Even today, North End has one of the most loyal and supportive followings in the Third Division and if the club did ever make it back to the First, then there is no doubt that Deepdale, with a modern-day capacity of around 19,000, would be packed for virtually every League or Cup fixture.

Whatever happens, however, it is doubtful if Deepdale will ever again echo to same level of excitement and expectancy that greeted Tom Finney as he stepped out onto the field of play. He was adored at Preston. The fans recognised and saluted his genius. Of course, the end of Finney's career coincided with the end of First Division football at North End. Not surprisingly, then, the fans look back upon the Finney era with great nostalgia. Nothing has quite gone right since the great man retired.

Through the pages of this book we have traced the career and life of a man who was unquestionably one of the best footballers of his generation and probably of all time. The statistics, which are impressive enough, cannot tell the full story of this remarkable player. For many, not just in Preston but across the footballing world, Finney was simply in a class apart. As one famous sporting journalist, Basil Easterbrook, once recalled:

'I remember covering a Preston away match at Portsmouth which North End won 5-2. Finney scored two and made the other three.

'The other twenty-one players trudged from the pitch at the end, caked in mud and stained in sweat. But Finney made for the dressing room with easy strides, his strip as little marked as the referee's. He was the match winner, the star, the wreaker of havoc and yet, in some indefinable way, he was detached from it all.

'I was conscious of a feeling of awe which touches ordinary mortals in the presence of a genius.'

Quite apart from his football skill, which was indeed prodigious, Tom Finney goes down in history as one of the truly great sportsmen of our time. Unlike many who sully their records with outbursts of annoyance, anger or violence, or the larger number still who take part in the 'normal, run-of-the-mill' tackling and physical encounters, Tom never went down that road. If an opponent was good enough to close him down, he did not try to break out physically. He bided his time and won through with skill, speed and intelligence, or not at all. He never retaliated. He was never booked or sent off. His temperament was sound and even. Nevertheless, he had a determination and ruthlessness which surprised many an opponent.

Any player who excelled during the 1950s and who has watched the progress of the game of football over the last thirty years might be expected to frown upon many of the developments he has witnessed. Tom does indeed criticise the obviously bad tendencies of crowd trouble and the 'win-at-any-cost' mentality which prevail today. But, unlike many, he does not hanker after a lost 'golden age'. He does not feel that the standard of play has deteriorated and he does not look back with embittered nostalgia. He still loves the game and stresses the good points, not the bad.

Finney was a product of his time. Brought up in an environment fiercely devoted to football, he has continued to enshrine many of the principles which were passed on to him by his father and the community in which he grew up. Down to earth, honest and hard-working, with a strong attachment to family life and his home town, Tom genuinely embodies all that was – and is – good about northern England.

Tom paused for a while, turned to me and said, 'You know something, I often get out of bed in a morning and think how damned fortunate I have been. Yes, that's exactly what I've been – very, very fortunate'.

Statistical Analysis

1. Preston North End career, 1946-60

Summary

TOM FINNEY played 433 Football League games for Preston North End between 1946 and 1960. He scored 187 goals for his club.
Preston North End's full League playing record in the Finney era reads:

Played	Won	Drawn	Lost	For	Against
588	262	124	202	1091	883

Finney played in several positions, mainly on the wings, but latterly at centre forward.

He won a First Division runners-up medal in both 1952-53 and 1957-58, when Preston North End finished behind Arsenal and Wolves respectively. He won a Second Division Championship medal in 1950-51.

He played just two seasons in Division Two following North End's relegation in 1948-49.

His full League debut came against Leeds United on the opening day of season 1946-47 at Deepdale. His final appearance came against Luton Town on the last day of season 1959-60, again at Deepdale.

He made his highest number of appearances in a season, 37, in 1949-50 and in 1959-60. His lowest number of appearances, 16, came in 1958-59.

His best season for goals came in 1957-58, when he scored 26. He reached double figures for goals in 10 of his 14 seasons for North End and he averaged a goal every 2.31 games. He never scored a League or Cup hat-trick and was North End's leading scorer once, during his last season.

Finney's FA Cup appearance record for Preston North End reads:

Played	Goals
40	23

He captained Preston North End in their losing 1954 FA Cup Final against West Bromwich Albion at Wembley.

His total number of appearances for his club, in both League and Cup reads:

Played	Goals
473	210

Preston North End's League record in the Finney era
1946-60

■ 1946-47 DIVISION 1

		P	W	D	L	F	A	Pts
1	Liverpool	42	25	7	10	84	52	57
2	Man. United	42	22	12	8	95	54	56
3	Wolves	42	25	6	11	98	56	56
4	Stoke	42	24	7	11	90	53	55
5	Blackpool	42	22	6	14	71	70	50
6	Sheff. United	42	21	7	14	89	75	49
7	**Preston**	*42*	*18*	*11*	*13*	*76*	*74*	*47*
8	Aston Villa	42	18	9	15	67	53	45
9	Sunderland	42	18	8	16	65	66	44
10	Everton	42	17	9	16	62	67	43
11	Middlesbrough	42	17	8	17	73	68	42
12	Portsmouth	42	16	9	17	66	60	41
13	Arsenal	42	16	9	17	72	70	41
14	Derby	42	18	5	19	73	79	41
15	Chelsea	42	16	7	19	69	84	39
16	Grimsby	42	13	12	17	61	82	38
17	Blackburn	42	14	8	20	45	53	36
18	Bolton	42	13	8	21	57	69	34
19	Charlton	42	11	12	19	57	71	34
20	Huddersfield	42	13	7	22	53	79	33
21	Brentford	42	9	7	26	45	88	25
22	Leeds	42	6	6	30	45	90	18

Games played

Beattie, A.	25	McIntosh, W. D.	40
Beattie, R.	37	McLaren, A.	14
Brown, W. F.	8	Mutch, G.	6
Corr, P. J.	3	Nuttall, W.	2
Dainty, A.	1	Robertson, W. J. T.	1
Dougal, J.	5	Scott, W. J.	42
Fairbrother, J.	41	Shankly, W.	41
Finney, T.	*32*	Simpson, R.	4
Garth, J.	21	Watson, W. T.	15
Gooch, J. A. G.	1	Wharton, J. E.	25
Hamilton, W.	37	Williams, E.	33
Horton, J. K.	10	Wilson, J. G.	14
Jessop. W.	4		

Scorers

McIntosh	26	McLaren	6 Dougal ...1
Finney	*7*	Shankly	6 Own goals ...2
Garth	7	Wilson	5 **Total** ...**76**
Wharton	7	Mutch	3
R. Beattie	6	Dainty	1

■ 1947-48 DIVISION 1

		P	W	D	L	F	A	Pts
1	Arsenal	42	23	13	6	81	32	59
2	Man. United	42	19	14	9	81	48	52
3	Burnley	42	20	12	10	56	43	52
4	Derby	42	19	12	11	77	57	50
5	Wolves	42	19	9	14	83	70	47
6	Aston Villa	42	19	9	14	65	57	47
7	**Preston**	*42*	*20*	*7*	*15*	*67*	*68*	*47*
8	Portsmouth	42	19	7	16	68	50	45
9	Blackpool	42	17	10	15	67	41	44
10	Man. City	42	15	12	15	52	47	42
11	Liverpool	42	16	10	16	65	61	42
12	Sheff. United	42	16	10	16	65	70	42
13	Charlton	42	17	6	19	57	66	40
14	Everton	42	17	6	19	52	66	40
15	Stoke	42	14	10	18	41	55	38
16	Middlesbr.	42	14	9	19	71	73	37
17	Bolton	42	16	5	21	46	58	37
18	Chelsea	42	14	9	19	53	71	37
19	Huddersfield	42	12	12	18	51	60	36
20	Sunderland	42	13	10	19	56	67	36
21	Blackburn	42	11	10	21	54	72	32
22	Grimsby	42	8	6	28	45	111	22

Games played

Anders, H.	20	Horton, J. K.	41
Beattie, R.	30	Jackson, H.	12
Brown, W. F.	1	McClure, W.	34
Calverley, A.	13	McIntosh, W. C.	34
Dougal, W.	10	McLaren A.	41
Finney, T.	*33*	Robertson, W. J. T.	6
Garth, J. R.	2	Scott, W. J.	31
Gooch, J. A. G.	34	Shankly, W.	32
Gray, D.	36	Walton, J. W.	11
Hall, W.	7	Waters, P. M.	13
Hannah, W. K.	11	Williams, E.	29
Hindle, J.	1	Wilson, J. G.	2

Scorers

McLaren	17	Beattie	5 Walton ...2
McIntosh	14	Jackson	3 Wilson ...1
Finney	*13*	Hannah	3 Own Goals ...1
Shankly	6	McClure	2 **Total** ...**67**

■ 1948-49   DIVISION 1

		P	W	D	L	F	A	Pts
1	Portsmouth	42	25	8	9	84	42	58
2	Man. United	42	21	11	10	77	44	53
3	Derby	42	22	9	11	74	55	53
4	Newcastle	42	20	12	10	70	56	52
5	Arsenal	42	18	13	11	74	44	49
6	Wolves	42	17	12	13	79	66	46
7	Man. City	42	15	15	12	47	51	45
8	Sunderland	42	13	17	12	49	58	43
9	Charlton	42	15	12	15	63	67	42
10	Aston Villa	42	16	10	16	60	76	42
11	Stoke	42	16	9	17	66	68	41
12	Liverpool	42	13	14	15	53	43	40
13	Chelsea	42	12	14	16	69	68	38
14	Bolton	42	14	10	18	59	68	38
15	Burnley	42	12	14	16	43	50	38
16	Blackpool	42	11	16	15	54	67	38
17	Birmingham	42	11	15	16	36	38	37
18	Everton	42	13	11	18	41	63	37
19	Middlesbr.	42	11	12	19	46	57	34
20	Huddersfield	42	12	10	20	40	69	34
21	*Preston*	*42*	*11*	*11*	*20*	*62*	*75*	*33*
22	Sheff. United	42	11	11	20	57	78	33

Games played

Anders, H.	15	Kane, L. R.	2
Beattie, R.	37	Knight, J.	16
Bogan, T.	11	Langton, R. J.	39
Brown, E.	7	McIntosh, W. D.	17
Brown, W. F.	28	McLaren, A.	14
Corbett, W. R.	19	Mattinson, H.	2
Davie, J. G.	18	Morrison, A. C.	19
Dougal, W.	12	Newlands, M.	26
Finney, T.	*24*	Robertson, W. J. T.	20
Gooch, J. A. G.	16	Scott, W. J.	19
Hannah, W. K.	3	Shankly, W.	6
Horton, J. K.	27	Walton, J. W.	38
Jackson, H.	6	Waters, P. M.	21

Scorers

Langton	12	McLaren	6	E. Brown	2
Beattie	9	Knight	4	Hannah	1
Morrison	8	Dougal	2	Own Goals	1
Finney	*7*	Jackson	2	**Total**	**62**
McIntosh	6	Anders	2		

■ 1949-50   DIVISION 2

		P	W	D	L	F	A	Pts
1	Tottenham	42	27	7	8	81	35	61
2	Sheff. Wed.	42	18	16	8	67	48	52
3	Sheff. United	42	19	14	9	68	49	52
4	S'hampton	42	19	14	9	64	48	52
5	Leeds	42	17	13	12	54	45	47
6	*Preston*	*42*	*18*	*9*	*15*	*60*	*49*	*45*
7	Hull	42	17	11	14	64	72	45
8	Swansea	42	17	9	16	53	49	43
9	Brentford	42	15	13	14	44	49	43
10	Cardiff	42	16	10	16	41	44	42
11	Grimsby	42	16	8	18	74	73	40
12	Coventry	42	13	13	16	55	55	39
13	Barnsley	42	13	13	16	64	67	39
14	Chesterf'd	42	15	9	18	43	47	39
15	Leicester	42	12	15	15	55	65	39
16	Blackburn	42	14	10	18	55	60	38
17	Luton	42	10	18	14	41	51	38
18	Bury	42	14	9	19	60	65	37
19	West Ham	42	12	12	18	53	61	36
20	Q.P.R.	42	11	12	19	40	57	34
21	Plymouth	42	8	16	18	44	65	32
22	Bradford P.A.	42	10	11	21	51	77	31

Games played

Anders, H.	19	Kane, L. R.	3
Beattie, R.	14	Knight, J.	23
Brown, E.	24	Langton, R. J.	16
Brown, W. F.	3	Mattinson, H.	12
Cunningham, W. C.	30	Morrison, A. C.	23
Davie, J. G.	10	Newlands, M.	19
Docherty, T. H.	15	Quigley, E.	20
Finney, T.	*37*	Ramscar, F. T.	14
Forbes, W.	16	Robertson, W. T. J.	24
Garvie, J.	5	Scott, W. J.	18
Gooch, J. A. G.	23	Walton, J. W.	32
Hannah, W. K.	1	Waters, P. M.	30
Horton, J. K.	31		

Scorers

E. Brown	12	Beattie	5	Anders	1
Finney	*10*	Knight	3	Own Goals	3
Morrison	9	Ramscar	3	**Total**	**60**
Horton	6	Langton	2		
Quigley	5	Cunningham	1		

■ 1950-51   DIVISION 2

		P	W	D	L	F	A	Pts
1	*Preston*	*42*	*26*	*5*	*11*	*91*	*49*	*57*
2	Man. City	42	19	14	9	89	61	52
3	Cardiff	42	17	16	9	53	45	50
4	Birmingham	42	20	9	13	64	53	49
5	Leeds	42	20	8	14	63	55	48
6	Blackburn	42	19	8	15	65	66	46
7	Coventry	42	19	7	16	75	59	45
8	Sheff. United	42	16	12	14	72	62	44
9	Brentford	42	18	8	16	75	74	44
10	Hull	42	16	11	15	74	70	43
11	Doncaster	42	15	13	14	64	68	43
12	S'hampton	42	15	13	14	66	73	43
13	West Ham	42	16	10	16	68	69	42
14	Leicester	42	15	11	16	68	58	41
15	Barnsley	42	15	10	17	74	68	40
16	Q.P.R.	42	15	10	17	71	82	40
17	Notts. County	42	13	13	16	61	60	39
18	Swansea	42	16	4	22	54	77	36
19	Luton	42	9	14	19	57	70	32
20	Bury	42	12	8	22	60	86	32
21	Chesterfield	42	9	12	21	44	69	30
22	Grimsby	42	8	12	22	61	95	28

Games played

Anders, H.	6	Marston, J. E.	19
Beattie, R.	27	Mattinson, H.	28
Brown, E.	5	Morrison, A. C.	42
Cunningham, W. C.	31	Newlands, M.	16
Docherty, T. H.	42	Quigley, E.	20
Finney, T.	*34*	Ramscar, F. T.	5
Forbes, W.	42	Scott, W. J.	31
Gooch, J. A. G.	27	Walton, J. W.	16
Horton, J. K.	37	Wayman, C.	34

Scorers

Wayman	27	Morrison	8	Ramscar	1
Horton	22	Beattie	4	Own Goals	3
Finney	*13*	Forbes	2	**Total**	**91**
Quigley	9	Brown	2		

■ 1951-52 DIVISION 1

		P	W	D	L	F	A	Pts
1	Man. United	42	23	11	8	95	52	57
2	Tottenham	42	22	9	11	76	51	53
3	Arsenal	42	21	11	10	80	61	53
4	Portsmouth	42	20	8	14	68	58	48
5	Bolton	42	19	10	13	65	61	48
6	Aston Villa	42	19	9	14	79	70	47
7	*Preston*	*42*	*17*	*12*	*13*	*74*	*54*	*46*
8	Newcastle	42	18	9	15	98	73	45
9	Blackpool	42	18	9	15	64	64	45
10	Charlton	42	17	10	15	68	63	44
11	Liverpool	42	12	19	11	57	61	43
12	Sunderland	42	15	12	15	70	61	42
13	W.B.A.	42	14	13	15	74	77	41
14	Burnley	42	15	10	17	56	63	40
15	Man. City	42	13	13	16	58	61	39
16	Wolves	42	12	14	16	73	73	38
17	Derby	42	15	7	20	63	80	37
18	Middlesbrough	42	15	6	21	64	88	36
19	Chelsea	42	14	8	20	52	72	36
20	Stoke	42	12	7	23	49	88	31
21	Huddersfield	42	10	8	24	49	82	28
22	Fulham	42	8	11	23	58	77	27

Games played

Anders, H ...7 Kaile, G. W. ...2
Beattie, R. ...33 Lewis, D. I. E. ...8
Cunningham, W. C. ...42 Marston, J. E. ...42
Docherty, T. H. ...42 Morrison, A. C. ...42
Dunn, J. ...13 Newlands. M. ...8
Finney, T. ...*33* Quigley, E. ...12
Forbes, W. ...29 Scott, W. J. ...34
Foster, R. J. ...17 Walton, J. W. ...8
Gooch, J. A. G. ...34 Wayman, C. ...41
Horton, J. K. ...15

Scorers

Wayman ...24 Horton ...5 Lewis ...2
Finney ...*13* Forbes ...3 Own Goals ...4
Morrison ...12 Quigley ...3 **Total** ...**74**
Beattie ...6 Foster ...2

■ 1952-53 DIVISION 1

		P	W	D	L	F	A	Pts
1	Arsenal	42	21	12	9	97	64	54
2	*Preston*	*42*	*21*	*12*	*9*	*85*	*60*	*54*
3	Wolves	42	19	13	10	86	63	51
4	W.B.A.	42	21	8	13	66	60	50
5	Charlton	42	19	11	12	77	63	49
6	Burnley	42	18	12	12	67	52	48
7	Blackpool	42	19	9	14	71	70	47
8	Man. United	42	18	10	14	69	72	46
9	Sunderland	42	15	13	14	68	82	43
10	Tottenham	42	15	11	16	78	69	41
11	Aston Villa	42	14	13	15	63	61	41
12	Cardiff	42	14	12	16	54	46	40
13	Middlesb.	42	14	11	17	70	77	39
14	Bolton	42	15	9	18	61	69	39
15	Portsmouth	42	14	10	18	74	83	38
16	Newcastle	42	14	9	19	59	70	37
17	Liverpool	42	14	8	20	61	82	36
18	Sheff. Wed.	42	12	11	19	62	72	35
19	Chelsea	42	12	11	19	56	66	35
20	Man. City	42	14	7	21	72	87	35
21	Stoke	42	12	10	20	53	66	34
22	Derby	42	11	10	21	59	74	32

Games played

Anders, H ...2 Lewis, D. I. E. ...29
Beattie, R. ...12 Marston, J. E. ...42
Baxter, J. C. ...33 Morrison, A. C. ...42
Cunningham, W. C. ...41 Newlands. M. ...12
Docherty, T. H. ...41 Robertson, W. J. T. ...1
Dunn, J. ...25 Scott, W. J. ...28
Finney, T. ...*34* Thompson, G. H. ...30
Forbes, W. ...17 Walton, J. W. ...14
Foster, R. J. ...11 Wayman, C. ...42
Horton, J. K. ...5 Wilson, J. R. ...1

Scorers

Wayman ...23 Baxter ...7 Beattie ...2
Finney ...*17* Foster ...4 Anders ...1
Morrison ...13 Horton ...3 Own Goals ...1
Lewis ...12 Dunn ...2 **Total** ...**85**

■ 1953-54 DIVISION 1

		P	W	D	L	F	A	Pts
1	Wolves	42	25	7	10	96	56	57
2	W.B.A.	42	22	9	11	86	63	53
3	Huddersfield	42	20	11	11	78	61	51
4	Man. United	42	18	12	12	73	58	48
5	Bolton	42	18	12	12	75	60	48
6	Blackpool	42	19	10	13	80	69	48
7	Burnley	42	21	4	17	78	67	46
8	Chelsea	42	16	12	14	74	68	44
9	Charlton	42	19	6	17	75	77	44
10	Cardiff	42	18	8	16	51	71	44
11	*Preston*	*42*	*19*	*5*	*18*	*87*	*58*	*43*
12	Arsenal	42	15	13	14	75	73	43
13	Aston Villa	42	16	9	17	70	68	41
14	Portsmouth	42	14	11	17	81	89	39
15	Newcastle	42	14	10	18	72	77	38
16	Tottenham	42	16	5	21	65	76	37
17	Man. City	42	14	9	19	62	77	37
18	Sunderland	42	14	8	20	81	89	36
19	Sheff. Wed.	42	15	6	21	70	91	36
20	Sheff. United	42	11	11	20	69	90	33
21	Middlesbrough	42	10	10	22	60	91	30
22	Liverpool	42	9	10	23	68	97	28

Games played

Baxter, J. C. ...42 Jones, E. ...7
Beattie, R. ...1 Kaile, G. W. ...5
Campbell, L. G. ...13 Marston, J. E. ...42
Cunningham, W. C. ...30 Mattinson, H. ...27
Docherty, T. H. ...26 Mitton, G. K. ...2
Dunn, J. ...21 Morrison, A. C. ...35
Else, F. ...1 Scott, W. J. ...4
Evans, R. P. ...3 Thompson, G. H. ...39
Finney, T. ...*23* Walton, J. W. ...37
Forbes, W. ...19 Waterhouse, K. ...1
Foster, R. J. ...28 Wayman, C. ...34
Hatsell, D. ...17 Wilson, J. R. ...4
Higham, P. ...1

Scorers

Wayman ...25 Hatsell ...11 Forbes ...1
Baxter ...15 Morrison ...7 **Total** ...**87**
Foster ...15 Kaile ...1
Finney ...*11* Evans ...1

■ 1954-55   DIVISION 1

		P	W	D	L	F	A	Pts
1	Chelsea	42	20	12	10	81	57	52
2	Wolves	42	19	10	13	89	70	48
3	Portsmouth	42	18	12	12	74	62	48
4	Sunderland	42	15	18	9	64	54	48
5	Man. United	42	20	7	15	84	74	47
6	Aston Villa	42	20	7	15	72	73	47
7	Man. City	42	18	10	14	76	69	46
8	Newcastle	42	17	9	16	89	77	43
9	Arsenal	42	17	9	16	69	63	43
10	Burnley	42	17	9	16	51	48	43
11	Everton	42	16	10	16	62	68	42
12	Huddersfield	42	14	13	15	63	68	41
13	Sheff. United	42	17	7	18	70	86	41
14	*Preston*	*42*	*16*	*8*	*18*	*83*	*64*	*40*
15	Charlton	42	15	10	17	76	75	40
16	Tottenham	42	16	8	18	72	73	40
17	W.B.A.	42	16	8	18	76	96	40
18	Bolton	42	13	13	16	62	69	39
19	Blackpool	42	14	10	18	60	64	38
20	Cardiff	42	13	11	18	62	76	37
21	Leicester	42	12	11	19	74	86	35
22	Sheff. Wed.	42	8	10	24	63	100	26

Games played

Baird, S.	15	Higham, P.	14
Baxter, J. C.	39	Jones, E.	6
Campbell, L. G.	11	Lawrenson, T.	1
Cunningham, W. C.	24	Marston, J. E.	40
Docherty, T. H.	39	Mattinson, H.	7
Dunn, J.	3	Morrison, A. C.	33
Else, F.	5	Thompson, G. H.	37
Evans, R. P.	2	Walton, J. W.	38
Finney, T.	*30*	Waterhouse, K.	8
Forbes, W.	38	Wayman, C.	6
Foster, R. J.	28	Wilson, J. R.	21
Hatsell, D.	17		

Scorers

Baxter	17	*Finney*	*7*	Baird	2
Foster	13	Wayman	6	Evans	1
Hatsell	10	Docherty	3	Own Goals	1
Higham	10	Waterhouse	3	*Total*	*83*
Morrison	8	Campbell	2		

■ 1955-56   DIVISION 1

		P	W	D	L	F	A	Pts
1	Man. United	42	25	10	7	83	51	60
2	Blackpool	42	20	9	13	86	62	49
3	Wolves	42	20	9	13	89	65	49
4	Man. City	42	18	10	14	82	69	46
5	Arsenal	42	18	10	14	60	61	46
6	Birmingham	42	18	9	15	75	57	45
7	Burnley	42	18	8	16	64	54	44
8	Bolton	42	18	7	17	71	58	43
9	Sunderland	42	17	9	16	80	95	43
10	Luton	42	17	8	17	66	64	42
11	Newcastle	42	17	7	18	85	70	41
12	Portsmouth	42	16	9	17	78	85	41
13	W.B.A.	42	18	5	19	58	70	41
14	Charlton	42	17	6	19	75	81	40
15	Everton	42	15	10	17	55	69	40
16	Chelsea	42	14	11	17	64	77	39
17	Cardiff	42	15	9	18	55	69	39
18	Tottenham	42	15	7	20	61	71	37
19	*Preston*	*42*	*14*	*8*	*20*	*73*	*72*	*36*
20	Aston Villa	42	11	13	18	52	69	35
21	Huddersfield	42	14	7	21	54	83	35
22	Sheff. United	42	12	9	21	63	77.	33

Games played

Baxter, J. C.	29	Hatsell, D.	23
Campbell, L. G.	13	Lewis, E.	11
Cunningham, W. C.	24	Mattinson, H.	27
Docherty, T. H.	41	Morrison, A. C.	19
Dunn, J.	21	Taylor, S. M.	15
Else, F.	8	Thompson, G. H.	34
Evans, R. P.	9	Thompson, T.	42
Finney, T.	*32*	Walton, J. W.	39
Forbes, W.	30	Waterhouse, K.	6
Foster, R. J.	15	Wilson, J. R.	24

Scorers

Thompson	23	Morrison	4	Forbes	1
Finney	*17*	Taylor	2	Own Goals	1
Hatsell	9	Lewis	2	*Total*	*73*
Baxter	7	Docherty	1		
Foster	5	Waterhouse	1		

■ 1956-57   DIVISION 1

		P	W	D	L	F	A	Pts
1	Man. United	42	28	8	6	103	54	64
2	Tottenham	42	22	12	8	104	56	56
3	*Preston*	*42*	*23*	*10*	*9*	*84*	*56*	*56*
4	Blackpool	42	22	9	11	93	65	53
5	Arsenal	42	21	8	13	85	69	50
6	Wolves	42	20	8	14	94	70	48
7	Burnley	42	18	10	14	56	50	46
8	Leeds	42	15	14	13	72	63	44
9	Bolton	42	16	12	14	65	65	44
10	Aston Villa	42	14	15	13	65	55	43
11	W.B.A.	42	14	14	14	59	61	42
12=	Birmingham	42	15	9	18	69	69	39
13=	Chelsea	42	13	13	16	73	73	39
14	Sheff. Wed.	42	16	6	20	82	88	38
15	Everton	42	14	10	18	61	79	38
16	Luton	42	14	9	19	58	76	37
17	Newcastle	42	14	8	20	67	87	36
18	Man. City	42	13	9	20	78	88	35
19	Portsmouth	42	10	13	19	62	92	33
20	Sunderland	42	12	8	22	67	88	32
21	Cardiff	42	10	9	23	53	88	29
22	Charlton	42	9	4	29	62	120	22

Games played

Baxter, J. C.	39	Lewis, E.	1
Campbell, L. G.	13	Mattinson, H.	10
Cunningham, W. C.	41	Milne, G.	5
Dagger, J. L.	25	Morrison, A. C.	6
Docherty, T. H.	37	O'Farrell, F.	18
Dunn, J.	37	Taylor, S. M.	37
Else, F.	42	Thompson, T.	38
Evans, R. P.	19	Walton, J. W.	42
Finney, T.	*34*	Waterhouse, K.	5
Foster, R. J.	2	Wilson, J. R.	1
Hatsell, D.	10		

Scorers

Thompson	26	Hatsell	5	Waterhouse	1
Finney	*22*	Dagger	2	Own Goals	3
Taylor	13	Foster	2	*Total*	*84*
Baxter	9	O'Farrell	1		

■ 1957-58 DIVISION 1

		P	W	D	L	F	A	Pts
1	Wolves	42	28	8	6	103	47	64
2	*Preston*	*42*	*26*	*7*	*9*	*100*	*51*	*59*
3	Tottenham	42	21	9	12	93	77	51
4	W.B.A.	42	18	14	10	92	70	50
5	Man. City	42	22	5	15	104	100	49
6	Burnley	42	21	5	16	80	74	47
7	Blackpool	42	19	6	17	80	67	44
8	Luton	42	19	6	17	69	63	44
9	Man. United	42	16	11	15	85	75	43
10	Nott'm. Forest	42	16	10	16	69	63	42
11	Chelsea	42	15	12	15	83	79	42
12	Arsenal	42	16	7	19	73	85	39
13	Birmingham	42	14	11	17	76	89	39
14	Aston Villa	42	16	7	19	73	86	39
15	Bolton	42	14	10	18	65	87	38
16	Everton	42	13	11	18	65	75	37
17	Leeds	42	14	9	19	51	63	37
18	Leicester	42	14	5	23	91	112	33
19	Newcastle	42	12	8	22	73	81	32
20	Portsmouth	42	12	8	22	73	88	32
21	Sunderland	42	10	12	20	54	97	32
22	Sheff. Wed.	42	12	7	23	69	92	31

Games played

Alston, A. G.	2	Hatsell, D.	10
Baxter, J. C.	37	Knowles, J.	2
Cunningham, W. C.	42	Mattinson, H.	4
Dagger, J. L.	10	Mayers, D.	34
Docherty, T. H.	40	Milne, G.	5
Dunn, J.	37	O'Farrell, F.	40
Else, F.	40	Taylor, S. M.	36
Farrall, A.	6	Thompson, T.	41
Finney, T.	*34*	Walton, J. W.	42

Scorers

Thompson	34	Baxter	5	Dagger	1
Finney	*26*	Hatsell	3	Docherty	1
Taylor	14	Farrall	1	Own Goals	2
Mayers	12	Alston	1	**Total**	**100**

■ 1958-59 DIVISION 1

		P	W	D	L	F	A	Pts
1	Wolves	42	28	5	9	110	49	61
2	Man. United	42	24	7	11	103	66	55
3	Arsenal	42	21	8	13	88	68	50
4	Bolton	42	20	10	12	79	66	50
5	W.B.A.	42	18	13	11	88	68	49
6	West Ham	42	21	6	15	85	70	48
7	Burnley	42	19	10	13	81	70	48
8	Blackpool	42	18	11	13	66	49	47
9	Birmingham	42	20	6	16	84	68	46
10	Blackburn	42	17	10	15	76	70	44
11	Newcastle	42	17	7	18	80	80	41
12	*Preston*	*42*	*17*	*7*	*18*	*70*	*77*	*41*
13	Nott'm. Forest	42	17	6	19	71	74	40
14	Chelsea	42	18	4	20	77	98	40
15	Leeds	42	15	9	18	57	74	39
16	Everton	42	17	4	21	71	87	38
17	Luton	42	12	13	17	68	71	37
18	Tottenham	42	13	10	19	85	95	36
19	Leicester	42	11	10	21	67	98	32
20	Man. City	42	11	9	22	64	95	31
21	Aston Villa	42	11	8	23	58	87	30
22	Portsmouth	42	6	9	27	68	112	21

Games played

Alston, A. G.	7	Mattinson, H.	8
Barton, J. B.	3	Mayers, D.	37
Baxter, J. C.	26	Milne, G.	30
Campbell, L. G.	6	O'Farrell, F.	33
Cunningham, W. C.	42	O'Neill, N. J.	2
Dagger, J. L.	6	Smith, J. A. G.	18
Dunn, J.	33	Sneddon, D.	1
Else, F.	37	Taylor, S. M.	17
Farrall, A.	11	Thompson, T.	34
Finney, T.	*16*	Walton, J. W.	36
Hatsell, D.	35	Wilson, J. R.	4
Lambert, J. G.	13	Wylie, J. E.	5
Lynne, M. G. A.	2		

Scorers

Thompson	20	Taylor	2	Cunningham	1
Hatsell	16	Campbell	2	Smith	1
Mayers	7	Alston	2	Own Goals	1
Finney	*6*	Lambert	1	**Total**	**70**
Baxter	5	Walton	1		
Farrall	4	Milne	1		

■ 1959-60 DIVISION 1

		P	W	D	L	F	A	Pts
1	Burnley	42	24	7	11	85	61	55
2	Wolves	42	24	6	12	106	67	54
3	Tottenham	42	21	11	10	86	50	53
4	W.B.A.	42	19	11	12	83	57	49
5	Sheff. Wed.	42	19	11	12	80	59	49
6	Bolton	42	20	8	14	59	51	48
7	Man. United	42	19	7	16	102	80	45
8	Newcastle	42	18	8	16	82	78	44
9	*Preston*	*42*	*16*	*12*	*14*	*79*	*76*	*44*
10	Fulham	42	17	10	15	73	80	44
11	Blackpool	42	15	10	17	59	71	40
12	Leicester	42	13	13	16	66	75	39
13	Arsenal	42	15	9	18	68	80	39
14	West Ham	42	16	6	20	75	91	38
15	Man. City	42	17	3	22	78	84	37
16	Everton	42	13	11	18	73	78	37
17	Blackburn	42	16	5	21	60	70	37
18	Chelsea	42	14	9	19	76	91	37
19	Birmingham	42	13	10	19	63	80	36
20	Nott'm Forest	42	13	9	20	50	74	35
21	Leeds	42	12	10	20	65	92	34
22	Luton	42	9	12	21	50	73	30

Games played

Alston, A. G.	10	Lambert, J. G.	3
Campbell, L. G.	8	Mayers, D.	19
Cunningham, W. C.	24	Milne, G.	38
Dagger, J. L.	14	O'Farrell, F.	10
Dunn, J.	29	Richardson, G.	13
Else, F.	42	Smith, J. A. G.	34
Farrall, A.	10	Sneddon, D.	40
Finney, T.	*37*	Taylor, S. M.	34
Fullam, J.	12	Thompson, T.	21
Hatsell, D.	3	Walton, J. W.	42
Heyes, K.	3	Wilson, J. R.	15
Humes, J. J.	1		

Scorers

Finney	*17*	Farrall	4	O'Farrell	1
Thompson	12	Alston	3	Walton	1
Sneddon	11	Smith	3	Cunningham	1
Taylor	10	Milne	2	Own Goals	1
Dagger	5	Lambert	2	**Total**	**79**
Mayers	4	Campbell	2		

Preston North End FA Cup Record, Finney era, 1946-60

	Preston North End						Finney	
	P	W	D	L	F	A	Games	Goals
1946-47	4	3	—	1	11	3	3	2
1947-48	4	3	—	1	7	6	4	1
1948-49	2	1	—	1	2	3	2	2
1949-50	2	—	1	1	2	3	1	1
1950-51	2	1	—	1	3	2	2	—
1951-52	1	—	—	1	—	2	—	—
1952-53	3	1	1	1	7	5	3	2
1953-54	8	5	2	1	20	8	8	3
1954-55	3	1	1	1	6	7	3	2
1955-56	1	—	—	1	2	5	1	1
1956-57	6	2	3	1	15	9	6	5
1957-58	1	—	—	1	—	3	1	—
1958-59	6	2	3	1	13	11	—	—
1959-60	6	3	2	1	14	9	6	4

Finney's record in Football League Representative Games

		Result	Goals
14 April 1948	v. Lg. of Ireland at Deepdale	W 4-0	—
23 March 1949	v. Scottish Lg. at Ibrox	W 3-0	1
15 Feb. 1950	v. Lg. of Ireland at Molineux	W 7-0	1
18 Oct. 1950	v. Irish Lg. at Bloomfield Rd.	W 6-3	—
29 Nov. 1950	v. Scottish Lg. at Ibrox	L 0-1	—
10 Oct. 1951	v. Lg. of Ireland at Goodison Park	W 9-1	1
31 Oct. 1951	v. Scottish Lg. at Hillsborough	W 2-1	1
26 March 1952	v. Irish Lg. at Windsor Park, Belfast	W 9-0	2
24 Sept. 1952	v. Irish Lg. at Molineux	W 7-1	—
17 March 1953	v. Lg. of Ireland at Dalymount Park	W 2-0	—
25 March 1953	v. Scottish Lg. at Ibrox	L 0-1	—
23 Sept. 1953	v. Irish Lg. at Windsor Park.	W 5-0	—
22 Sept. 1954	v. Lg. of Ireland at Dalymount Park	W 6-0	—
26 Oct. 1955	v. Scottish Lg. at Hillsborough	W 4-2	1
7 Dec. 1955	v. Lg. of Ireland at Goodison Park	W 5-1	—
13 March 1957	v. Scottish Lg. at Ibrox	L 2-3	—
26 March 1958	v. Scottish Lg. at St. James Park	W 4-1	—

	English League record						Finney record	
	P	W	D	L	F	A	Games	Goals
TOTAL	17	14	—	3	75	15	17	7

2. Tom Finney's international career, 1946-58

Summary

Tom Finney won 76 caps in the first 101 internationals after the Second World War. He played against 23 different countries and visited 21 countries in the process. His full record of games was:

Played	Won	Drawn	Lost	Abnd.	For	Against
76	51	12	12	1	227	102

Finney scored 30 international goals. He played in three positions: outside right 40 times; outside left 33 times; and centre forward 3 times.

He scored from 3 penalties and missed one. He played 21 times with Stanley Matthews also in the side.

He played in 29 home internationals, scoring 10 goals; 11 World Cup ties, scoring twice; and 36 friendly matches, scoring 18 goals. He played most frequently against Wales (11 times) and Scotland (10 times). His best goal-scoring was against Portugal, totalling 6, four of which came in one game.

He played in 30 home games, 46 away games and 16 of his international appearances were at Wembley.

His 76 England games are summarised below:

1

v. Northern Ireland in Belfast   28 September 1946
Result: won 7-2; Finney played at outside right and scored once.
57,000 people watched Finney's debut, when Raich Carter, Wilf Mannion (3), Tommy Lawton, Bobby Langton and Finney himself scored the goals. Tom had a super game and repeatedly tore gaping holes in the Irish defence with his skills. His link up with Carter was outstanding.

2

v. Eire in Dublin   30 September 1946
Result: won 1-0; Finney played at outside right and scored once.
Another fine performance by Tom which climaxed in his goal described thus: 'Bobby Langton gave Wilf Mannion a through pass down the left. Mannion cut in and unleashed an angled shot which the goalkeeper could only parry. The ball ran loose and Finney ran in to slot the ball home.'

3

v. Wales at Maine Road   13 November 1946
Result: won 3-0; Finney played at outside right
Tom did not score in this one but again played well, linking up superbly with his highly talented teammates. He was always involved and started the move for Wilf Mannion to score the third goal.

4

v. Holland in Huddersfield   27 November 1946
Result: won 8-2; Finney played at outside right and scored once.
This was a one-sided game in which all the England players excelled. Tom's goal came just before the interval, making the score 6-1 at half-time! He also had a hand in several of the other goals.

5

v. France at Highbury   3 May 1947
Result: won 3-0; Finney played at outside right and scored once.
Another influential game for Tom, who was always dangerous. His goal broke the deadlock after 51 minutes and followed a sparkling move between Bobby Langton, Raich Carter, Tommy Lawton, and Wilf Mannion, who then passed to Tom to shoot home.

6
v. Portugal in Lisbon   **25 May 1947**
            Result: won 10–0; Finney played at outside left and scored once.
Tom was in exquisite form for this game and he and Stanley Matthews ripped Portugal apart. Finney's goal
was the fourth and probably the best of the match. Picking up a ball on the half–way line he beat one man,
then another, before reaching the bye–line. As he turned towards goal, a third opponent came at him only to
be beaten as well by the Finney footwork. The Preston man then shot past the goalkeeper from the narrowest
of angles.

7
v. Belgium in Brussels   **21 September 1947**
            Result: won 5–2; Finney played at outside left and scored twice.
England were inspired by the magic of Stan Matthews on this day and both of Tom's goals, the third and
fourth, were set up by the Blackpool star. Both were clinically scored from close in.

8
v. Wales in Cardiff   **18 October 1947**
            Result: won 3–0; Finney played at outside left and scored once.
Tom and Stan were again weaving their spells down the wings in this game and all the goals came in a
blistering first fifteen minutes. Tom's goal was the first and came after a swift passing movement between
Peter Taylor and Matthews left Wilf Mannion the chance to pass to Tom. The goal came with a sweet left–
foot shot.

9
v. N. Ireland at Goodison Park   **5 November 1947**
            Result: drew 2–2; Finney played at outside left .
Finney had another excellent game on this day giving his marker, Martin, a torrid afternoon. But all the
honours went to the battling Irish on a day when Peter Doherty's late goal gave them a much deserved draw.
It was the first of Finney's internationals that didn't end in victory.

10
v. Sweden at Highbury   **19 November 1947**
            Result: won 4–2; Finney played at outside right.
This was Stan Mortenson's match. The Blackpool star scored a hat–trick to shine in a game where Finney
was rarely involved.

11
v. Scotland at Hampden   **10 April 1948**
            Result: won 2–0; Finney played at outside left and scored once.
Finney scored one of his best goals for England in his first match against the Scots. It was England's first and
came just before the interval. A superb move began with Frank Swift's clearance finding Tommy Lawton.
The centre forward flicked the ball to Stan Pearson who, in turn, found Finney with the perfect through ball.
The 'Preston Plumber' took the ball in his stride, beat Young and Govan by balance and footwork before
shooting magnificently past goalkeeper Black.

12
v. Italy in Turin   **16 May 1948**
            Result: won 4–0; Finney played at outside left and scored twice.
One of Tom's own favourite internationals and a superb display by the whole England team. His goals were
the third and fourth and came in the 71st and 73rd minutes. The first was volleyed in from a clever lobbed
pass by Wilf Mannion and the second came after good work by Henry Cockburn and Stan Mortensen.

13
v. N. Ireland in Belfast   **9 November 1948**
            Result: won 6–2; Finney played at outside left.
For a long spell in this game Finney was well held by his marker Johnny Carey but after an hour's play
Finney began to get the better of him and towards the end ran riot. Despite this, he neither scored, or had a
direct part in the goals.

14
v. Wales at Villa Park   **10 November 1948**
            Result: won 1–0; Finney played at outside left and scored once.
In a poor match Finney scored the all important goal after 39 minutes. Jackie Milburn, lively throughout,
made a strong run down the middle and, as he was desperately challenged by the Welsh defenders, the ball
ran loose to Finney and he did the rest giving the keeper no chance.

15

v. Scotland at Wembley   9 April 1949
Result: lost 1–3; Finney played at outside left.
The first time Finney had been on a losing England side. He rarely had the chance to make an impact on the tough Scottish defence, despite a rousing finish which almost saved the game.

16

v. Sweden in Stockholm   13 May 1949
Result: lost 1–3; Finney played at outside right and scored once.
The impressive Swedes scored a famous victory this day and despite Finney scoring the England goal and featuring in several other near misses, Sweden thoroughly deserved their win. 3–0 down at the interval, Finney's goal came in the 67th minute when he rounded off a fine dribble by Roy Bentley. It started a revival but bad luck and some poor finishing failed to save the visitors.

17

v. Norway in Oslo   18 May 1949
Result: won 4–1; Finney played at outside right and scored once.
Finney struggled to produce his best form in this game but still scored the best goal of the match. It came in the 38th minute and was England's second. Billy Wright, John Morris, Wilf Mannion and Stan Mortensen were all involved in a superb move which ended with Finney shooting home a fine goal.

18

v. France in Paris   22 May 1949
Result: won 3–1; Finney played at outside right.
Finney was the best forward on view in this game and his clever wing play continually opened up the French defence. He overcame some fierce tackling to create some wonderful chances for his colleagues.

19

v. Eire at Goodison Park   21 September 1949.
Result: lost 0–2; Finney played at outside left.
An historic victory by the plucky Irish who became the first 'foreigners' to win on English soil. Finney was always in the action but on this day was guilty of some bad misses in front of the goal. He was not alone, though, and the Irish scored from their only two real chances and thus deservedly won the game.

20

v. Wales in Cardiff   15 October 1949.
Result: won 4–1; Finney played at outside-right.
A devastating 12-minute spell in the first half gave England three goals, with Finney making two of them. The Preston man had one of his best games, cutting down on the over-elaboration he had been guilty of in a couple of previous appearances. He rounded off his fine display by combining with Len Shackleton to set up Jackie Milburn for the fourth goal in the second-half.

21

v. N. Ireland at Maine Road   16 November 1949.
Result: won 9–2; Finney played at outside right.
One of Finney's best ever internationals. He conjured up some sheer magic as he teased the whole Northern Irish defence with his balance, poise, speed and footwork. His marker, McMichael, just didn't know which way to turn. Although he did not score himself, he had a hand in no fewer than six of the goals on a day when even the persistent Manchester rain could not dampen the Preston star.

22

v. Italy at White Hart Lane   30 November 1949.
Result: won 2–0; Finney played at outside right.
Finney continued his fine form and produced another excellent display against a very good Italian side. Only the brilliance of goalkeeper Bert Williams kept England in the match at times but when the home side did attack, then Finney was the key. His wing play did much to unlock the defence for Jack Rowley and Billy Wright to score.

23

v. Scotland at Hampden   15 April 1950.
Result: won 1–0; Finney played at outside right.
Another splendid performance by Finney, whose combination with Wilf Mannion was the highlight of England's attack. It was a good game, with England continuing their fine record at Hampden.

24

v. Portugal in Lisbon   **14 May 1950.**
Result: won 5–3; Finney played at outside right and scored four times.
Finney had gone six games without actually scoring an international goal but in the lovely setting of the National Stadium in Lisbon he changed this state of affairs with a stunning four-goal display. It was a thrilling performance. After one shot had skimmed the bar, he was then brought down in the penalty area. He coolly slotted home the spot kick and then scored England's third goal after good approach work by Jackie Milburn and Roy Bentley. As Portugal then hit back, Finney stopped them in their tracks with a brilliant dribble and fierce shot to complete his hat-trick and settle the result. Finally, after Stan Mortensen had been felled, Finney again stepped up to convert the penalty.

25

v. Belgium in Brussels   **18 May 1950.**
Result: won 4–1; Finney played outside left.
After being a goal down at the interval, England stormed back with four second-half goals. Finney played his part as usual and his perfectly flighted free kick was headed in by Stan Mortensen to give England a 2–1 lead.

26

v. Chile in Rio de Janeiro, Brazil   **25 June 1950.**
Result: won 2–0; Finney played at outside right.
This was England's first ever World Cup Finals match and Finney was there in the number-seven shirt. It was a disappointing match played in pouring rain, but after a hard battle Finney's centre midway through the second half was converted by a low shot from Wilf Mannion to make it 2–0.

27

v. U.S.A. in Bel Horizonte, Brazil   **29 June 1950.**
Result: lost 0–1; Finney played at outside right.
Probably the most infamous England international of all time. Along with the rest of the side, Finney had a nightmare. Chance after chance went begging and all the players were guilty of some bad misses.

28

v. Spain in Rio, Brazil   **2 July 1950.**
Result: lost 0–1; Finney played outside left.
In their last World Cup game of 1950 and needing a good performance to end the memory of the U.S.A. defeat, England played very well against Spain but could not score the vital goals needed. They also had to endure some dreadful tackling. Finney played well but he and Stan Matthews bore the brunt of the dubious tactics of the Spanish defenders. Twice Finney was hauled down in the penalty area for the referee to wave play on and in the end Lady Luck refused to smile on England.

29

v. Wales at Roker Park   **15 November 1950.**
Result: won 4–2; Finney played at outside right.
Finney featured in several flowing moves during this splendid match and had a hand in two of the goals. Wales gave a good account of themselves in what was one of their best displays but in the end they were beaten by the combined genius of England's star players.

30

v. Scotland at Wembley   **14 April 1951.**
Result: lost 2–3; Finney played at outside left and scored once.
England, hampered by an injury to Wilf Mannion which led to England being one man down after only eleven minutes, put up a fine performance; Finney was outstanding. His dribbling skills set up Harold Hassall for their first goal and ten minutes from the end he brilliantly combined with Stan Mortenson before lobbing a superb goal over the goalkeeper.

31

v. Argentina at Wembley   **9 May 1951.**
Result: won 2–1; Finney played at outside right.
Argentina almost produced a shock win in this game. Having led from the 18th minute, they were pegged back by England for much of the rest of the match. The home side could not find a way through until the 79th minute when Finney's corner was headed in by Stan Mortenson. With just four minutes to go Jackie Milburn scored the winner.

32

v. Portugal at Goodison Park   **19 May 1951.**
Result: won 5–2; Finney played at outside right and scored once.
How Finney loved to play against Portugal! He was in one of his devastating moods on this day and it was his stunning goal in the 76th minute which finally killed off Portugal's stubborn challenge and put England 3–2 up. He picked the ball up on the touchline and hit a spectacular swerving shot from the same position. It was worthy of the name 'match winning goal'.

33

v. France at Highbury   **3 October 1951.**
Result: drew 2–2; Finney played at outside right.
Finney had a quiet game at Highbury but it was from his firm cross that was diverted by French defender Firoud for the opening goal. Should that have given Finney 31 goals, one wonders?

34

v. Wales in Cardiff   **20 October 1951.**
Result: drew 1–1; Finney played at outside right.
This was a scrappy game which also featured the debut of Tommy Thompson. Finney's best contribution came when he took a pass from Billy Wright, moved through the inside–right channel, and then laid off the perfect square pass to Les Medley. Medley's lobbed pass was headed in by Eddie Bailey to level the scores.

35

v. N. Ireland at Villa Park   **14 November 1951.**
Result: won 2–0; Finney played at outside right.
Another poor game which had only two worthwhile attacks in the first half. Both were inspired by Finney. In the first, a fine cross-field pass by Len Phillips sent Finney away and split the Irish defence. Finney's pass then found Nat Lofthouse and only a desperate dive by the goalkeeper saved the day. Then in the 44th minute a fine move ended with Finney's lovely cross being headed home powerfully by Lofthouse.

36

v. Scotland at Hampden   **5 April 1952.**
Result: won 2–1; Finney played at outside right.
Finney produced another of his brilliant performances against the Scots and his combination with Ivor Broadis was one of the outstanding features of the victory. The pair repeatedly tore large holes in the Scottish defence and they generally caused havoc as England's fine record continued.

37

v. Italy in Florence   **18 May 1952.**
Result: drew 1–1; Finney played at outside right.
The star of the first half of this match was the Italian goalkeeper Moro. Several times he defied the best efforts of England's attack, with Finney being thwarted more than once. Despite Ivor Broadis' early goal they could not beat Moro again and eventually the Italians equalised.

38

v. Austria in Vienna   **25 May 1952.**
Result: won 3–2; Finney played at outside right.
This was the match in which Finney's good friend Nat Lofthouse won the nickname of the 'Lion of Vienna'. Finney played his part in the great win but his game was stifled by some harsh challenges by the ruthless Austrian defenders.

39

v. Switzerland in Zurich   **28 May 1952.**
Result: won 3–0; Finney played at outside left.
England were always in control of this game and none of the players had to work particularly hard for victory. Finney had a quiet but efficient match.

40

v. N. Ireland in Belfast   **4 October 1952.**
Result: drew 2–2; Finney played at outside right.
A dramatic match with a late goal saving England from defeat. Finney featured in the move taking a pass from Jack Froggatt, flicking it on to Billy Wright who returned it to Froggatt. The Portsmouth player then centred for Billy Elliott to head home that face-saving goal.

41

v. Wales at Wembley   12 November 1952.
Result: won 5–2; Finney played at outside right and scored once.
This was vintage Finney again and he really turned on the style for Wales' first visit to Wembley. He was England's most influential player, scoring the first goal after also being involved in the build up with Redfearn, Froggatt, Nat Lofthouse, Roy Bentley and Billy Elliott. Finney's marvellous finish was sheer delight. He then helped to create two other goals for good measure as England won a memorable victory.

42

v. Belgium at Wembley   26 November 1952.
Result: won 5–0; Finney played at outside right.
Finney produced another influential performance without hitting top form and he had a hand in four of the five goals. Nat Lofthouse was outstanding and a real powerhouse. Finney missed chances himself but his passing was brilliant.

43

v. Scotland at Wembley   18 April 1953.
Result: drew 2–2; Finney played at outside right.
Just look at the descriptions of England's two goals. Finney conjured up some wonderful magic as he twisted his way in field past Steel, Cowie and Cox before sending Ivor Broadis through the middle with an inch-perfect pass. The number eight switched the ball from right to left foot under pressure from Brennan before unleashing a thunderbolt wide of the diving Farm. Then in the 70th minute Billy Wright sent Broadis away just inside his own half. A long dribble ended with a square pass to Finney. The Preston player suddenly moved into second gear and, with a breathtaking piece of footwork, a slight feint and a change of pace, left Cox in his wake before finally pulling back a diagonal pass to Broadis again who hit home a low first-time shot. All the talent of Finney was on view.

44

v. Argentina in Buenos Aires   17 May 1953.
Result: drew 0–0 (Abnd.); Finney played at outside right.
This was an amazing match of only 25-minutes duration. By then the pitch was awash as a monsoon-style rainstorm hit the stadium. The referee had no option but to abandon the game. Contrary to popular belief, this was not where the famous picture of Finney called 'The Splash' was taken!

45

v. Chile in Santiago   24 May 1953.
Result: won 2–1; Finney played at outside right.
The 1953 summer tour continued with another good win for England in front of a packed house of 70,000 people. Unfortunately reports of the game lack detail so there are few memories of Finney's performance.

46

v. Uruguay in Montevideo   31 May 1953.
Result: lost 1–2; Finney played at outside right.
A visit to the current World Champions ended this part of the tour. The visit was hampered by many players suffering from stomach upsets or 'Chile Belly!' Finney played well in a good display and went close to scoring several times. However, in the end the team's missed chances cost England the game.

47

v. U.S.A. in New York   9 May 1953.
Result: won 6–3; Finney played at outside right and scored twice.
Finney had a good second half, scoring two goals and being much more direct. He had a hand in some of the other goals, too, in what was a vengeful England victory after the humiliation of the 1950 World Cup defeat.

48

v. Wales in Cardiff   10 October 1953.
Result: won 4–1; Finney played at outside right.
Finney looked well below par in this flattering victory against a battling Welsh side. Wales could easily have been well clear at half–time but for inspired goalkeeping by Gil Merrick.

49

v. Scotland at Hampden   3 April 1954.
Result: won 4–2; Finney played at outside right.
Finney loved Hampden. Having missed three internationals, he was brought back for this clash and played like a man inspired. An inch-perfect pass gave Ivor Broadis a fine goal and then Finney turned Cox inside

out before crossing for Johnny Nicholls to head home in spectacular fashion. The fourth goal, too, was Finney-inspired as, once again, he sent Cox in all directions with his superb footwork before crossing, this time for Jimmy Mullen to head in.

50
v. Yugoslavia in Belgrade 16 May 1954.
Result: lost 0-1; Finney played at outside right.
A disappointing performance by England and a quiet match for Finney. Yugoslavia were formidable opponents and it was a game where only the England defenders came out with credit. One chance was created by the Finney/Broadis combination but the goalkeeper saved brilliantly from Jimmy Mullen's header. It was a sad day for Finney to celebrate gaining his 50th cap.

51
v. Hungary in Budapest 21 May 1954.
Result: lost 1-7; Finney played at outside left.
Finney had missed the famous game at Wembley between these two teams seven months previously but was definitely in this one, although he probably wishes he hadn't been. England were totally outclassed. Finney worked hard but missed a sitter in one attack and it was a day he will want to forget.

52
v. Belgium in Basle, Switzerland 17 June 1954.
Result: drew 4-4 a.e.t.; Finney played at outside left.
The second World Cup finals which Finney had appeared in and a dramatic match this turned out to be. England were 3-1 up with 15 minutes to go, only to lose their lead and then go into extra-time. Finney had made the second goal and was always in the action. The defensive lapses cost them dearly, though, and Gil Merrick had a nightmare match in goal.

53
v. Switzerland in Berne 20 June 1954.
Result: won 2-0; Finney played at outside right.
On a hot summer's day England's second game in these finals came against the host country. It was a mediocre affair. Finney caused Switzerland some anxious moments, especially when he moved along the inside-right channel. The home crowd were not too happy with the result.

54
v. Uruguay in Basle, Switzerland 26 June 1954.
Result: lost 2-4; Finney played at outside left and scored once.
One of the best games of the tournament and England were unlucky to lose. They were always in the match and when Finney was on the spot to follow up after a Nat Lofthouse shot was blocked to make it 3-2 in the 65th minute, it set up a pulsating finish which was ruined when Uruguay snatched another breakaway goal ten minutes from the end. Again, Gil Merrick's goalkeeping was not all that it should have been. If it had been better England might have gone on to greatness. As it was, their challenge was over for another four years.

55
v. West Germany at Wembley 1 December 1954.
Result: won 3-1; Finney played at outside left.
The undoubted stars of this famous win against the new World Champions were Stan Matthews and Tom Finney on the wings for England. Whereas Matthews hugged the touchline, Finney preferred to cut inside to create havoc. Several times Finney saw shots blocked. When Len Shackleton put Finney in, only a fine save prevented a goal, but the ball ran loose for Ronnie Allen to score the second England goal. This was another of Tom's super displays.

56
v. Denmark in Copenhagen 2 October 1955.
Result: won 5-1; Finney played at outside left.
Finney was brought down for an obvious penalty just under half an hour into the game after an amazing dribble had left Danish defenders in his wake. Don Revie scored from the kick. However, on this day Finney tended to overdo the dribbling and often ran into trouble. With the King and Queen of Denmark present, he was obviously trying to impress. He did have a part in one of the other England goals though.

57
v. Wales in Cardiff 22 October 1955.
Result: lost 1-2; Finney played at outside left.
This was the first Welsh victory over England in 17 years of trying and on the day they thoroughly deserved it.

England were disappointing, despite hard-working performances by Finney and Stan Matthews on the wings. The nearest they came to an equaliser was when Don Revie backheeled a volley from Finney's cross on to the crossbar.

58

v. N. Ireland at Wembley   **2 November 1955.**
Result: won 3–0; Finney played at outside right and scored once.
A mixed performance by Finney. Though not at his best in a poor England showing, he still managed some nice touches. He helped make the second goal and in the 88th minute he rounded off the victory with a good goal himself. Johnny Haynes and Bedford Jezzard combined well to give Finney possession. His quick change of direction and acceleration took him inside Graham before his fierce diagonal shot beat Uprichard and nestled in the far corner.

59

v. Spain at Wembley   **30 November 1955.**
Result: won 4–1; Finney played at outside right and scored once.
Finney missed a penalty in this game but ended with an excellent performance under his belt. After only seven minutes a lovely through ball by Johnny Haynes sent Finney away, but as he entered the penalty area a Spanish defender brought him crashing to the ground. Finney took the kick but it was far too timid and Carmelo saved easily. Later on, however, Finney featured in the build-up to two of the goals and then scored the third himself. His goal came after a slip by a defender gave him the chance to make ground before cutting inside and planting a lovely diagonal shot just inside the far post and just before a crunching Campanal tackle stopped him!

60

v. Scotland at Hampden   **14 April 1956.**
Result: drew 1–1; Finney played at outside right.
This was the best Scotland showing at Hampden against England for years and only a late goal by man–of–the–match Johnny Haynes saved England from defeat. Finney was rarely seen, although a couple of typical bursts sent shivers down the Scottish fans' spines as they remembered previous performances by the maestro.

61

v. Wales at Wembley   **14 November 1956.**
Result: won 3–1; Finney played at centre forward and scored once.
Finney had missed five more internationals before regaining a surprise selection in the number-nine shirt for the first time. The ball playing role he played was not a total success but he did enough to warrant another attempt. Wales took the lead in this game but were then hampered when their goalkeeper Kelsey was injured diving at Finney's feet. Before half–time Finney hit the post with a header and, after the break, with full–back Sherwood in goal, the extra strength of England told and they scored three goals. The third one was decisive and came from Finney. Johnny Brooks and Stan Matthews combined at a short corner and, when Matthews centred, Finney nipped in to flick the ball delicately wide of the stand–in keeper.

62

v. Yugoslavia at Wembley   **28 November 1956.**
Result: won 3–0; Finney played at centre forward.
Finney was back to his brilliant best in this superb performance by England. With Stan Matthews also outstanding, the Yugoslavs resorted to dubious tactics to stop the duo; they did not work. The visitors' goalkeeper made an outstanding save from Johnny Haynes after lovely play by Matthews and Finney, and then the same three combined to give Johnny Brooks the chance to strike a fine goal. When Haynes was injured Tommy Taylor came on as substitute and took up the centre-forward role, with Finney switching to inside right and Brooks to the left. With Finney now partnering Matthews on the right, they produced some marvellous play. With 25 minutes left Finney, who continually left Horpat stranded, set off on a long run, holding the ball and evading some desperate challenges. He then weaved his way to the right-hand byeline before turning the ball neatly inside where Taylor was left with a simple scoring chance. It settled the result and England could even afford a missed penalty by Roger Byrne.

63

v. Denmark at Molineux   **5 December 1956.**
Result: won 5–2; Finney played at outside left.
Another vital World Cup win and a fine first half for Finney. After only two minutes, a darting run and a slide-rule pass set Taylor up for the first goal. Then, on 20 minutes, Finney produced some clever body swerves and electric pace which left Larsen groping and again Tommy Taylor was on the end of the final pass to score. Two special goals by Duncan Edwards were also fondly remembered from this game.

64

v. Scotland at Wembley   **6 April 1957.**

Result: won 2–1; Finney played centre forward.

Finney again teamed up with Tommy Thompson for this match, although the latter was well held by another clubmate Tommy Docherty. The Doc was visibly shaken after one crunching tackle on Finney, however, when the winger had to go off for a few minutes for treatment and Docherty was so upset that he faded from the game. Finney and Thompson both featured in the build–up to Derek Kevan's equaliser and then stood in awe of a tremendous 25-yard shot by Duncan Edwards which almost ripped the net off for England's winner. It was a goal remembered long after the game was!

65

v. Eire at Wembley   **8 May 1957.**

Result: won 5–1; Finney played at outside left.

Another vintage display by Finney, who laid on all but the first of England's five goals in this World Cup match. Young Drumcondra star Alan Kelly was the Eire goalkeeper under fire and Finney's skills kept him very busy. It was especially so with the third goal, as Finney cut inside to unleash a fine shot which Kelly could only parry upwards for John Atyeo to follow up and score. Finney's combination with Johnny Haynes was lethal at times.

66

v. Denmark in Copenhagen   **15 May 1957.**

Result: won 4–1; Finney played at outside left.

The World Cup again and the second leg of the tie against Denmark. Johnny Haynes and Tom Finney's partnership again inspired all the best moves from England. Denmark ran their hearts out and made it difficult but after the home side went ahead early on England struck back with Haynes, Finney and Duncan Edwards combining superbly for Haynes to score. The Haynes/Finney duo also made the fourth goal, giving Tommy Taylor the chance to score his tenth goal in only 3½ appearances since the Yugoslavia match.

67

v. Eire in Dublin   **19 May 1957.**

Result: drew 1–1; Finney played at outside right.

With Eire needing to win and England needing just a draw to qualify for the World Cup Finals in Sweden in 1958 you could imagine the tension as the game slipped into injury time with Eire leading 1–0. The 47,000 crowd were willing the referee to blow his whistle when suddenly Finney, who up till then had had a quiet game, picked up a fine pass from Jeff Hall and set off down the right wing. He cut inside Saward's tackle and then swerved outside Cantwell. Saward ran back for another try but was beaten on the bye-line. Finney then produced the perfect centre for John Atyeo to leap like a salmon to head home. The England players jumped for joy and the Eire fans just could not believe it.

68

v. Wales in Cardiff   **19 October 1957.**

Result: won 4–0; Finney played at outside left and scored once.

Finney had another fine game and once more with Johnny Haynes and Duncan Edwards caused havoc in the Welsh ranks at a rain- soaked Ninian Park. England's third goal was scored by Finney and was the best of the match. Billy Wright found Haynes, who was outstanding, and his plans in turn sent Finney away. As the winger approached the defenders, Haynes made a super decoy run which allowed Finney to cut inside and hit a screamer into the far corner of Kelsey's net.

69

v. France at Wembley   **27 November 1957.**

Result: won 4–0; Finney played outside left.

One of Tom Finney's biggest fans was the star of this win and that was little Brian Douglas of Blackburn. In the last international before the terrible tragedy of Munich, England produced a memorable show. Finney missed some good chances but was always in the thick of things and two goals each for Tommy Taylor and debutant Bobby Robson were ample reward for an excellent display.

70

v. Scotland at Hampden   **19 April 1958.**

Result: won 4–0; Finney played at ouside left.

This was Bobby Charlton's debut international and when a brilliant run and cross from Finney came over in the 20th minute Charlton hit a volley that will be remembered by all who saw it as one of the best goals seen at Hampden. All Charlton could say was how honoured he was that Finney passed to him! This was a super win for England at Hampden and kept up Finney's fine record of never having been on the losing side there.

71
v. Portugal at Wembley   7 May 1958.
Result: won 2–1; Finney played at outside left.
Two marvellous goals by Bobby Charlton lit up this match and though England deserved the win in the end,
Portugal had given a good account of themselves. Finney's best moment came towards the end when a
superb run was unceremoniously ended by a crude challenge by a defender. Penalty! Again, though, Finney
did not take the kick and this time it was Jim Langley's turn to miss from the spot, his shot hitting the post.

72
v. Yugoslavia in Belgrade   11 May 1958.
Result: lost 0–5; Finney played at outside left.
England were thoroughly thrashed in this World Cup warm-up friendly and to make it a miserable
afternoon for Finney he was treated to some diabolical tackling from the ruthless defenders. He was totally
stifled by this tactic.

73
v. Russia in Moscow   18 May 1958.
Result: drew 1–1; Finney played at outside left.
Finney was back to his brilliant best for this prestigious friendly and several times he came close to adding to
his international goals total. Linking superbly with Johnny Haynes, he created havoc with a header from Brian Douglas's cross which struck the post. Bobby Robson also headed against
a post from Finney's corner and on the hour the Preston player forced the save of the match from the great
Lev Yashin. Combining well with Haynes, he cut inside to hit a fierce shot which looked a goal all the way.
Somehow, though, Yashin extended one of his seemingly telescopic arms to turn the ball away for a
wonderful save.

74
v. Russia in Gothenburg (World Cup)   8 June 1958.
Result: drew 2–2; Finney played at outside left and scored once.
In their first group match of this World Cup, England often left Finney on his own in attack for the first hour
of play. Russia powerfully built up a two-goal lead as a disappointing England looked down and out. But
with thirty minutes left they began a fine fightback. Inspired by Finney they clawed their way back into the
tournament. Derek Kevan pulled one goal back and then, after Bobby Robson had a goal disallowed, Finney
sent Haynes through, only for him to be felled in the area. Penalty! What a situation, five minutes to go, 2–1
down and a penalty. Finney was the man given the responsibility to take it and he coolly fired wide of even
Yashin's famous reach for the equaliser.
    One sad postscript was that Finney was injured in the game and sadly was unable to take any further part
in the competition. His World Cup experience was over.

75
v. N. Ireland in Belfast   4 October 1958.
Result: drew 3–3; Finney played at outside left and scored once.
Three times Northern Ireland led and three times England levelled in this exciting international played in
unrelenting rain. Bobby Charlton was brilliant for the visitors and it was from his pass that Finney scored
the thirtieth and last of his England goals. A burst through the middle into Charlton's pass and a clever shot
under the advancing Gregg gave Finney a new goalscoring record.

76
v. Russia at Wembley   22 October 1958.
Result: won 5–0; Finney played at outside left.
The last international for Finney in a glorious career that had won him friends at every venue. After the
World Cup disappointments a win against the Russians was desperately wanted and England obliged with a
vintage performance. Bobby Charlton, Finney and Brian Douglas gave Johnny Haynes his first goal of a
hat-trick and Ronnie Clayton, another Finney fan, was the inspiration of a four-goal second half. Finney
could have had another penalty but let Charlton take it and the irony was that Nat Lofthouse scored
England's fifth goal which enabled him to equal Finney's 30-goal record set up in the previous international.

Acknowledgements

A GREAT number of people have extended the hand of assistance to make this book possible and I would like to dedicate the book to my wife, Elisabeth, for her patience, understanding and support.

I must also single out several others for their help, namely Mike Payne, Joan Eckton, David Kay (of Thwaites Brewery and a North End fanatic), David Bell (of W. H. Smiths in Preston), Dave Swanton, Mrs Gornall, Ted Griffith, Ian Rigby, David Jones and Kenneth Whalley.

I would also like to thank Dave Russell for much valuable information and comment regarding the role of soccer in England between the wars. The section in Chapter One on this subject is his.

It goes without saying that the help and support of the entire Finney family has been necessary for this book to see the light of day. Tom has been magnificent, being on call at all times of the day to answer questions and look out old photographs. Many of the pictures in the book are from his own private collection. Tom's wife, Elsie, as well as all of the family, have been superb. Thank you all.

The staff of Preston North End Football Club, particularly the Commercial Manager Wayne Dore, have been most helpful at all times.

Also of crucial importance has been the contribution of the *Lancashire Evening Post,* who have kindly allowed us to use so many of their excellent library photographs. *The Lancashire Evening Telegraph, The Bolton Evening News* and *Cumbrian Newspapers* have also been of great assistance.

Finally, I would like to thank all of Tom's team-mates and colleagues who have volunteered memories, opinions and viewpoints on Finney's life and career. When I began writing this book I had no idea of the depth of esteem in which he was held and, in truth, Tom's reputation as the 'gentleman footballer' has been the single most important factor making my job as his biographer so pleasurable.

Note on the illustrations

MOST of the illustrations in this book have come from the archives of the *Lancashire Evening Post* or the personal collection of Tom Finney. Every effort has been made to trace the copyright owners; in some cases, however, the original provenance of some of the older prints is unclear or unknown. Where we have not been able to trace the copyright owners, we would like to apologise. Our sincere thanks are extended to those who have granted permission to reproduce photographs:

The Lancashire Evening Post, 10, 11, 17, 18, 21, 22, 25, 28, 30, 39, 42, 43, 46, 49, 51, 52-56, 66, 71, 81, 84, 87, 93, 94, 101, 104, 105, 111-121. Henry Melling, 5, 19, 35. Phil Waine, Preston, 6. Provincial Press Agency, 24, 26, 29, 31, 103. *Leicester Evening Mail,* 32. *Daily Herald,* 27, 33. John Bull, 34. Thomas Kidd, 37. Colorsport, 44, 45. *Daily Express,* 63. *Cumbrian Newspapers,* 64. *Lancashire Evening Telegraph, Blackburn,* 65, 70. *Bolton Evening News,* 67. Provincial Newspapers, Preston, 74, 76, 92. Brock Photography, Manchester, 78. Fox Photos Ltd., 95. Peter G. Read, Preston, 96. Harry Bamber, Preston 99. D. C. Thomson & Co. Ltd., Manchester, 102. D. N. Hall, Nairobi, 108. *Manchester Daily Mail,* 110.

Index